Life to Death

Life to Death

HARMONIZING the TRANSITION

RICHARD W. BOERSTLER, PH.D. AND
HULEN S. KORNFELD, R.N., M.A.

HEALING ARTS PRESS
ROCHESTER, VERMONT

To Claire M. Hinman,
who has been both a dear friend and a generous benefactor.
Without her continuous encouragement and support,
our research and educational work could never
have been accomplished.

Healing Arts Press
One Park Street
Rochester, Vermont 05767

Copyright © 1995 by Richard Boerstler and Hulen Kornfeld

Note to the reader: This book is intended as an informational guide. The remedies, approaches, and techniques described herein are meant to supplement, and not to be a substitute for, professional medical care or treatment. They should not be used to treat a serious ailment without prior consultation with a qualified health care professional.

LIBRARY OF CONGRESS CATALOGING-IN-PUBLICATION DATA
    Boerstler, Richard W.
        Life to death : harmonizing the transition : a holistic and meditative approach for caregivers
          and the dying / Richard W. Boerstler and Hulen S. Kornfeld.
        p.   cm.
        Includes bibliographical references and index.
        ISBN 0-89281-329-6
        1. Death—Psychological aspects. 2. Death—Religious aspects. 3. Meditation. 4. Terminally
        ill—Psychology. 5. Terminally ill—Home care. I. Kornfeld, Hulen S. II. Title.
        BF789.D4B64   1995
        155.9'37—dc20   95-38850
                                                           CIP

Printed and bound in the United States

10 9 8 7 6 5 4 3 2 1

Type design and layout by Electric Dragon Productions
This book was typeset in Garamond with Cuento as the display typeface

Healing Arts Press is a division of Inner Traditions International

Distributed to the book trade in Canada by Publishers Group West (PGW), Toronto, Ontario

Distributed to the health food trade in Canada by Alive Books, Toronto and Vancouver

Distributed to the book trade in the United Kingdom by Deep Books, London

Distributed to the book trade in Australia by Millennium Books, Newtown, N. S. W.

Distributed to the book trade in New Zealand by Tandem Press, Auckland

Distributed to the book trade in South Africa by Alternative Books, Randburg

CONTENTS

ACKNOWLEDGMENTS

This book is the product of many years of sustained commitment by the authors, each of whom has been dedicated to adapting emerging body-mind theories to chronically and terminally ill patients. We are most grateful to the many people who have encouraged our work, including our families and clients. We could not have considered this project without home support, especially from George Kornfeld and Dorothy Boerstler. We have addressed, and been touched by, many people from all walks of life and all levels of health and need in our workshops and lectures and through direct client care. We have been encouraged by advocates within patient-care and support groups, hospital-based programs, hospices, home-care agencies, long-term-care facilities, university classrooms, and many professional conferences, as well as by private-counseling and care-management clients, who have all provided us with opportunities to share our approaches. In turn, our own lives have been enriched as our many contacts opened themselves to us.

We are grateful to all who have contributed to our personal and professional development, and especially to those whose challenges and aggravations have provided the foundation for our work. We have experienced our greatest rewards as our professional and lay teachers have become our friends. Because we have benefited from such a diverse population and have had such broad-ranging experiences, we have sought to blend these influences into our work with clients and into our public presentations.

Without the experiences we shared with our very special clients, we would have nothing but theory. Many people are described in these pages, but we have used other names and varied some details to protect our patients' right to confidentiality.

We want to offer our deepest appreciation to our publisher, Ehud Sperling, and the Inner Traditions International staff. We especially wish to acknowledge the helpful guidance of Cannon M. Labrie, our editor. His patience and thoughtful suggestions have been invaluable.

We are especially indebted to the many professors and program planners who have invited us to present our lecture-demonstrations to receptive and responsive groups throughout the last sixteen years. The process has been reinforcing and professionally maturing, and we often feel we walk away with as much as we have given. Those programs have served as the foundation of our text.

We particularly want to thank Caroline Jo Dorr, our mentor, friend, and advocate, under whose guidance our studies in thanatology developed; and Professor Joseph G. Green and his wife, Patricia, who have consistently encouraged our work, stimulated our thoughts, and joined our ventures. In addition, we are thankful to have had the support and intellectual camaraderie of a very special group: "The Associates." Each member has contributed to our perceptions and our visions of the possible. Most notably, we recognize the late Anne Wallens, L.I.C.S.W., whose wisdom and sharing consistently reinforced us; and Arlene McGrory, D.Sc.N., who has shared our vision of a holistic approach to terminal care.

Glora Winstock, Professor Dan Baer, Professor Bodo Reichenback, Lucille Mullaly with her Cape Cod group, Professor Alan Anderson, Alan Parker, Edward Bednar, and Ann Duncan-Treviranus have each encouraged our work and our musings throughout the years. Our professional growth has developed because we have been influenced by the pioneering work as well as the encouragement of Dr. Avery D. Weisman, Dr. Therese A. Rando, Professor Kenneth Ring, Dr. Patricia Norris, Rabbi Earl A. Grollman, Dr. David Meagher, Professor Kenneth Kramer, Professor Jonathan Earle, and Anya Foos-Graber. These distinguished scholars, and many others, have inspired us through both their published works and their personal validation. We hope to prove ourselves worthy.

INTRODUCTION

～

*The wise man looks at death with honesty, dignity, and
calm, recognizing that the tragedy it brings is inherent in the
great gift of life.*
—Corliss Lamont, Issues of Immortality

This book is as much about life as it is about death and dying. It is about
easing the process of illness and dying, and reducing anxiety and stress. It is
for everyone who is concerned about coping with emotional and physical
changes as vital issues. It reflects on concepts of immortality as they affect
fears and provide solace. This book differs from others about death and
dying and the body-mind, because it is intended for caregivers of many levels and for people from different backgrounds as they develop their own attitudes and health plans. Practical issues as well as philosophical questions
are presented, because both are necessary in life and death.

We present in this book a technique called comeditation, which can relieve the pain and anxiety felt by any individual, even one who is seriously
ill. Most especially, it can ease the transition experienced by one who is
dying. Though an ancient practice originally developed in Tibet, the technique is entirely suitable for use in our time and society. Comeditation is easily learned and practiced, and its benefits are experienced not only by the ill
or dying person but by that person's family and other loved ones.

Unlike meditation as it is commonly understood, comeditation requires
two participants: the ill or dying person who is referred to in this book as the
recipient, the subject, or the primary meditator, and the person giving the
comeditation, referred to as the helper, the assistant, the facilitator, or the
comeditator.

Harmonizing the Transition

Each of us acts as an instrument within our world's ensemble. The tones, the pitch, the nuances from one influence the others. In turn, we each respond with periods of silence and crescendo that are stimulated by the modulations and discords that resonate within ourselves. Anxiety, distraction caused by pain, and many other rambling thoughts interfere with the process of rebalancing the body, a process that takes place in deep relaxation or with a good night's sleep.

Comeditation—a method by which a person who wishes to relax is aided by a companion who vocalizes specific sounds, approved or chosen by the first person, in exact synchrony with that person's exhalations—allows the body to completely relax, with consequent release of both physical and mental tension. The mind becomes clearer and more able to focus calmly; the fully relaxed body regulates itself through natural rebalancing. Pain lessens, anxieties can be viewed more objectively, relationships become richer, and a deeper assurance of personal values may emerge. Physical discomfort and emotional unrest become soothed, uniquely, through social support and spiritual awareness.

When inner anxiety prevails, it causes turbulence in every other aspect of a person's life. Various relaxation methods have been shown to improve overall mental and physical function. We particularly advocate comeditation as a vehicle for calming the mind, relaxing the body, and easing the spirit, because the assistance of another helps to override a mind that spins when discomforts or distractions inhibit focusing. As an adjunct to care, comeditation may be combined with any treatment method, and it may be expected to complement the effects of other treatments.

Anyone can learn the comeditation technique, and, with practice, anyone can apply it safely by learning just a few basic principles. Children, college students, athletes, middle-aged caregivers, acute- or chronic-pain patients, the physically challenged, those who are dying, and grieving loved ones may all use the comeditation method to relax the body and calm the mind. Numerous health problems are related to emotional stress, muscle strain, and distortions of posture, and the recipient can learn to transfer the sensations of reduced tension from the comeditation to daily activities. Once an individual understands that stress is the result of the body's reaction to certain postures and intensities, he or she can learn to interrupt a muscle pull or a strained nerve before a spasm causes a full-blown pain reaction. By using this special method of letting go, many have found an effective component in anxiety and symptom management. A seeker of inner wisdom may also use this technique to pursue an evolution of consciousness, regardless of her or his state of health or philosophy.

While we advocate using a body-mind approach to resolving health issues, that is only one aspect of a complete program of total health-care management. Exercise, nutrition, hygiene, medical treatment, family counseling, rest and relaxation, and spiritual support are all necessary to good health care. The case examples provided in this book discuss patients who were confronted with a full range of problems. The many aspects of coping with serious illness and death are explored, and we have identified challenges and responses that resonate throughout the human condition. While most of our clients have used comeditation to help them cope, it is always proposed as just one portion of a complete care plan.

We strongly advocate the use of comeditation in many situations, because we recognize the amazing effects obtained by just one session and have witnessed profound improvements in coping as the method has become part of a patient's daily routine. We have used it ourselves and have experienced every benefit we have seen with others. But comeditation is like a medication that has been given over time in the proper dosage. When symptoms are disturbing, the remedy is viewed as miraculous, but as the situation improves, the treatment is taken for granted. We all tend to emphasize the troubling factors of our lives while identifying the soothing moments as a reinforcement of who we really are. To bring the entire unit (identified as each life) into a harmonious work of art, each of us must balance all aspects of our lives, including the quieting, lyrical connections within.

Those who are healthy, but who want to explore a range of common problems associated with living in an extended family, may gain personal insight as well as a better understanding of others by using comeditation techniques. Professional caregivers who are seeking a holistic guide, family members of seriously ill patients who wish to provide care but who also need support, and those who have symptoms of a progressive illness daily face the issues we present here. The suggestions we offer in this book are intended to help and support patients, caregivers, and others. Work, strength, and courage come from within.

Our purpose in encouraging any form of relaxation is to enable each person to maintain his or her ideal status as much as possible. If one feels in control of oneself, rational decisions may be considered and expressed effectively. Modern medical technologies have allowed many people to survive severely debilitating conditions that would have meant death fifty years ago. Whether the increased time seems precious or painful may depend on the individual's attitude as much as on the treatments and discomforts associated with the affliction.

On the other hand, it is necessary for us, individually and as a society, to face the issues implicit to our time. Many people are now family caregivers of their own elderly and infirm. As health-care costs continue to rise and the population ages, this problem will affect every family. While spiritual development may require perfecting the inner being, if those who are developing remain inward, then society will be dominated by the anxious and self-centered. Moral responsibility will fall to those eager for selfish gain.

Issues of medical ethics are not obscure intellectual exercises but involve every one of us as potential subjects affected by circumstances, as taxpayers, and in our moral positions. Our present society devotes its resources to prolonging life by advancing hospital technologies but is hesitant to investigate the mysteries of death and the promises of an afterlife. Near-death experience studies have appeared in the popular press, but grants for academic study have been meager. On the other hand, certain policies and attitudes have emerged: ethical debates are capturing headlines, medical providers are informing clients of their rights, and hospice-care policies are being required by medical insurers for their terminal-care patients in many areas. We hope that these recent changes demonstrate progress in acknowledging respect for the individual rather than reflecting financial concern.

The Authors' Backgrounds

When Richard was an insurance investigator, he felt the need to counsel people who had been traumatized or who had progressive illnesses. He was inspired to return to his studies in psychology, but he felt compelled to expand his interests in religious practices as well, because he found that even many who considered themselves "good" Christians seemed to gain only shallow comfort when they were under emotional distress. He delved into the oriental philosophies believing that if he could find clues to his own peace of mind he could share his knowledge with others.

He had been searching for years in an effort to control his own "spinning mind," and a tendency to ruminate over his concerns. He had spent hundreds of hours trying to meditate regularly, but continued to feel far away from the goals of "clear mind, peaceful heart." In 1977, before a general audience at Harvard Divinity School in Cambridge, Massachusetts, a method was presented that took a person who had never meditated before and showed that person breathing slowly, muscles free of tension, emerging with a radiant face while speaking of pain relief and inner tranquility. Richard knew he had to devote himself to learning, teaching, and adapting this technique so everyone could benefit from it. Within a few days he arranged to begin work with the presenter, Patricia Shelton, director of the Clear Light Society in Boston, Massachusetts. Richard published a small pamphlet and began to present this special technique to nursing programs and psychologists' conferences.

As a head nurse in a hospice-oriented, chronic-care hospital, Hulen had been searching for a way to teach relaxation to patients who were anxious and in pain. She discovered that there was a disparity between a patient's actual symptoms and the patient's behavior. One patient in particular inspired her decision to combine traditional medicine with holistic practices in further studies.

Several patients in the hospital were unable to tolerate discomfort without loud and bitter complaint, but Hazel, who had an extensive spinal metastasis, discovered a way to transcend her pain. Although analgesics were given on a regular schedule, the pharmaceutical advances that are now common practice had not yet evolved.

The nursing staff scheduled a morphine injection before Hazel's bathtime, but often she would say, "I just can't deal with being turned now. Come back in ten minutes and I'll be ready for you." Watching from her doorway, one could see that she lay perfectly flat and still. When the staff returned after ten minutes, not only was she able to be touched and moved but she exchanged pleasantries about their interests and lives, and she expressed concern about other invalids whom she had haughtily avoided several weeks before. Hazel was able to reduce the intensity of her own pain and she changed the way she viewed society as well as her outlook on death. According to Hazel, "It's a little like praying, but don't tell my Aunt [a traditional Catholic] because she won't understand." Hazel had learned to meditate. Through this experience, Hulen realized that meditation was the key to pain management. But how could she develop the skill and teach others?

Hulen's graduate-studies advisor had suggested that she meet Richard, and Richard's discovery of the Tibetan method of combining the meditator with a guide was the solution Hulen sought. Hulen and Richard joined together to teach comeditation in 1979.

We both became interested in thanatology, the study of death and dying, because we wanted to help those who seemed to be in the most need. Although the many debilitating processes cannot be altered, we know that small comforting efforts do make a difference to anyone in physical or emotional pain. If the distress can be relieved somewhat, even for a short time, the effort is worthwhile.

We have all sat beside a loved one feeling that there must be some way to translate our own caring into a form of comfort for that person. Whether you are a parent caring for a child with a tummyache; an adult child who has reversed roles with an aged parent; or a patient, or the spouse of a patient, with a progressive illness, doing something to ease the suffering for a few moments does seem worthwhile. Similarly, when we are confronted—privately and professionally—with a friend or a loved one who is very sick or dying, and when we are threatened by our own problems, do we not question mortality? Do we not wonder about the meaningfulness of our own lives? These are natural issues for us all. Although discussion may seem difficult at first, a supportive exchange will become strengthening.

The concept of holistic living recognizes that each of us must balance every aspect of ourselves. Even Hazel, a person who found inner peace on her own, had to attend to her complex physical needs. She required extensive support and friendship from others, and she sought philosophical counseling from several sources. It is this whole person, like notes combining in unique harmony, that resonates into an unforgettable memory. The question "Who am I?" is appropriate for each of us to ponder throughout every stage of life, for a total life is like a progression of chords, developing with underlying tones, rests, and surprises.

We have found that the questions stimulated by our clients' spiritual unrest are frequently withheld until our relationships with them are well established. Neither author holds a degree in theology, so we do not approach our clients as pastoral counselors. But, we have found that when those we treat are ready to share their innermost anxieties, fears and misconceptions (often harbored since childhood) may emerge. Some people are haunted throughout life by strict rules and vicious treatment disguised as religious training. But even gentle nurturing may have been distorted by careless expressions and rare but fearful childhood experiences. Frequently, evaluative judgment may be clouded when threatening stories from biblical origins have been used to manipulate the young and the uncertain. Part of any counseling is to help those who are obsessed with certain fears to see old impressions as imagery or allegories that may or may not apply to current life. It is not the theological origins but the manner in which the ideas have been presented that may prove most harmful. By diffusing fears and rectifying attitudes that limit inner growth, a positive and inspiring philosophy may emerge. Our society tends to avoid such issues in spite of the fact that one cannot move on emotionally until confrontation occurs.

Overview of Chapters

Chapter 1 is entitled "Death and the Spirit." Whether or not the reader is religious, everyone recognizes that when death occurs, the spiritual essence of the person no longer emanates from the body. Fear of the unknown is at the core of many anxieties, whether it is the fear of death or the fear of what life will become amid physical insults and major disruptions in daily living. There may be concern about one's mortality, or intense feelings may be related to the impact of loss and grief. These ageless questions have been addressed by many philosophies demonstrating humankind's common identities. By recognizing that change is a universal fact that may be accepted, we can build on the past, deal with the present, and prepare for the future while calmly accommodating uncertainties.

Chapter 2 defines meditation as a way of settling the mind while relaxing the body. Rather than a mysterious influence from foreign heresy, meditation is nature's provision for rest and personal revitalization. This inner quiet is within everyone but has been ignored in humankind's modern tendency to worry, hurry, and fill time with noise. When meditation is deep, connection with the profound may occur. This is an act of prayer that has been used in some form by every major religion. As a biological process, meditation stimulates specific natural chemical responses that modulate pain and anxiety and enable self-control.

Chapter 3 describes the comeditation technique and gives examples of its uses. The practice of comeditation was developed by Tibetan lamas to be used when attending those who were sick and dying. Modern adaptations preserve the basic form but adapt it to individual physical and philosophic considerations. We consider this process to be a sacred trust and insist that the person who is receiving it never be violated by the intrusion of undesired religious concepts or instructions. Only the procedure and words or sounds reviewed and agreed upon may be used.

Chapter 4 is entitled "A Holistic Approach to Health Care." Holistic principles embrace all aspects of a person, including her or his environment. Whereas wellness is considered a normal state, the hospice philosophy emphasizes holistic principles while applying them to maintain normal balance as much as possible while a patient is dying. Each person must determine his or her own direction as the family members provide support and experience their own effects. We have made some practical caregiving suggestions, because most people who are looking for guidance during this difficult period are fundamentally concerned with the ordinary tasks that need to be attended to from one day to the next. Most popular books ignore basic caregiving problems, and while nursing texts are available, they are difficult for the layperson to use.

Chapter 5 asks "What Is Help? What Is Hope?" Home care provides the lure of one's personal haven, but problems loom regardless of the setting. Practical challenges continue to require time and attention. However, any major change is a security threat, and coping is an emotional problem more than a functional one. It is the emotionally vulnerable person who suffers the most, regardless of physical symptoms. Denial and a hopeless-helpless attitude are two extremes of the spectrum of responses that complicate the situation for patient, family, and caregivers; yet, there is a tendency—not entirely bad—for every human to have to deal with these feelings. Hope is a sustaining concept that is available in many forms and that can adjust to any condition if given a chance.

Chapter 6, "The Patient and the Family," relates to the changes that occur in all family members when their roles change as the result of a progressive illness or death of another. Anticipation is often worse than the experience. Anticipatory grief is viewed from the various perspectives of the patient and family. When certain emotions seem unrelenting and tasks seem overwhelming, anyone can become subject to burnout. This phenomenon is explained and suggestions are provided for brief time-outs. The use of organizations and professional caregivers has been considered because such support is appropriate and invaluable for a stressed family. Grief itself is a normal response requiring "work" as well as time. Research conducted over the last fifty years supports the belief that each person's mourning has its own course. The support of friends and relatives is helpful throughout any adjustment to change, regardless of the culture or the time.

Chapter 7 is entitled "The Rollercoaster Experience of Leukemia, AIDS, and Other Devastating Diseases." The reality of life as we approach the twenty-first century is that most diseases may be viewed as chronic conditions. Dramatic medical responses rescue patients from life-threatening situations; after recovery, a period of near-wellness allows normal activity and planning. Then there is another illness flare-up, fear of death and loss, recovery, and then another flare-up, and so on. The patient and his or her loved ones experience traumatic emotional changes, including cycles of disinvestment and reinvestment. Relationships are strained by uncertainty when AIDS, leukemia, and most other diseases cycle through aggressive and remissive periods.

Chapter 8, "Community Concerns," asks whether self-determination is a right or a freedom. Inner peace may sometimes be found more easily as the illness becomes more severe, but many in our society believe that the amount of pain and physical deterioration one must experience should be the individual's own choice. Should our laws be lenient toward the person who chooses suicide and the persons who provide assistance? Near-death experiences may be partially explained as biochemical phenomena. Will this research influence society's view of death? In a changing culture in which health-care reform is an ongoing issue, our views of serious illness and death determine our humanitarian as well as our economic directions. We can all make a difference in the way physical and emotional difficulties affect our lives.

Each life transition must be a combination of circumstances and intentions, and the climax (dying) reflects all of the influences of that life. Each variation affects the quality of each transition; therefore, it is worth our while to seek a variety of methods to try to make it a little better. We each play a valuable role as we contribute to the harmony experienced within one another. Comeditation is one means of helping another person to harmonize the transition.

I

DEATH AND THE SPIRIT

~

The student learns by daily gain.
The way is gained by daily loss.
Loss after loss until at last comes rest.
By letting go all gets done.
The world is won by those who let go.

—Lao-tzu, Tao te Ching

Perceptions of Change

The great sages of ancient China believed that water represents the passage of human life, that birth was just one bend or turn in the eternal stream of life. After cascading over rapids, waterfalls, and other obstacles, the water of the river enters the last bend before flowing into the ocean. According to the sages, a human life could be compared with a droplet of water: The drop serves its purpose, joins with other drops, merges with the ocean to become waves, and then becomes vapor and clouds. Nothing is lost.

The fear of being lost, of losing that stage of being that is familiar, is the common fear of death. While most religions teach the belief in an afterlife, such teachings do not necessarily reassure the dying person. But identifying with nature and its constant changes is a personal experience that can bring comfort to one who is contemplating his or her own mortality.

In our urbanized culture, we have lost touch with the lessons and comforts of the natural world and focus more on visible achievements and maintaining our status. We try to ignore our fears because vulnerability does not command respect from others.

In daily living we do not focus on spiritual anxieties. Instead, we submerge our fear of death in the excitement of television shows and movies.

Most of us are complacent about the way we conduct our business and how we use our free time because we do not feel an urgency to make the most of every minute. Then, when death is imminent, we suppose it is too late to change. Our tendency is to treat death as an enemy. Nevertheless, we know that every life ends.

The liturgy of any faith repeatedly reminds its practitioners of death. The message inspired by many religious traditions is that through faith, proper conduct, and divine forgiveness the prayerful may have "everlasting life." Some patients use portions of various quotations or images to provide comfort when they meditate. Their health status is irrelevant to the inspiration of the thought. Some who have no terminal-disease diagnosis and therefore no physical reason to think of death nonetheless experience extreme pain and are engulfed by despair. Long- and short-term illnesses affect sensitive nerves and cause suffering; this suffering is felt by the individual within his or her origins and experiences.

The image of the sacrifice of Jesus Christ as he died on the cross has served as an inspiration to millions as they have reminded themselves that their pains are minor compared with those suffered by Christ. In this respect, the power of·faith can be thought of as a lesson in letting go. When we tighten to defend ourselves, we suffer; when we relax in trust, we share our vexations with the creative source. Many scholars believe that the lessons of the cross are those of acceptance and the resolve to yield to the inevitable. Christ knew that love is more powerful than fear.

During the Middle Ages there were many texts that discussed the subject of death, such as *The Craft to Know Well to Die: Know Well How to Die for Ye Shall Not Learn to Live Unless Ye Learn to Die*. They provided guidelines for faithful Christians seeking the everlasting peace of God, including instructions on repentance, examinations of the value of good works rather than the acquisition of fortune, and discussions about the impermanence of all earthly conditions. *The Rule and Exercises of Holy Dying*, written in 1652, advised that when a child's teeth fall out, the child has experienced the death of those teeth, and that baldness, like dim eyes, stiff limbs, and wrinkled skin, "is but a dressing to our funerals."[1]

Such teachings advised the lay public to follow the monastic practice of holding death in constant awareness. Through such acceptance of death, the penitent is always ready for it and is constantly aware of the precious details surrounding life. A beautiful affirmation of life and death can be found in the writings of Chuang Tzu (399–295 B.C.), who believed that life and death are human distinctions made by those who do not understand the unity of things.

> The ten thousand things are one with me. Nothing is not acceptable, not even death. The sage leans on the sun and the moon, tucks the universe under his arm, merges himself with things and achieves simplicity in oneness. For him the ten thousand things are what they are and thus they enfold each other. Life is the companion of death, death is the beginning of life. Who understands their workings? Man's life is a coming together of breath. If it comes together, there is life; if it scatters, there is death. If life and death are companions to each other, then what is there to be anxious about?
>
> The great clod [the earth] burdens me with form, labors with me in life, eases me in old age, and rests me in death. So if I do think well of my life for the same reason I must think well of my death. You have the audacity to take on human form, and you are delighted, but the human form has ten thousand changes that never come to an end. Your joys must then be unaccountable. Therefore, the sage wanders in the realm where things cannot get away from him and are all preserved. He delights in early death; he delights in old age; he delights in the beginning; he delights in the end.[2]

From this view, what we consider death is a concept—a concept deduced from observation of an external event. As long as we experience anything, we are not dead; yet we are governed by our own egos. It has been said that the two things each of us cannot experience are our own egos and our own deaths. Japanese author Mokusen Miyuki suggests that death is simply the lack of life. He notes that in the East dying and death are regarded as one's last enterprise in life. Death exists inside as a part of life, not outside, as the negation of life.[3]

The Easterner is concerned with the inner attitude, or readiness to confront death. Even in anticipated horror it is important to conduct oneself well in these last moments of life, although we all fear such a challenge. The reality of death and dying is integrated in one's efforts to live meaningfully. In life's journey, each stage of the journey is equally important. Thus, one "dies" at the end of each critical stage of life. In this tradition, aging is regarded not only as physical change but also as moral and spiritual growth.

The German-born Tibetan lama Anagarika Govinda offered the following definition of death:

Life means giving and taking; exchange and transformation. It is a breathing in and breathing out. It is not taking possession of anything, but the taking part in everything that comes in touch with us. It is neither a state of possession nor of being possessed. Neither a clinging to the objects of our experience nor a state of indifference, but the middle way, the way of transformation.

We are transformed by what we accept, we transform what we have accepted by assimilating it. We are transformed by the act of giving, and we contribute to the transformation of others by what we are giving.

He who opposes this process will die the slow death of rigidity; he will be expelled and rejected from all that lives, like dead matter from a living organism. Death is a deficiency in the faculty of transformation.

In the acceptance of this definition of death, we must see that we are talking about life! To live we must go through continual change, which might be called continual death. Thus we are courting death when we refuse to accept it. We enjoy a waterfall or a cloud formation—in spite of its impermanence: The changing forms heighten our delight.[4]

Another eloquent description of life and death was written by D. T. Suzuki, who described how Zen Buddhists view death.

Zen is right in the middle of the ocean of becoming; it shows no desire to escape from its tossing waves. Just because things are constantly changing, breaking, dissolving, decaying, and dying does not mean they are to be despised or shunned in favor of things judged to be eternal and immutable. Plum blossoms and cherry blossoms, as the Japanese appreciate almost to the point of a national passion, are beautiful despite the fact, and in a sense because of the fact, that their beauty is so fragile and brief. Thus it is said that if a man were never to fade away like the dew, never to vanish like the smoke over the mountain, but lingered on forever in the world, how things would lose their power to move us.[5]

A pre-Hindu view of the universe as "the diamond net of Indra" provides us with an even more descriptive understanding of life and death. In this metaphor each of us is represented by a thread with a diamond light center. The thread of one life is interwoven with the threads of all others through identity and interdependence. In reality this is true: we are all dependent upon the whole of humanity for our existence. Consequently, there is not a single one of us who does not affect the other. In this universe each of us contains the past, present, and future; in turn, all of time includes ourselves.

For hundreds of years various pantheistic sects have embraced this "imagined" universe as a living, breathing reality. Important directions to the modern world lie within those legends. Our planet's fragility and its demands are now being demonstrated by scientific studies identifying the earth as a living body, affected by its lifeforms.

Brother David Steindl-Rast, a Benedictine monk, defines a *religious* person as one engaged in the quest for ultimate meaning. When we recognize the many little deaths that we experience in daily life through changes and losses, our activities acquire more meaning and provide purpose. Our society has taught us to equate purpose (the job or a relationship) as our primary reason for living; therefore, we tend to believe that without that identity of purpose, life has lost its meaning.

Even when death approaches and we can no longer control what is happening or be assured that specific goals will be met, there are aspects of both life and death where meaning can be found. Brother Steindl-Rast points out that we must learn "to die not only our final death, but those many deaths of daily living by which we become more alive whenever we give ourselves to whatever presents itself instead of grasping and holding it . . not to give [something] up means to exclude ourselves from that free flow of life."[6] We cannot have our cake and eat it too, but if the cake is not consumed it will eventually dry up and disappear as dust.

Except for those who have learned Native American tribal customs, most of us lack appropriate rituals and perspectives through which to view the transition from this life to the next. We may have difficulty relating to the Sioux saying, quoted by Sioux medicine man, John Fire Lame Deer, "It's a great day to die."[7] This statement, often made when one is viewing a glorious summer day, may or may not be associated with confronting conflict. It is an acceptance of fate.

Searching for Meaning

Many of us find that we can choose the direction of our life and death. Prisoners have reported that the meaning of life was never so vivid as when deprivation forced them to ponder questions they had ignored in normal life. Dr. Viktor Frankl, a survivor of the German concentration camps, defined freedom as the continuous right to take a stand toward one's preferred choice regardless of the circumstances.[8] In his book *Markings,* Dag Hammarskjöld, former Secretary General of the United Nations, offers a caveat that applies to Frankl's interpretation of choice: "Life only demands from you the strength you possess," he says. "Only one feat is possible—not to have run away."

How can we prepare ourselves for death, which could come at any time in the form of an external or internal assault? The event that most troubles us may be that of our own parting or the loss of a loved one. It is difficult to achieve and sustain a balance between devotion to our loved ones and readiness to withdraw from them by dying or letting them die.

The exact moment between life and death is always unpredictable, even during a bedside vigil. If suffering is involved, anticipation of the death is invariably confused. Sadness over the loss of the dying person's virtues and expectations mingles with wishes for the pain to end. Neither the dying person nor the bystanders wish to be overcome with feelings of regret, guilt, or anxiety, but it is equally difficult to admit relief and anticipate moving on. We want a path: some direction that will lead us through this important event in our lives. Yet, feelings are often so complex and confusing that well-meant expressions of condolence frequently don't reach a desolate person.

It is as though one's basic being must be ripped apart in order to be discovered. What is the purpose of life, joy, pain, daily struggles, involvement with others, planning an uncertain future, death? Whether from spiritual certainty, scientific doubt, or existential questioning, the modern, self-absorbed mortal yearns for purpose and meaning to life. We fail to acknowledge that this search requires a fuller understanding of death. The preciousness of each moment is more real when we are able to identify with the transitory nature of all things while being aware of continuity. Acknowledged interrelationship with the God-source is found in the Upanishads:

> *He who, dwelling in all things,*
> *Yet is other than all things*
> *Whom all things do not know*
> *Whose body all things are,*
> *Who control all things from within—*
> *He is your soul, the inner controller, the immortal.*[9]

Excerpts from a paper written by a brother of a patient with whom we consulted demonstrate how meaningfulness can unfold as life evolves into death:

He did not want to think of himself as a cancer patient or a dying person. Then, about six weeks before he died, my brother began to acknowledge the reality of his condition. He, with the family, admitted that our home care system was reaching a breaking point. He looked out the window, at the big maple tree Dad had planted when he was a boy. Then, he reluctantly turned away and packed his bags ready to be transported to the [local inpatient] hospice. . . . The rest of this paper will be concerned about the events which took place during that final six-week period. Once he said, "I feel like my bags are packed, and now I am waiting for a train to take me on a long journey." I said, "Yes. And I am here to take you to the station." Looking back on his life, my brother said to me, "I am a failure. I have no wife, no children, nothing to show for the time I was here." I disagreed, saying, "You are not a failure. All your life, you have been a kind and a gentle person. You have loved many people. And many people have loved you—including me." To reinforce this message of acceptance and affirmation, I joined forces with our local parish priest, who guided him through a review of his entire life and stressed God's unconditional love. An old friend who usually stopped to speak with him before going to work brought him fresh flowers from her garden. The hospice staff offered kindness, comfort, and extremely competent management of pain.

Father S. helped my brother come to terms with his past life. But a gut-churning fear of the unknown, of total annihilation was triggered by the proximity of death. I was stuck on the strong feeling that there was something I could do to help him. But I did not want to impose my own personal practices on him. Precious time was passing quickly when I realized that I needed someone who really understood the consciousness of a dying person and how to work with it.

I remembered an earlier association I had had with Dr. Richard Boerstler, and called him at his home. He explained five stages which we could adapt for our comeditation practice; the first two were particularly helpful when my brother was having discomfort or was restless. (1) Relaxation of the body is aided by systematically reviewing each part of the body, (2) relaxation of the mind occurs by repeating the sound *ahhh* in conjunction with the recipient's outbreath, as you would heave a sigh of relief at the end of a long, hard day. By occasionally interjecting words such as "just listen" or "nothing else is necessary," the caregiver is able to suggest a growing sense of peacefulness, of being cradled by the soothing effect of the slow, rhythmic sound.

The other steps followed when he was relaxed, or they could be said alone while watching him breathe when he was in coma. (3) Deepening the process of meditative stabilization is accomplished by the simple technique of repeatedly counting, one to ten, as the recipient exhales. While doing this, the caregiver watches the chest of the person very closely, saying each number as the chest falls. Each number thus becomes like the stroke of an oar, rowing the person deeper and deeper into [peacefulness]. (4) Envisioning the moment of death with images of light and energy can be a potent antidote for fear and anxiety. The recipient was invited to listen to a sequence of light visualizations in the same manner as with the numbers. (5) The practice concludes with a selected phrase chosen by the recipient for its special personal significance. My brother chose "Hail Mary, Full of Grace." During our first demonstration session in the hospice chapel my brother responded by looking more and more relaxed and peaceful. When we came to the meditation in which he visualized a clear light, the sweetest smile came over his face. The atmosphere in the chapel reflected that feeling. Afterwards one observer said it was as if there was a fire being kindled in his heart, filling the space with sweetness, light, and warmth. After that first comeditation session, more people got involved, including the doctor, several nurses, a social worker, friends, and our father. For the next two and a half weeks, he went in and out of consciousness as we kept vigil at his bedside. The last night of his life, I stayed with him until midnight. The thought came to me that he was worried about our father because my brother had come home to care for Dad when Mom died. His breath was very slow and quiet, but I sensed he would not leave while I was there with him. I kept doing the meditation anyway. There was such a sense of peace and serenity in the room. Then, I kissed his forehead and whispered in his ear several times, "Don't worry, I promise you I will take care of Dad." A few minutes after I returned home, the night nurse called to say that my brother had died peacefully in his sleep just a while after I left.

This experience bridged our two religious paths. The Tibetans, which I have studied, believe that the suffering before dying is like the turbulence of a passing thunderstorm. At the moment of death, the clouds dissipate, and the sun shines brightly in the clear sky of eternity. In many of the world's religions, the meeting of the soul with God at the moment of death is likewise depicted in much the same way.

My brother was helped in the process of dying by being lovingly affirmed by a network of friends and caregivers as he approached and entered a dimension of reality that is infused by a magnificent, ecstatic luminosity. [Our family] would suggest that comeditation be made more widely available, so that more people, like my brother, can be helped in the process of their dying.

E. B., August 1994

Preparing for Death

Few of us are prepared for death, whether our own death or the death of someone close to us, whether predictable or not. We must recognize that "letting go" is a psychological as well as a physiological process. The caregiver who is fearful of death cannot accept a client's dying any better than the unprepared patient or family can. Everyone who deals with death and dying must address the following questions:

1. What is a good death?
2. What are the fundamental needs of the dying person?
3. If your own consciousness is to become part of the universe at the time of transformation, what state do you wish it to be in at the moment of passage?

What Is a Good Death?

Most of us, if given a choice, would prefer to die suddenly and without awareness of pain. When we watch people we love wasting away, consuming their own bodies because they cannot retain foods, and living in fear of interrupted nights and confused days, we are enraged that someone we care about must suffer such indignities. Yet, this period of suffering may impel the person to direct his or her failing energies toward issues that must be resolved. Both the dying person and the loved ones must face these essential components of grief: physical distress, feelings of helplessness, anger, and despair. Full awareness of these issues can lead to touching and nurturing and making preparations aimed at reducing everyone's loneliness and confusion, as well as to preparing for withdrawal.

As nurse, doctor, therapist, cleric, friend, or family member, none of us can decide the best way for a terminally ill patient to die. In fact, not even the person who is dying knows all the factors that influence his or her life and death experiences and how those experiences influence others.

Death (not dying) may be the one thing that humans have not corrupted. The "passage"—that brief moment between the body's fullness with life and then the absence of life—happens today just as it happened in prehistoric times.

What Are the Fundamental Needs of the Dying Person?

A dying person's needs are not much different from her or his requirements through life. While we are each subject to certain fundamental drives (identified by Abraham Maslow in 1954 as "the hierarchy of needs"), we emphasize one aspect over another depending upon who we are, our past learning experiences, and our recognized goals. Individual needs vary from person to person, but certain human needs are universally shared. Dr. Maslow described them as a "hierarchy" on the basis that if the first needs are not met, life cannot proceed fully enough for the realization of the latter.[10]

The first set of needs, physiological needs, embraces the basic drive to obtain nourishment and other basic requirements—such as water and air. For example, a newborn mammal first gasps or cries to fill the lungs, then struggles to reach the breast. To an exposed infant, safety is synonymous with maternal nourishment; in obtaining protection, love is also conveyed. As development allows independent actions, self-acknowledgment or self-esteem reassures the individual. The recognition of the human needs beyond physical satisfactions was referred to by Maslow as self-actualization. Self-actualization occurs when a person feels a sense of inner identity linked with true inspiration, when consciousness bursts beyond the boundaries of space and time. When examining one's own needs (or the needs of someone with whom you are involved) it is clear that anything identified as a need is "fundamental." But we may alter priorities as serious illness or threats strike.

These high priorities serve as the basis for nursing care, whether it is administered by family members or professional caregivers. Self-esteem requirements continue as long as there is life. Guilt and forgiveness may become issues the person must resolve before dying. The person's self-worth, when affirmed, may be identified as an eternal quality that can be expanded in spiritual awareness.

What State Do You Wish Your Consciousness to Be in at the Moment of Passage?

Superficial consideration of this question might prompt some to say, "I want to be in my own bed" or "I want to be in the hospital where experts are responsible" or "I want to be at my favorite resort" in the mountains or the oceanside. The external surroundings are not important, however; it is the inner territory that evades identification and requires development. The greatest physical and emotional challenges an individual faces are often associated with the failing health of one's self or of a loved one. Although death may be the eventual outcome of an illness, in our modern world it can take a long time to die. For most of us the diagnosis of a progressive illness may be made on the basis of early symptoms that are easily treated. Hypertension with cardiovascular disease, arthritis, emphysema, many early-stage cancers, and diabetes are examples of conditions that require medication and lifestyle adjustments during the early stages, but their immediate effect is mostly anticipatory anxiety. As problems arise we begin to realize how much these illnesses can affect what we do and how we are changing. Often anxiety and stress affect our physical responses, resulting in a vicious cycle of increased stress, unrelenting symptoms, more stress, more symptoms, and so on. Confusion and loneliness are often intensified as the illness becomes prolonged.

The perfect state of consciousness is found in the "clear mind, peaceful heart" of meditation; it is the basis of the discovery of the true self. Identity with the transcendent soul is possible for both the healthy and the dying.

According to modern usage, psychology implies the study of mental processes, emotions, desires, and behaviors. But the term developed from the Greek word psyche, meaning "soul." The psychiatrist or psychologist who ignores the life spirit of the individuals he or she treats may recognize but not truly understand their fundamental aspects.

One approach to self-actualization is for an individual to recognize the indivisibility of life and death. In life it is the ego that continually tries to predominate, but the altruistic self identifies with all of nature. It is this death of the ego, or the self-centered inclination, that is the purpose of spiritual and moral codes. Whenever we are patient with another, when we express cheerful caring instead of complaints of our own discomfort, when we do something we dislike to please another, no matter how small, a little of our selfishness and self-will has died. By giving of ourselves and extending to others, we let go and expand beyond our own boundaries, simultaneously.

Perhaps when Saint Francis said, "It is in dying that we are born again to eternal life," his understanding of spiritual completion came from his own experiences in giving of himself. As Saint Francis related to other creatures, he opened a greater joy of being within himself. Little by little as we are able to surrender everything—not under duress but entirely by free choice—we become enriched while desiring nothing. Once we are established in this state of unity, it transcends time or conditions. From the Christian point of view, this is what Jesus meant when he offered everlasting life: Our constant awareness of the unity of life, our constant awareness of God, is not interrupted even when the physical body dies.

While it has been said that we are a death-denying society, those who confront serious illnesses think about their mortality. It is our natural inclination to wonder what happens when we die. Is there life after death? If so, what sort of life will it be? History and literature provide us with numerous philosophic and religious discussions about death. The immortality of the soul and the resurrection of the body have been central to the Christian legacy of the West's cultural foundation. These attitudes have influenced funeral practices and laws regarding suicide. Images of purgatory and damnation are displayed in museums and churches and are studied in art courses that represent both Eastern and Western cultures. But these dramatic masterpieces have little influence on everyday life.

Even people who regularly attend a church, a temple, or a mosque question their faith when they face their own death or the death of a beloved partner or family member. Most of us lack appropriate rituals and perspectives to satisfactorily guide us through the transition from one life to the next. We pray petitionary prayers, and we grieve while following the funeral and mortuary customs of our society, but few of us have much preparation for the actual "crossing over."

By living a life of achievement, one can hope to leave it willingly. The question is one of timing. That is, if we don't prepare soon enough, we may die before we are ready. If we are so resigned to death that we ignore the necessities and possibilities of daily living, life will be incomplete, even though it continues.

Emotional Responses to Loss

Dr. Elisabeth Kübler-Ross found in her studies of the dying that "denial, anger, bargaining, depression, and acceptance" were the common sequence of feelings experienced by someone who has been suddenly taken ill or who has been diagnosed with a terminal condition.[11] Although these emotional states do not follow any order, and they all may merge with each other at various times, fear mixed with confusion is usually the first emotion experienced, while hope is a sustaining gift.

There is no "right" way to feel or behave when the body and emotions are in crisis. It is not uncommon for a spouse or parent to express these emotions more vividly than the patient. Usually, each member of a family has different feelings in a different pattern from those of the other family members. Each loss, whether it is a change in certain roles, a loss of comfort and companionship, or threatened life security, is felt personally.

As bold areas within a painting or unexpected tones in a musical score can enhance the quality of the work, a life must have variations of happiness and trials. It is the ability to integrate the challenges with the softer experiences that makes life harmonious. Attitude and the many influences of a person's life combine to form the whole being—the physical, psychological, social, and spiritual aspects that constitute the individual. During the experience of loss undergone by the ill or dying person, holistic nurturing reinforces the total person and enriches the caregiver, for we are all affected by our experiences with one another. The goal is to harmonize life in all its stages, including the ultimate transition: death.

An unrelenting, progressive illness is stressful for the patient, the family, and the caregivers. It is difficult to see this trying period as a blessing. But as the process unfolds, there may be many tender periods of serenity and peace. There is the opportunity for all concerned to "put their houses in order," that is, to complete those activities and share the words that have been neglected, if there is the heart to do so.

Death and Time

In the mother's body man knows the universe, in birth he forgets it.

Old Jewish Saying

There are two Greek words for the meaning of time. One is *kairos*, which can be defined as quality time, subjective time, time that is unique to each person. *Kairos* involves accomplishment and fulfillment, emotion and richness. It is the time that makes an hour spent with a dear friend seem only a single minute. This *kairos* time is distinct from *chronos,* or objective time. *Chronos* is the strict time of the clock between medications. It is the television or radio marking the passage of the day, the linear concept of time as a succession of discrete events with no apparent meaning. The hospice program, which will be discussed in chapter 4, has been developed to support and promote quality time, or *kairos.*

Imagine that regardless of any interventions or plans, you are fated to live until a certain date and then fated to die on that day. You do not know when that date is or where death will happen. How would your time be different if you expected to live another thirty years? thirty months? thirty days? thirty minutes? In *Is There an Answer to Death?* Peter Koestenbaum says, "The person who sees death as external is fragmented. He who perceives death as part of life is integrated and whole. . . . I am at this moment moving to my death in essentially the same way that I always have and always will be."[12]

The Body-Mind Connection

We feel very fortunate to have learned and worked with the process we call comeditation because it gives us the opportunity to link an ancient, sacred Tibetan practice—following the breath through a sharing of sound and concentration—with the latest medical achievements. In the study of consciousness, the goal is "clear mind, peaceful heart." This is a status that we all desire, whether we are physically well or declining.

Studies of the autonomic nervous system response and the physiology of pain indicate that stress reduction is a necessary feature of modern health care. Dr. Herbert Benson of Harvard University has been instrumental in investigating and disseminating information about this phenomenon. He found that the "relaxation response" causes a decrease in sympathetic nervous system activity and thereby in the level of stress.[13] Relaxation therapies, such as meditation in various forms, hypnosis, and biofeedback, induce parasympathetic (modulating) reactions. This results in decreased levels of some of the body's irritating natural substances and decreased responsiveness to others; therefore, the person is aware of less pain, is less anxious, and learns to be calm in a crisis. Thus, our most progressive biologists have determined that the ancient seers were right. The meditative mind transcends the body; "clear mind, peaceful heart" may be achieved. This holds the key to the third question about death: "If your own consciousness is to become part of the universe at the time of transformation, what state do you wish it to be in at the moment of passage?"

The "secrets" we share in this book were once passed from master to disciple. But, in the second half of the twentieth century, distinguished medical institutes have encouraged studies to define the connection between the mind-body interaction and the treatment of disease. Along the way, many people have personally experienced, and some have clinically identified, the transcendent capabilities of a mind-body practice. Historically, various religious groups have incorporated some of these principles in their claims of miraculous healing. This "mystery of the spirit" may be perceived by anyone, through religious striving or through inner awareness alone.

The following case study is an example of how some people are able to use the final moments as an opportunity to verify the richer aspects of one's life even when the situation seems to be a tragedy of loss and suffering. It is never too early or too late to seek inner clarity.

～

Randy was thirty-one, with metastasized cancer of the spine, living in his parents' summer home, bitter that he was suffering with so much pain. His mother was caring for him with the help of a home nursing aide. His mother had been referred to our organization, Associates in Thanatology, because her own physician thought she should learn to meditate to control her own high blood pressure. Randy had already developed contractures of his legs and back, so he rested in a near-fetal position.

The day we met Randy, his face rarely showed emotion, although he had been a poet. He seemed as cynical about people as he was about his fate. After getting acquainted and explaining the comeditation method, we helped prop Randy with pillows to support his bent legs and back to enable his spine to be as straight as possible when he relaxed. Hulen did a comeditation session with Randy's mother while Richard did a session with the son. Richard felt that Randy was very close to reaching out for comfort of any sort, and as he let go as much as he could, his position eased. Hulen recognized that he needed better management of his pain-controlling medication, and she recommended that the family and doctor consider some appropriate alternatives and use comeditation to enhance the effect of the medicines. We also recommended that gentle range of motion exercises be given when his body was relaxed to help gradually release his limbs.

Soon after his new regimen began, Randy was making wisecracks to the aide, was willing to be moved during the day to a view of the water, and restored his relationships with his siblings. In the meantime, while thinking of relaxing herself while giving her son comeditation, his mother's blood pressure went down and her doctor decreased her medicines.

Because of a special request from Randy, Richard taught him a light visualization. Randy was particularly fond of the light image because it reminded him of the reflection of light on the sea. Thoughts of the sea blended easily for him into concepts of the clear light of eternity. One early morning when death was near, he asked his mother to just stay there to repeat this refrain. For some time she said his special words to him on his exhalation until he stopped breathing. His transition was peaceful, serene and without anxiety.

In addition to the fact that Randy's passage was so gentle, this event became beautiful to the family because the mother was involved by saying the chant to her son at that precious moment. Thus, she became an intimate part of his evolution. She was involved, caringly, both with his birth and his death. The fact that she could participate in this major event was most important to her and all those in her household. Their acceptance and appreciation of the way he gently slipped from life to death verified the ancient statement, "Death is always the great teacher," because they felt that they had learned that death was not a fearful enemy but a natural release to another phase.

An Appropriate Death Requires Safe Conduct

For the dying person to be enabled to drift from life to death with an unencumbered mind has been a goal of the Tibetans. It also addresses the basic principles of modern terminal caregiving. The research on death by the psychiatrist Dr. Avery Weisman set the tone for thanatology to be seen as a source of important contributions to psychology. Dr. Weisman developed two principles: "safe conduct" and "appropriate death." He stated, "It is safe conduct that the doctor and other concerned professionals must promise, even pledge to those patients who are obliged to surrender their autonomy as time goes by and they must yield essential control to someone else."[14]

When the terminal patient must endure physical and emotional insults with major losses, trust becomes the one factor that others can sustain. While the actual "crossing over" is a private function, being guided through the harbor provides security. This is the role that the Tibetan lamas perfected and that anyone can take, but the process is appropriately practiced throughout life, especially when stresses and pains mount.

In addressing the second principle, Dr. Weisman wrote, "An appropriate death is one that a person might choose, had he a choice." He understood that while no one can choose the disease or the progression of the symptoms, many other choices occur daily. While hope for recovery is not realistic, hope for certain conditions, such as improved pain management, communication with a beloved, and obtaining a clear mind and peaceful heart, are obtainable and can be supported.

It is intriguing to speculate about life after death. The different traditions have many and varied stories giving impressions of heaven, paradise, hell, and the fate of the soul after death, but most say little about what happens at the moment of death. However, *The Tibetan Book of the Dead* provides extensive details about the passage.[15] It describes what Tibetan Buddhists believe happens during and immediately after death. No other literature, East or West, is so explicit.

From the Tibetan Buddhist viewpoint, the last moments of consciousness are crucial in the passage. *The Tibetan Book of the Dead* provides a system of yogic exercises to enable the practitioner to enter the death experience before dying. Thus, the Tibetans maintain that what happens at death is determined by the awareness of the nature of consciousness. They teach that the process of dying begins with the dissolution of the "basic elements of life": earth, water, fire, and air. Then the person may awaken to the clear light of the void. Near-death experiencers in our society consistently report being acutely aware of bright loving light; so these actual, private events, without prior knowledge, correspond to ancient concepts.

We do not have space to detail the entire progression described as the *bar-do-tho-dol* (literally, the "liberation by hearing in the *bardo*," which is the intermediate state between life and death). The title of *The Tibetan Book of the Dead* is directed toward the passage between death and rebirth. In the dream state that the Tibetans believe arises in the mind at death, visions and images offer the individual opportunities for awakening or rebirth. In essence, the book is meant to assist the student to die consciously and to know how to choose a proper rebirth. Special emphasis is placed on how to avoid one's own projections and unconscious tendencies. Death is seen as the last chance in life to transform all conditions and confusions into peace and serenity.

In this respect, *The Tibetan Book of the Dead* is really a manual for the living. It is concerned with the intermediate states between birth and death as well as with those between death and rebirth.

Ancient philosophies address the same mysteries that each individual contemplates when questioning mortality and meaningfulness today. In our Western culture, we may feel alienated from unfamiliar words and concepts that have been defined in abstract terms and obscure parables. But the texts that have been preserved and developed through the early Eastern religions introduced basic philosophic ideals and goals that define spirituality. They are the aspects of divinity on which we speculate when we acknowledge our own limitations and wish for unconditional harmony.

2

MEDITATION

~

*Let your life lightly dance on the edges of time like dew
on the tip of a leaf.*

—Rabindranath Tagore

Why We Need Meditation

It is a human tendency to dwell on the things that bother us, even when we are not in a position to correct the problems. Strife, conflict, and achievement expectations drive us all. Tension that results from anxiety, risky body movements, and strain from overtaxing efforts can cause pulled muscles, headaches, and emotional irritability in anyone—in those who are physically well and in those who are enduring illness. The effects of an injury are often exaggerated and prolonged because the body stiffens and habitually guards itself when the person is under constant stress. Symptoms from a pulled back or environmental exposure that occurred when one was distracted by emotional pressure can serve as long-term reminders of a bitter situation. In the midst of anxiety, doubts tend to magnify, and we can become uncertain about ourselves and our abilities, generating more guarding and stress-related tension.

When we feel physical or emotional anguish, we tend to endure the experience and then review the pain over and over again. The memory holds not just the event but also the related factors associated with the episode—how the original pain felt, the present discomfort, actual losses, memories of past ideals and achievements, and the anticipation of future pain and losses. Such irritants lead to a buildup of resentment and hostility and complicate relationships and activities. When destructive influences are harbored, they have an impact on the persons we will become.

Many of us magnify our difficulties with coping by choosing behavior that creates more problems. We mislead ourselves by adopting addictive patterns, such as using alcohol on a daily basis, taking chemical substances to alter self-perception, or overworking to the point of physical and mental burnout. These behaviors are likely to be selected at the expense of the other people and activities in one's life, and the new habits become even greater obstacles in obtaining success.

Medical prescriptions, over-the-counter drugs, health-food supplements, legal stimulants and calmatives (such as caffeine-containing beverages, tobacco, and alcohol), and illegal drugs are common choices for handling stress, and they comprise a significant portion of our annual gross national expenditure. According to a 1990 survey, "Americans made 425 million visits to providers of alternative therapy, roughly the number of visits to all primary care physicians, and they spent $13.7 billion on such care, comparable to out-of-pocket costs for all hospitalizations."[1] Alternative and conventional treatments are used by people who want to counter both actual and perceived physical and mental deficiencies as easily and as quickly as possible. Outpatient workshops and programs and stress-management seminars are helpful aids to becoming healthy, but changes must occur on the inside as well. One's day-to-day pressures, roles, and expectations do not change, and family problems, such as the care of a sick child or spouse or the responsibility for an elderly parent, can significantly increase a person's duties and stresses.

We all need a means of calming ourselves when anxiety builds upon itself. When a concern causes muscles to tighten, we are gearing for action; but emotional and intellectual calm are necessary for exchanges within a polite society. Although defensive reactions are usually inappropriate, we tend to carry those body-guarding behaviors into everything we do. We all need to learn some method to soften these reactions, not only for social comfort but also for personal health.

If the body is tight, it usually is accompanied by mental and emotional thrashing, which causes the autonomic nervous responses to increase in agitation. Methods that work within, such as meditation, are far more effective in releasing tension than a temper tantrum. And those who are able to manage internal strife are less likely to suffer from organic effects of hyperreactivity such as more rapid use of body insulin, increased demand on kidneys, increased digestive reactions, and so on.

Many diseases—such as heart and vascular diseases, hypertension, lupus, multiple sclerosis, arthritis, colitis, asthma, and diabetes—are directly aggravated by emotional strain. It is wise to learn methods to manage our emotions as a means of also managing our bodies, because each of us will undoubtedly develop a medical diagnosis with chronic implications if we live long enough. An early start may delay nature's advances, but it is never too late to benefit from relaxation techniques.

What Is Meditation?

Our fast-paced, goal-oriented society creates stress rather than relieving it, and even the ill and dying are not exempt from its physical and emotional effects. But even under these conditions, humans have the innate capacity to achieve serenity. Relief from the outside world is felt when a person settles into a calm, secure atmosphere. This quietness of the inner spirit, this natural silence, is a form of meditation common to us all. A parent who holds a sleeping baby after a feeding is luxuriating in their mutual contentment. One who settles into a favorite chair after a successful day at work or after completing a vigorous outside chore is receiving a well-earned reward. A fisherman who is happy just drifting with the current, not really wanting to be disturbed by a nibble, merges with the natural world surrounding him.

We all have experienced the basic elements of inner peace. Physical and mental tension is relieved when the body relaxes. Both internal and external noises recede as the mind drifts into a comfort mode. Three factors—a place of security (imagined or actual), physical relaxation, and mental quiet—are the primary factors that determine tranquility.

While in a state of total harmony, the body's chemicals normalize, and it may feel as though communion is exchanged with a deep, inner factor (variously identified as perfect peace, God, the inner being, or universal consciousness). While the results of absolute body relaxation are similar to those of a good rest, meditation may have faster and more physically and emotionally unifying effects than the same amount of time in sleep. Insights may occur without effort, and physical complaints may be relieved. When the deepest phases are experienced, the individual realizes purity within. No connection with any philosophy or teaching is implied, but the person feels a reinforcement of inner spiritual strength.

Meditation is a simple process with far-reaching consequences; there are very few people who have not experienced some periods of spontaneous meditative consciousness. One's most profound memories are often based upon those moments of inspirational quiet during which life seems to be on hold. Time is transformed from *chronos* to *kairos;* a simple period of rest can evolve into meaningful timelessness. Yet, because the short period of rapture is so captivating, everything else is easily brushed aside. As the focus provides peace, even that focus is lost to a deeper inner awareness. With this expanded perspective, worries, overtaxing concepts, and physical tension seem to fade. The person feels renewed. Thus, with a consciousness one wants to sustain, letting go is eased.

We were asked to consult with a colleague's elderly client, and the patient had agreed to see us with the hope that we could help him address the pain and extreme fatigue he constantly experienced as the result of advancing cancer of the lung. Our threefold purpose with this client was to teach him a relaxation method that would allow his body to reduce tension and, consequently, reduce pain; to deepen his respiration, thus improving his lung function so supplemental oxygen could be more effective; and to help him with his anxiety, which was provoked by inadequate lung function, pain, and emotional distress.

The client met us with apprehension, saying, "I'll bet you're going to try to teach me some kind of meditation. Well, I'm too old to learn something new like that." A quick glance around his apartment revealed religious artifacts throughout, so our answer was, "Are you too old to pray?" Surprised, he replied, "Of course not, I've been praying all my life." We then made the point that no one is ever too old to learn but that most learning involves building upon experiences of the past. What had kept him praying throughout his life? If he had faith, why was he feeling upset?

We then pointed out that there are two kinds of prayer. The first, petitionary prayer, is the common practice in which God is called upon to address the supplicant's needs. It is like giving God your shopping list. If the petition isn't answered during this kind of prayer, the person may feel abandoned and become estranged if the requests, viewed as one's desperate necessities, appear to be disregarded. Sorrow and despair may be the result. The second form of prayer, contemplation, is to assume an attitude of worship during which one opens oneself to listen. This is the prayer of the spirit: "Thy will be done." When a person lets go, and is totally present, he or she is meditating, regardless of religious faith or practice. A prayer of listening inwardly opens the self for comfort. As this comfort occurs, tension lessens, all movements become easier, and thoughts are less frantic.

Our discussion had struck a sensitive chord in the patient. We were trying to help him reinforce a faith that he had practiced all his life. Because of his personal history and a shift in perspective, he was able to apply something that seemed new but was actually old knowledge to him. His treatment period became his prayer time, and he became able to deal with his illness physically, emotionally, and philosophically.

Types of Meditation

While writing *Freedom in Meditation,* Patricia Carrington extensively researched studies on meditation as well as people who were long-term meditators and people who, as test subjects, had been taught different forms of meditation techniques. She investigated many different alternative-care methods, such as body rhythm and transpersonal psychology approaches. According to Carrington, "Meditation is a conglomerate word. . . . There are literally hundreds of practices which can be listed under the heading of 'meditation'." She found that the primary common feature of these hundreds of forms was that the meditating person becomes completely absorbed by the object (or focus) of meditation.[2]

While formal meditation was originally developed as a way toward spiritual growth, recent approaches are used most often for practical goals such as improved health and stress management. People who attend health-related programs, however, may find that they also achieve a kind of inner enrichment. Those who meditate for religious purposes have a greater sense of well-being and deal with stress more easily. Because they are able to relate to all people and circumstances, they do good works and are often capable of extraordinary accomplishments. Mother Teresa is a living example of such a person.

Yoga, oriental exercises such as t'ai chi, and various martial arts emphasize breath control, balance, posture, and mental concentration combined with relaxation. They promote awareness of every sensation and the reduction of anxieties to patterns of thought. Practices to improve movement and function, such as various aerobic exercises and martial arts, have used inhalation-exhalation as the foundation for achieving both inner control and external power. The movements are executed in coordination with inhalations and exhalations to augment physiological and psychological balance.[3] Martial-arts students learn to strike on their own exhalation because it maximizes their strength. Watching for the opponent's moment of inhalation provides even more advantage.

The Hindus developed concepts of energy movement and body-mind training with the chakra system, from which most Eastern practices evolved. Many physical-therapy systems have incorporated theories of energy enhancement and body balancing as well. But the common factor in Eastern disciplines, which have been shown to effectively improve both body function and mental outlook, is that they all engage the entire body through deep breathing, full circulation, and mental concentration on the action alone. These principles, which are also aspects of meditation, are used by major sports figures and world Olympic winners. And as maintenance of the body through exercise has become a major emphasis in Western modern health care, millions of avid joggers, aerobic-exercise participants, and weight trainers find they are improved, overall, when they exercise routinely. A major benefit of exercise is that it promotes deeper respiration. It seems logical that something that works well for athletes would be beneficial for common people with myriad aches, pains, and infirmities. People like our elderly patient who was apprehensive about learning "something new" may be put off by the unfamiliarity of teachers from Eastern disciplines such as gurus, swamis, yogis, and meditation masters.

Breath Awareness Connection

Some practitioners of meditation have referred to the process as breathing thoughtfully, being aware of the breath, just breathing (with no other thoughts). In any culture, when a chant is repeated or a hymn is sung, the expression of sound is made as the breath goes outward. As the sound is sustained, spreading beyond the self, a full breath is taken deeply. The attention is only on the breath, the sound, and the intent.

Everyone carries the basic tool for meditative awareness because everyone breathes. The practice of meditation generally involves some relationship with the physiology of respiration. It is a simple way of engaging the voluntary nervous system to affect positive self-control, because respiration is the one vital function that responds to both voluntary and involuntary nervous system commands. While voluntary choices allow us to vary our breathing rates, breath is automatic when the will is relaxed.

There is an ancient Hindu saying: "We come into this world on an in-breath, and we go out of the world on an out-breath." An infant must open its airway to live; we commonly recognize death as a cessation of respiration and circulation. In ancient Greek, Hebrew, and other languages, one word meant both "breath" and "spirit."

The Chinese thought of *ch'i* or *qi* as breath and related it directly to the body's energy. When an infant cries, the sound is made during the exhalation. Babies naturally engage their diaphragms, employing belly as well as chest movements when breathing. The baby discovers the ability to make sounds on the out-breath and develops stronger exhalations and vocal skills at the same time. Both crying and gurgling become focus factors for the baby.

An adult suffering from compromised respiratory function must also use the abdominal muscles to effectively empty and fill the lungs. Often, a moan becomes a comforting device for both adult and child. Thus, through physiological demands, nature provides an innate physical and conscious connection that is especially advantageous to the most vulnerable.

The complex nature of lung dysfunction may provide insight into the relationship between respiration and stress. A respiratory crisis escalates like a strong wind blowing over an ocean. As the ocean sweeps into a storm and then becomes a hurricane, the turbulence mounts, a circular pattern develops with self-feeding aggression and the destructive path broadens if the momentum is sustained. Fear, which stimulates rapid breathing, also signals cardiovascular pumping, supplying fluid for the lungs to process. The cycle escalates as the rapidly beating heart provides a greater volume of blood for the lungs to treat (that is, to get rid of carbon dioxide and provide oxygen) in any given minute. The breath is so rapid that the oxygenated air cannot get into the deeper lung recesses, while the short breath cycle prevents the carbon dioxide from being fully expelled. Lung patients are challenged to separate from the anxiety of distress in the midst of crisis to become observers. Through detachment, fear is reduced and the lungs are freed to breathe more slowly and more deeply. Then the respiratory cycle can perform at its best potential. The act of calming promotes more effective breathing efforts; consequently, the accompanying improvement in blood oxygenation reduces the demand for faster breathing and relieves the feeling of anxiety. In the meantime, appropriate medical treatment can be provided.

While severe lung disease serves as a dramatic example, it demonstrates a universal pattern of behavior. We all develop inappropriate responses to tension. Most of us overwhelm our minds with racing thoughts and reactions to anxieties throughout each day. Part of our instinctive reaction to anxiety is to restrict our lungs' capacity by breathing less deeply and more irregularly.

Immediate fear may result in holding the breath; succeeding breaths are then shallow and rapid, and they are unable to carry oxygen into narrowed lower lung areas.

The Physiological Effects of Meditation

Many physiological changes have been observed in subjects who meditate. The best-known effects, especially among hypertensive patients, are lower blood pressure and lower heart rate. Another classic finding is a decrease in respiration rates. Studies have shown that oxygen consumption might be reduced as much as 55 percent, and carbon-dioxide elimination may be lessened by as much as 50 percent, because during meditation the body needs less energy and less oxygen to metabolize energy.[4] Although dramatic changes in breathing occurred, all those studied were without ill effects.

In Western medicine, a well-trained physician or nurse often feels justified in doubting a patient's claim of pain if the source of the pain is not clearly evident. The body's chemical reaction to stress and relaxation has been largely ignored. The endocrine and nervous systems have now been shown to be closely integrated. Together they affect the body's response to all stimuli, and it has become clear that a person reacts physiologically to disturbances or to calming influences.

Our bodies naturally produce receptors, called neurotransmitters, that are ever ready to hook on to the molecules of similar chemical substances. Whether the similar molecules are those of acquired substances such as alcohol, food, coffee, tobacco, morphine, or various narcotics and pain relievers, the body responds by sending tiny messengers from head to toe searching for a match. Thus, our emotions and reactions affect our own body chemicals through our neuroendocrine systems.

For decades researchers have published data that establishes stress as a cause of structural and chemical changes in the body, but this knowledge has only recently begun to change common medical practice. Our bodies respond not only to immediate dangers but to long-term aggravation. Hans Selye identified the "general adaptation syndrome" to stress as completing the "stress syndrome" in three phases: alarm, resistance, and exhaustion. Selye found that after the sudden gearing to respond to physical trauma the body goes into an accommodation cycle, but when the stress continues for a long time, the exhausted body returns to the initial stress stage as a final effort of resistance while becoming overwhelmed by the attack.[5] The course of most chronic diseases falls within this pattern: crisis, plateau, crisis.

Fear and apprehension serve to protect us, but our bodies' guarding mechanisms become habits that build up layer by layer as the years go by. The cellular changes of normal aging compound the effects: tension, reduced elasticity, narrowing function, more tension. Conditioning factors such as heredity, previous exposure, and acclimatization influence the sensitivity of a particular body to certain stimuli at a particular time.

Even though the biological effects of stress on the body have only recently been recognized in the laboratory, quieting methods have been used to reduce the wear and tear of health hazards throughout history. In earlier times, extended bedrest would be recommended. More recently, sedatives or tranquilizers have been prescribed to help the body to forget its hyperreactivity. In addition to these measures, we have learned that we can make a difference within our own bodies by taking time to understand ourselves and retrain our automatic reactions.

This is the foundation of biobehavioral psychology and the use of biofeedback as a self-monitoring device. In biofeedback, sensors are attached at one or more points to provide information about changes in the body's electrical energy as relaxation occurs. When certain muscle or skin-temperature changes indicate the desired stage of relaxation, the monitoring screen or sound signals to the client that he or she has achieved the objective level of tension release. Full muscle relaxation, as achieved in a meditative state, is the best way for a tense person to affect the signal positively. After learning how this feels, the person can transfer this sensitivity awareness to activities and interactions.

Meditation provides the same natural comfort-giving effects whether or not a sensory unit is involved. The soothing natural neurotransmitters are released as tension is dropped from the muscle fibers. The bone structures align with equalizing balance, and the body and mind become aware of calming factors. Thus, discomfort and discontent are eased.

If a physician's full analysis of the problem establishes a basic organic or structural cause, meditation will relieve the symptoms but cannot be expected to entirely correct the flaw. When medicines are prescribed, those medicines may be more effective if meditation is practiced as well. In fact, many patients plan their meditation time just after taking certain medicines so they can receive the full benefit. In such cases, they inform the doctor because it may be advisable to gradually reduce the prescribed dosage.

Is Meditation Entirely Safe?

These days, it seems that some investigator will find danger in everything we consume or do. It is not surprising, then, that a few reports of negative experiences with meditation have been widely circulated, alarming some people.

Not everyone who meditates will have a profound experience. But, if the person surrenders to the process with the intent to grow spiritually, devotion to the quest requires a great deal of time and inward reflection. Almost all documented psychiatric side effects associated with meditation have resulted from overindulgence in time and intensity.[6] A fanatical attitude should be avoided and a certain amount of judgment must be applied. The most important human survival tool has always been intelligence. The unique quality of meditation is the guidance into awareness; therefore, no effects should ever be out of the participant's control. A meditation session will be more beneficial if you can stay with it for at least twenty minutes, but if you want to shorten the session, you can always stop at will.

If, by rare chance, a frightening vision or feeling occurs, recognize it. If you let go of something disturbing and then have another unpleasant impression, note that also. When you return to normal consciousness, the events during meditation should be viewed as subconscious messages, which may provide clues to your situation. They should not be given any greater weight than vivid dreams, however. And, like dreams, they may serve as important windows into the subconscious and thus facilitate therapeutic counseling. There is no more reason to expect that meditation will be harmful than to fear that sleep may be harmful.

Sometimes people who have nightmares are too frightened to fall asleep, but their bodies must have rest. Because meditation provides relaxation while the mind is not wandering, a sleep-deprived person can benefit from meditation. Clearly, however, disturbed sleep or disturbed meditation periods are clues to the need for expert spiritual or psychological guidance. A preexisting psychiatric problem may show itself through subconscious channels; that is a reason to address the condition, not to "kill the messenger."

Meditation training includes disregarding attention-getting distractions that confuse or seduce the practitioner away from the goal of pure consciousness. These events have been referred to since ancient times. Saint John of the Cross, for instance, wrote of his despair as "the dark night of the soul" before he perceived the divine light.[7] But these impressions occurred when the mystical searcher, single-focused, felt emotionally barren while working through inner conflict.

In all forms of meditation, the practitioner is always in control. Some people may fear meditation because they believe it is similar to hypnosis. Some instructors refer to "autohypnosis" when they teach meditative techniques. But while hypnosis and meditation have certain features in common, such as relaxation of the body and reduction of cascading thoughts, the two states vary in brain activity. In hypnosis, thoughts change continually according to the instructions or activity taking place.[8] But in deep meditation, thoughts are suppressed.[9] In neither meditation nor hypnosis is any part of the brain "turned off," or nutritionally deprived.

If the meditator is concerned about undesired occurrences he or she needs only to decide to become more aware of the environment and body, and slowly come out of the meditation and posture. At the end of any fully relaxing period, it is advisable to move the body slowly at first, because the blood pressure has accommodated to the posture, and dizziness may occur if movement is forced before the blood pressure is redistributed. This is not a sign of danger: it is the same adjustment that the body needs after a deep sleep. If the restfulness of full relaxation is even more effective following meditation than it is after sleep, it should be expected that the body's circulation will respond similarly.

Never, in more than fifteen years, has either of us had anyone experience a harmful reaction in giving comeditation. This excellent record is probably due to the comfort the subject derives from the assistant's presence, vigilance, and adaptability. The assistant is entirely focused on the recipient's breathing and overall appearance. Sensitive observations influence the decision to make changes such as sound intensity, inserted phrases to draw back wandering attention, switching sections, or concluding the session.

Pain or paralysis can follow prolonged sitting meditation. If certain nerves are compressed and circulation is limited for long periods of time tissue damage can result. This is why we recommend moving even a dying patient slightly at least every twenty minutes, whether the person is meditating or not. We have frequently observed slight, brief tremors or twitching, especially of a hand or leg, which are of no consequence. Such motions should be ignored because the meditator is probably not aware of them.

The story of Barbara demonstrates how meditation can help a person access forgotten traumas that unknowingly affect daily life. Barbara felt that her experience with comeditation must have been "bad" because when her session was concluded she just felt like weeping. She was assured that she was just being touched by deep feelings. After being encouraged to let those feelings flow and express the grief she had suppressed, she realized that she was experiencing a wonderful breakthrough. At the conclusion, she recognized that she had gained an important perspective on an old problem.

By viewing an event in an atmosphere of safety and objectivity the person can try to understand and deal with his or her reality. Anxiety is more manageable if a trusting relationship can provide a calm overview with support and encouragement. It is not uncommon, however, for a particularly anxious or phobic person to be intolerant of lying down or remaining quiet in the presence of another. We have willingly modified our approach, often to include exercise (such as walking together) while counting or saying chosen words. By teaching the recipient the basic method, he or she can later apply those same principles privately.

In working with Barbara, we know that we actually taught meditation because she had no intention of ever letting her vulnerability be so exposed. But the client would often say how valuable comeditation was in controlling anxiety. Sometimes she would add that no other form of meditation would ever work because her mind could not quiet down enough, but it did with the comeditation instructions. The influence of a teacher-caregiver made the difference.

Body-Mind Management

As we face many small concerns throughout each day we may concentrate on everything but our breathing and the accumulation of tension. We all are subject to the effects of fear and apprehension, even when the source of intimidation is barely perceived. But Patricia Carrington reviewed studies to determine whether meditation changed the dreams, self-perceptions, and personality dynamics of students over a three-month period. She found that "practical meditation does reduce tension and improve functioning on a number of levels. This may lead to startling changes in behavior and the way the meditators view themselves even if deep-seated emotional problems remain unchanged."[10]

"Clear mind, peaceful heart" is a commonly used meditation refrain. Relieved of the expectation of solving problems, the meditator is temporarily freed from worldly concerns. The mind is in a clear state, waiting for inner awareness. Mind and heart can become calmer. Thoughts come only one at a time, and they can be brushed aside so they do not interfere with the focus. The heart pumps perhaps a little more slowly; the demands on both blood pressure and lungs are reduced. The body begins to feel rested, and the mind develops a fresh perspective.

This is not a state of unconsciousness or sleep but a period of heightened lucidity. Consciousness swings back to the here-and-now quite easily. Those who have any knowledge of the subject speak of meditative *practice,* however, because the practitioner must deliberately intend to stay within the meditation and undertake regular sessions over time to effectively achieve a true meditative state at will.

The goal of sitting meditation is to become fully aware. When this happens, ideational thought waves become sporadic, body energies are tempered and enhanced by a quiet mind. In explaining the need for meditation, Anodea Judith said, "While few of us would eat dinner on yesterday's dirty dishes, we think nothing of tackling a new problem with yesterday's cluttered mind. No wonder we feel tired, confused and ignorant!"[11] The image is of cleansing the mind while providing a smoother flow of thoughts between the areas of the brain.

During meditation the yogi may take only one or two breaths a minute. But circulation is maintained, and there is more actual control over essential body functions than our medical physicians ever dreamed was possible before recent studies were undertaken. Following up on their interest in brain function and variations in perception, Elmer and Alyce Green, at the Menninger Foundation, began in 1964 to study autogenic training as it had already been introduced in Berlin by Johannes Schultz in 1932. They demonstrated with electronic feedback that a subject, by means of autonomic (muscle tension) control, could warm his hands when he was deeply relaxed.[12]

The first widely circulated report on the physiology of meditation was an article in *Scientific American* in 1972.[13] Zen masters, yogis, and practitioners of transcendental meditation (TM) were monitored for metabolism, heart rate, brain-wave patterns, oxygen consumption, and blood pressure. Tests indicated that meditation produced effects in the body through the control of an "involuntary" mechanism: the autonomic nervous system. Since then, many investigators have confirmed these findings.

In these early studies, breath was used as a link between the voluntary and involuntary nervous systems. Through the ages, awareness of the breath has been a means of practicing yoga or sacred devotion. Research over the last twenty-five years has determined the physiological effects of these ancient practices. Elmer and Alyce Green, for instance, have documented a deliberate increase in the temperature of one hand over the other as well as voluntary control of heart action.[14] These researchers and many others have validated the range of effects that can occur by linking consciousness and breath with altered body-mind states.

At hospitals associated with Harvard University and the Menninger Institute, and in numerous other sites throughout America as well as other parts of the world, research practitioners have applied these principles to patient care. They have created the new field of biobehavioral medicine through blood-pressure clinics, pain-management clinics, and cancer-treatment programs, treating both organic and psychogenic diseases. Today, few state-of-the-art hospitals do not offer wellness programs that promote relaxation principles. Whether or not the process of reducing stress and gaining more conscious control of undesirable reactions is called meditation, the principles are similar.

The Quest for Perfectibility

Norman Cousins, in an article titled "The Mysterious Placebo: How Mind Helps Medicine Work," says, "Labels are not important; what is important is the knowledge that human beings are not locked into fixed limitations. The quest for perfectibility is not a presumption or a blasphemy but the highest manifestation of a great design."[15] Our attitude toward our own perfectibility may be based on training, need, or personal experiences that occur with or without planning. Cousins himself decided that he was not going to let an advancing disease with a terminal prognosis determine how he would suffer and die. He sought guidance from many sources and incorporated many unusual treatment approaches, especially humor and attitudinal changes. Cousins' immune system became revitalized. He recovered from his illness and led an active life writing, lecturing, and inspiring others.[16]

Carl and Stephanie Simonton first began in 1971 to work with patients who successfully used relaxation, combined with mental imagery, to combat confirmed cancerous tumors.[17] Since then, they have been joined by other highly qualified physicians and psychologists advancing the premise that by changing their attitudes and by practicing body-mind stress reduction, patients can recover from devastating diseases. Dr. Bernie Siegel's study of "exceptional patients" led him to state, "I believe that with more emphasis on spiritual growth and availability of [psychologically reinforcing] therapy programs, there would be an even higher survival rate among the highly motivated patients."[18] Dr. Siegel teaches that destructive habits are sustained when low self-regard reduces a person's natural defenses.

While patients may blame themselves inappropriately when they are told that their attitudes have shaped their diseases, it has been determined that a patient's approach to treatment and ability to manage anxiety does make a difference in the course of the illness. Vast populations in India and elsewhere in the Orient have incorporated meditation into health-maintenance systems by combining relaxation principles with theories of energy enhancement. Many religions consider an open, prayerful heart to be the key to relying upon God's grace and power to heal. In each case, health is improved and sustained when one lets go of anxieties while assuming responsibility through unwavering personal participation.

Kenneth Pelletier, in *Holistic Medicine,* credits Johannes Schultz for early, extensive research data and case histories on the use of autogenic training. This self-induced relaxation therapy, based on a proven method of meditation, was not presented by anyone in an instructive training form until 1977, however. Pelletier notes that in autogenic training "the emphasis is not in trying to control the natural system, but rather on helping natural systems use their inherent potentials of self-regulatory adjustment more fully."[19] This principle of inherent self-regulation identifies the curative qualities of meditative practices, regardless of the meditation style chosen.

Jeanne Achterberg and Frank Lawlis used meditative imagery combined with art therapy for cancer patients, for patients with diabetes mellitus,[20] and for people with autoimmume conditions such as rheumatoid arthritis.[21] Dr. Jon Kabat-Zinn describes patients at the University of Massachusetts Medical Center's Stress Reduction Clinic who were helped by meditative methods after diagnoses of cerebral aneurysm, cerebral palsy, chronic obstructive lung disease, various cancers, heart disease, depression, headaches, psoriasis, and sleep disorders.[22] We rank among our closest friends a person with whom we worked when a cerebral aneurysm in the temporal lobe caused bizarre and disorienting thoughts and images. The process took several years, essential medical adjustments, and people who cared, but the determination to regain balance through inner control helped our friend to emerge enriched by those experiences.

In modern health care the quest for perfectibility has been centered on physical correction. Few unmotivated people, whether they are functionally well or not, will take time from their busy schedules to learn and regularly practice a technique without a strong incentive, such as a chronically sore back, cardiovascular disease, cancer, or an addiction that must be broken. People following a twelve-step program for addiction frequently believe that their recoveries stem from effectively stripping themselves, relinquishing everything, and opening themselves in meditation.

Breath and Change

The body's respiration is one constant process between life and death, regardless of the span of time. The infant becomes a developing child; the youth will become old. The body may become diseased or distorted; joyfulness may be displaced by agony or vacant awareness. Throughout each life, both desirable and undesirable events will usher in change, but breath will be a continuing part of that life.

As breathing goes on whether one is aware of it or not, the breath is always available to use as a device for meditation focus. All meditative practices throughout the world have adapted this principle. One's life may be full of suffering or joy, difficulties or achievements, complications or simplicities; but during breathing meditation it is possible to simply become an observer of the breath and to realize that thinking is not required. Mulling over and fretting over one's problems only cause more suffering. The art of gaining control is to let everything pass—to avoid stagnation by not dwelling on any one thought. "Like a dragon slipping into the water," or "like a tiger entering the mountain" were ways the ancient Chinese likened the merging of an individual into the universal awareness.

Not dwelling on a problem is not the same as not solving it. It has been said that an anxious mind is like a wild monkey jumping from tree to tree. The fearful monkey is acting on anxiety; creating a commotion and shaking the trees will warn other creatures of danger, whether they are at risk or not. The monkey will also bring about the consequences of fear and destruction, such as lost eggs and nests, dropped fruit, and broken limbs without actually dealing with the problem. Less excitement might provide better cover and be less harmful.

Everyone can relate to the wild monkey image, for we have all felt it. The person preparing a job presentation, a student about to take a test, a patient in a well-equipped hospital observing the dying person in the next bed, and a parent fearful of losing the family shelter all contend with anxious thoughts jumping uncontrollably about. We know we cannot think clearly or function smoothly when there are so many impressions and ideas bombarding our minds. But we can remind ourselves that respiration reflects the state of the mind and that the effort to slow the breath will allow the mind to settle. Conversely, a calmed, meditative state of mind will evoke a slower, deeper rate of respiration.

Sound

Meditation is commonly practiced in the chanting of prayers, the use of rosaries, the recitation of mantras, and other devices to link the functional with the spiritual. The physical and emotional aspects of each participant become enriched by the experience of listening as well as by the experience of creating the sound. In contemporary life, anyone who is a member of a choir or band knows this. The rituals developed by the culture or religion with which a person can best identify are likely to be most helpful because sound and meaningfulness are combined.

Chants developed by religions of the past and those used in contemporary worship set up fundamental vibrations when practiced en masse or when allowed to resonate within one's head. *Alleluiah, Om* (sounded *ahh-ouu-mmmm*), *Amen, Aum, Kyrie Eleison, Sh'Ma, Om Mani Padme Hum,* the repeated phrases of American spirituals—all such chantings create internal vibrations that the practitioners find spiritually expansive. When the human ear "hears," it responds to vibrations as they produce sound. As the sound is repeated, the intellect acclimates. Rather than thinking about the sound, the body allows the vibrations to resonate throughout. Each cell is freed to be bathed in the sound, to be stimulated responsively. Through such reaction to an outer source, deep inner awareness may occur.

Modern particle physics has shown that the molecules of the universe (that is, the basic structures of the stars, the planets, and all living matter including ourselves) are composed of electronic particles with vibrational motion to maintain the structure. Too tiny to be seen, but detected electronically, these vibrations may be identified as sounds.

As we are composed of such atoms ourselves, it is not surprising that humankind has always found sound to be a means of linking with the inner force believed to be associated with the creator. The most ancient Hindu texts are founded on a philosophy that originated before recorded history and that incorporates change, destruction, and re-creation with the concept of dynamic rhythm.

Vibrational movements do cause the units (whether atomic particles or human emotions) to expand their potential and to develop an attraction to others. Through a physical resonance or a mental connection, the use of sound in meditation may realign the body and stir the soul. Such creative force connects the most minute to the encompassing whole.

The Growth of Consciousness

Psychotherapy has developed some methods using meditative principles, pychosynthesis and hypnotherapy. But the primary focus in psychotherapy has been to change the contents of consciousness. By contrast, meditative traditions have been concerned with transforming consciousness itself. Even though the root of *psychotherapy* is *psyche,* meaning "soul," the modern psychologist focuses more on behavior. The separation of psychology from the recognition of the soul may be one of the most dangerous dichotomies of our civilization because it creates the illusion that we have progressed beyond the spiritual wisdom of earlier times.

We cannot ignore the spiritual aspect of ourselves any more than a maple tree can deny its sap. In the quest for perfectibility we cannot be wholly completed unless our bodies remain aware of the inner surge as a response to nature's connection with the eternal.

While most of us are not able to obtain sainthood, nor do we expect to, we are concerned about peace of mind, control of fear and distress, and inner fulfillment. The tug at one's basic core, which might be interpreted as vague anxiety even when there is no specific reason for discontent, suggests that we have merely pursued purposes. We have not found the source of stimulation, that surge of meaning to complete one's identity, the inspiration leading into fulfillment. We may experience brief periods of time in which all factors combine to form the perfect whole we each know we can be. Those are the supreme experiences of self-actualization described by Abraham Maslow (see chapter 1). This is what Viktor Frankl discovered in the Nazi prison camps when he became aware that the meaningfulness of one's personal dedication can be greater than extreme suffering and hopelessness.[23] It is the peacefulness that "passes all understanding." All philosophies are at home in this understanding of transcendence.

Such communion with the sublime may be achieved in a meditative state. Various religious works have described these experiences as prayer in a contemplative mode, and certain forms of prayerfulness are referred to as the spirit praying unceasingly within (the blessed).[24] Sometimes unfortunate circumstances cause a person to withdraw from normal activities. If the time is spent in periods of thoughtful relaxation, unhappiness may be replaced by renewed confidence.

Herbert Benson, in *Your Maximum Mind,* describes the emotional transformation of a woman he calls Gail, who had lost everything—job, husband, mother, brother, and her own health—within a few months. Feeling "unworthy" and in despair, she could not hold a job and withdrew from the company of others. But after spending many hours reading a book on positive thinking and the Bible, and lingering in meditative prayerfulness, "Gail had a distinct feeling . . . that her life could be turned around. Along with this feeling, she had an overwhelming sense of God's presence with her." She resumed her job search, her symptoms of back pain diminished, and her vibrant personality returned, newly matured.[25]

This unity of body and spirit is believed to have been exemplified by Saint Francis of Assisi. In discussing prayer and the unconscious mind, Dr. Larry Dossey refers in his book *Healing Words* to one description of Saint Francis, that he "seemed not so much a man praying as prayer itself made man." Dossey describes extraordinary rescues and recoveries that he has seen occur when the threatened person turned quietly inward, let go, and trusted the unseen power of the unconscious mind. He explains the phenomenon as "not so much praying as 'being prayed.'"[26] This concept of "being prayed" is the essence of all mystical striving.

How Does One Meditate?

From the beginning of this book we have talked about using relaxation with some awareness of the breath as a means to meditation. But as we all know, a person can be aware of breathing throughout a lifetime without discovering a profound sense of peace. The clue is, of course, attention. If the mind leaps from one point to another, considering three or four issues and their multitude of interactive complications, the mind is not centered on breathing. Problems may be solved and decisions may be made because the person has allowed a quiet time to just think things through, but meditation has not actually occurred. We need experience to discover the golden period of awareness between thoughts.

The opening vignette in *One Minute Wisdom* by Anthony DeMello begins with the student asking the Master, "Is there such a thing as One Minute Wisdom?"

"There certainly is," said the Master.

"But surely one minute is too brief?" replied the student. "It is fifty-nine seconds too long," answered the Master.

The student asks, seeking discussion, "Then why all these years of spiritual endeavor?"

The Master teaches silent awakening: "Opening one's eyes may take a lifetime. Seeing is done in a flash."[27]

Many meditation guides speak of "mindfulness" as any moment of quiet awareness, whatever the focus, that contains the elements of meditative peace. The Buddhists refer to "mindfulness" as a meditative state, in which one attends only to the process of involvement whether it is sitting, walking, working at a chore, or preparing for sleep. In this way, one is in a prayerful state regardless of the activity. Mindfulness means being attentive while letting go. It means suspending judgment while identifying with the object or activity at hand, sensing deeply while remaining uninvolved.

The Vietnamese monk Thich Nhat Hanh speaks of employing the heart of an artist when viewing an almond tree for open communion with the tree. He recommends this technique: Become cognizant of the tree's nature. In meditation, if an intruding thought persists, continue to recognize it but do not chase after it. Shift back to the breath or the sound as the continuing focus, let go even of that, observe a new thought, shift back to the focus, and so on. By using breath as a tool for aligning mind and body, one keeps consciousness in the present reality while "seeing into the great body of reality."[28]

In *Wherever You Go, There You Are*, Dr. Jon Kabat-Zinn speaks of the bloom of the present moment.[29] This simple concept implies that each moment is to be honored as rare, precious, and filled with potential. It offers an opening into mindfulness, or the observational awareness of whatever the mind embraces. There is no reason for evaluation, no need to link one thought with another. There is the open mind, the thought as it enters, admission of the thought, return to the breath, release of the thought, open mind. The cycle may continue for as long as desired. Sessions of twenty minutes to half an hour, once or twice a day, are usually recommended for beginners.

In meditation a posture is taken to promote an unhurried flow of the meditative cycle. The person may lie down on the back with arms alongside the body (as we recommend in comeditation) if sleep is not likely or if the purpose of relaxation is to prepare for sleep. Traditionally, a sitting posture with no support is favored because after many practice sessions the challenge of maintaining perfect alignment provides sufficient stimulation to keep the person alert while, through habit, the posture is monitored by the body instead of the conceptual mind.

A point of focus is selected: meditators may choose a consistent sound, an object or spot in the room, or the person's own breath. The breath is overwhelmingly favored because it is always with you. In comeditation—as we will explain further in the next chapter—the assistant provides a stimulus by making a sound as the meditator's exhalation occurs, and we advise the recipient to keep eyes closed throughout the session.

Dr. Jon Kabat-Zinn has shown that intensive "mindfulness training" may produce long-lasting physical and psychological benefits as well as deep, positive changes in attitude behavior. In *Full Catastrophe Living: Using the Wisdom of Your Body and Mind to Face Stress, Pain and Illness,* he wrote, "another common mistake people make when they first hear meditative instructions about breathing is to assume we are telling them to think about their breathing—but this is absolutely incorrect. Focusing on your breath does not mean you should think about your breathing. It means you should be aware of it and attend to the changing qualities."[30] There is no reason to fear that physiological problems will develop from this exercise because you are totally aware of how you feel and can calmly make a correction by breathing more deeply. Allow yourself to monitor your body, and if you want to continue, you may resume the relaxation. Reengage or reactivate the meditation slowly to retain the easy posture and movements and the calm outlook.

This is the important lesson in meditation. Becoming an observer, an experienced meditator will watch for the body to breathe. No distress is felt; when oxygen is needed the lungs expand fully, because nature abhors a vacuum. This fundamental principle of physics, the readiness of space to fill, applies both to the body and to the active mind. If a person is suddenly caught off guard, as when an unprepared child is questioned by a teacher, the mind seems to go blank. There are cascading thoughts that cause unintelligible static; the mind is active but not communicating. If attention is directed to a nonthreatening issue, normal function resumes.

If you release the air in your lungs, you will automatically breathe in cleaner, purer air from your environment. You breathe because the atmospheric pressure outside your body does not allow your lungs to create a vacuum. Shallow, rapid, anxious breathing (which we all tend to do when emotionally upset) exchanges air primarily within the upper part of the lung, and the higher concentration of oxygen in that area signals that an abundance of oxygen is coming in. So, when the body is anxious, believing it has more good air than it needs, the body restricts the depth of the respiration; consequently, the lungs do not use their full capacity.

If the meditator notices the exhalation and allows the inhalation to come when it is ready, diaphragmatic breathing will use the lungs more fully. In pushing aside apprehension while allowing the breathing to come when the body is ready, the meditator is calmed, and the body equalizes. According to age-old yoga teachings, there is a direct correlation between breathing rate and the generation of ideas, which reflects the body's adaptive capacities. A person need not deliberately try to change a breathing speed but only to utilize the potential depth. When this occurs, a meditator may breathe six breaths a minute or less, be fully oxygenated, and still feel that the breathing is more rapid than necessary.

Mastery of breathing leads to mastery of anxiety. Control of anxiety will allow a person to breathe more fully and more effectively. An anxious person can become calmer by deliberately breathing slowly and deeply. A rapid breather will become anxious, engulfed by rushing thoughts. By extending the feeling of relaxation while the breath flows outward, any exhalation can serve as a mini-meditation.

Joan Borysenko, former director of the Harvard Medical School Mind/Body Clinic, advises in *Minding the Body, Mending the Mind*, "Don't worry about how you are doing."[31] Most meditation teachers acknowledge that the most difficult obstacle in meditation is learning detachment. Thoughts that come into the mind do not break your meditation unless you become disturbed while trying to control them. Zen master Thich Nhat Hanh tells students not to create a battle within themselves: "Whenever a wholesome thought arises, acknowledge it: 'A wholesome thought has just arisen.' And if an unwholesome thought arises, acknowledge it as well. . . . Don't dwell on it or try to get rid of it. . . . To acknowledge it is enough."[32]

Borysenko provides an excellent image in discussing everyone's natural tendency to be troubled by a wandering mind. She paraphrases Saint Francis' advice, "You can't stop the birds from flying back and forth over your head, but you can stop them from nesting in your hair." Sogyal Rinpoche, in *The Tibetan Book of Living and Dying,* suggests that the mind is like a container of muddy water: "The more we leave the water without interfering or stirring it, the more particles of dirt will sink to the bottom, letting the natural clarity of the water to shine through."[33] The important message here is that calming will occur with practice, and mastery will develop as the process is integrated into daily life.

Establishing a routine and maintaining it—providing time for meditation (with or without prayer), time for exercise, time for work, and time for enjoyment—balances a full day with activities, challenges, and quiet that can improve function, tire the body, and promote problem solving. Someone who dedicates each moment to mindfulness is able to engage in every activity while also maintaining a meditative perspective, thereby eliminating extreme fatigue and frustration while experiencing each period as harmony. But no skill can be acquired without effort. Starting and continuing with a plan, even when distractions or discouragements interfere, is the first step.

In the West, when we say "I will meditate on it," we mean "I will think about, or contemplate, the problem." Meditative practices in most Eastern traditions require transcending all conceptual thinking: "I will free my mind from encroaching thoughts." The stresses in modern life overwhelm us when we dwell on our worries. Meditation allows consciousness without the active mind—an open sky with no walls surrounding it. It is a subtle, short-term death of the "I," "me," "mine"—that is, a release of the ego and all that defines you or me as separate and possessive. The yogi believes that his mind is merging with the universal consciousness. Then, all that remains is pure consciousness. Nothing is lost; rather, the deeper self is exposed. Our technique of comeditation is an explicit sharing of these benefits.

The Quest for Mystical Awareness

While becoming aware of our own immateriality, we may become free of expectations. It is then possible to gain the insight that this life offers one potential and that death offers another potential. Like the seasons, neither is more powerful than the other. Winter, spring, summer, fall—the seasons come within their own times, bearing their own purposes, within the flow of nature. This awareness may become the first step in the final transformation of consciousness. The "letting go" process becomes a part of daily awareness of nature. Thus, when death does occur, it is a gradual process, acceptable for the body's transformation. Physiological factors are not "thieves in the night" but signals to act upon medically if postponement of death is appropriate.

Meditation can be thought of as a "mini-death" of the mind, which may be a more profound experience than physical death. Mind with a capital "M" goes on living; mind with a small letter "m" vanishes or dies, according to Buddhist thought. That is: the Mind associated with the essence of being is realized as the true self and is indestructible; the mind associated with desires, ownership, and importance is dropped as being no longer appropriate. As the innermost consciousness is identified with an expansive quality of being, the pettiness of self-indulgence becomes easier to control. This is why modern therapies for addiction have been so successful. The addict recognizes his or her personal powerlessness while surrendering to a higher power. Universal love diminishes anxiety through the warmth of all-encompassing peacefulness. Thus, fear of life is reduced as well as the fear of death. The most significant transition in the span of anyone's life, whenever it occurs, is the neutralization of fear.

With practice anyone can discover that the space between the inhalation and the exhalation provides a special opportunity for communion with the higher power, or the inner self. In extending that period, one may realize transcendence while gaining more, rather than less, control over organic function. Yet, the essence of the process is "letting go." When tension is reduced, the body functions more easily. When tension cannot be relaxed, it is necessary to identify the fears provoking the on-guard state. This is the foundation of the premise that in order to live or to die well one must lose the fear of death. This principle has been recognized for thousands of years, and it guides the search for inner calm.

Beyond change and the promise of "everlasting life," however, is the discovery of "undifferentiated unity" which is identified as "nothingness" or the fading away of distinctions. This same sacred emptiness (to the Buddhists "the fertile void") is recognized as fullness, which envelops all love—personal, charitable, and divine. This mystical bliss encompasses every person, every creature, and every part of the environment. Even when there is separation because an individual is so small and acknowledges unworthiness, being united with the One by experiencing an awesome presence is yearned for as a completion of being. It is an experience sought by many Hindus, Buddhists, Jews, Christians, Moslems, Native Americans, and others throughout history. It is a goal that is commonly expressed by mystical searchers, both in living and in dying.

Few people who are caught up in modern life will admit to mystical aspirations. But when life is fading, a person's regrets may surface, along with feelings of despondency and hopelessness. Meditation can provide an opening into this hidden suffering. Comeditation, especially, is useful when time and energies are waning and when a helper is near and eager to be of use. Comeditation offers an opportunity to bridge the aches and pains of physical infirmity to the awareness of peace if the recipient and assistant wish to try.

3
COMEDITATION

~

*When our attention is on giving and joining others, fear is
removed and we accept healing for ourselves.*

—Gerald G. Jampolsky, Teach Only Love

What Is Comeditation?

Comeditation can be simply described as a method in which one person
helps another to relax. Concepts about consciousness, life, and death are not
needed by the person who is physically and/or emotionally tense and wants
only to relax. No psychological interviews are required. The person may be
completely healthy or in any stage of ill health. The only requirement is that
another person be available to act as a facilitator and that both are willing to
spend twenty to thirty minutes uninterrupted by any distractions. They may
adapt the method in any way to accommodate the recipient's physical con-
straints or preferences. The facilitator tells the recipient about the standard
routine and invites the person to make any alterations desired and to choose
special words or sounds preferred by him or her.

On completion of the comeditation experience the person feels completely relaxed and usually peaceful; some may experience a transformation
of consciousness. Use of the guide for comeditation (see appendix A) will
allow any two people to perform a relaxation exercise to ease the recipient's
tension. The practice is nonsectarian. It involves no dogma and no belief system, except as the recipient chooses, and the entire process is determined by
the recipient.

Recall from our earlier discussion that the relaxing person is referred to
here as the recipient or the subject, and the person giving the comeditation
is referred to as the helper, the assistant, the facilitator, or the comeditator.

The word *comeditation* signifies meditation with another. In actual practice the primary person is the one who receives the method. The primary meditator—the recipient—assumes a position as nearly straight and flat on the back as is comfortable. The second person—the assistant—serves as a guide to prompt a progressive muscle-relaxation process and to make sound cues when the recipient exhales. Following progressive relaxation, the recipient and the assistant make the sound *ahhh* together. The exhalation of old air clears the lungs of both participants, while the echoing effect of the doubled sound provides reinforcement. The assistant watches the recipient's chest, making the chosen sounds exactly as the recipient exhales. As the session proceeds the recipient only listens, but by hearing the expected words or sounds is able to sustain a focus that would otherwise be disturbed by a stream of thoughts.

This sound on the exhalation is the key to the rapid manner in which the recipient is able to let go. As a direct link with the recipient's body, the sound serves to assure the recipient that another cares in a very special manner. Through this process the recipient's mind is freed because the assistant is maintaining that link between body function and awareness; the recipient simply listens, perhaps slipping into a state between wakefulness and sleep in which the mind lets go of anxieties. As body tensions are released, musculoskeletal distortions that cause pain relax. In addition, a special comforting is experienced through this sharing. If the recipient finds a sense of peace, inner enrichment occurs. Spiritual growth may occur as the individual chooses and as spiritual reinforcement is searched for.

Because comeditation involves two people, the assistant may also experience calm and comforting if he or she is in a relaxed position. The act of focusing on the recipient provides a point of concentration beyond one's own personal agenda. By opening himself or herself, the assistant becomes uniquely aware of the other. When such a caring relationship is given a chance to evolve, both participants become fortified. Fear is less threatening as they are calmed. With inner quiet they become more able to accept their status, even when it includes infirmity and death.

One of our close friends rejected the religious teachings of his family and their church when he was fourteen. All of his subsequent education and private reading made him more skeptical of theological thought. He tolerated our interest in philosophy only if he did not have to participate. He was, however, impressed when we shared with him examples of patients who had experienced pain relief and improved function through comeditation.

Soon he began to understand for himself how tension can affect the body—when he developed cardiac irregularity during his company's near collapse. Once, following a day of personal stress, we accompanied him to the hospital emergency unit because he had unrelenting chest pain and a rapid heart rate. He was attached to a cardiac monitor, seen briefly by a nurse and a doctor, then seemed to be forgotten.

The heart rate continued between 148 and 164 beats per minute, accompanied by anxiety and discomfort. With nothing else to do, we thought it was appropriate to offer a comeditation session. He replied, "Can't hurt, go ahead." Within twenty minutes, his heart rate was seventy-six beats per minute with no skips, and he was free of pain. The doctor came in and said, "You converted yourself!" Our friend answered, "The comeditation did it." At that point he admitted that our studies had been well directed, and he wanted to tell others about our work.

When a patient is approaching death, comeditation is the ideal vehicle for nurturing the person's body, emotions, and spirit. As meditation serves as an aid in dealing with physical symptoms and myriad anxieties during day-to-day living, the meditative state is even more valuable during the dying process, when variations in body chemistry bring about additional and challenging physical and mental changes.

The Benefits of Comeditation

- Physical pain diminishes when tension is released
- Emotional anguish lessens when one opens oneself to listening.
- Presence in listening allows one to receive.
- Shared words and sounds that are comforting and nonjudgmental strengthen relationships.
- The spirit is reinforced through the word and sound choices of the recipient.

Comeditation Provides

- Help with symptoms such as pain, nausea, shortness of breath.
- Alleviation of anxiety symptoms such as anger, panic, insomnia.
- Comfort through another, which can be recalled when one is alone later.
- Activation of spiritual centering, directed by personal choices.

In day-to-day caregiving, comeditation may be used one to four times a day for periods of twenty to thirty minutes each to provide comfort without interfering with the essential tasks of the daily routine. During the last stages of dying, comeditation may be used as a continuing background to other caregiving activities, to maintain contact and help the patient stay centered on his or her chosen sounds.

When the terminal phase changes the patient's responsiveness, extended or more-frequent comeditation sessions, as planned earlier with the patient, may be given. If the patient is semicomatose, assume that the hearing continues to be competent. Vigils may be maintained to keep continuity of the specifically desired sounds.

The goals for use of comeditation during the dying process are to ease the letting go of bodily afflictions and sensations, to release mental attachments and allow worldly intents to yield to spiritual changes, to complete one's philosophic plan, and to provide a safe passage when the spirit is ready to depart.

The Origins of Comeditation

It is impossible to determine who first devised the practice of sharing a meditation directly with another. The cross-breathing practice originated in India as a Vedic tradition, probably more than three thousand years ago. Group chanting has been used since the earliest civilizations to provide a show of force—as many voices join, the harmonics multiply the sound, suggesting that this is a crowd worthy of notice. By using sound alone, some people have been able to go into states of ecstasy.

The procedure we call comeditation was originally transmitted from teacher to student through the centuries in Tibet. The uncompromising tradition of oral transmission restricted communicating sacred exercises—a legacy of the early Hindu principles that spread with Buddhist practices. The advanced teacher could share certain instructions only when the student proved to be ready. Since consciousness at the time of death is believed to determine a person's afterlife progression, a Tibetan Buddhist sect developed the procedure whereby one monk works directly with another when the second is critically ill, to aid the dying monk's advancement in the *bardo,* or the transition (in this case, the period after death).

These Buddhist monks understand that a teacher is needed throughout their lifetimes to guide the individual monk in philosophy and mediation. Although they are among the most advanced practitioners of meditation in the world, the Tibetan monks' pursuit of enlightenment causes them to have the attitude that they are always students. This exchange with another is particularly welcomed when the troubled mind has difficulty in concentrating, or when critical illness affects the ability to focus.

Historically, Hinduism developed in India about the same time Moses received the Ten Commandments. Siddhartha Gautama, who rejected his princely heritage in the search that led to his becoming the Buddha, was born in India about 563 B.C., and his followers were initially linked with Hinduism.[1] While the most sacred practices were forbidden to be recorded, it is believed that comeditation evolved from ancient Hindu traditions. The ancient Vedic teachings were classified by Patañjali about 200 B.C. but were probably a fundamental aspect of Hindu practices long before that time.[2] Although it was the Hindus who refined the many yogic systems, certain yogic postures described by Patañjali have been passed from learned teacher to ready student as part of Buddhist practice since those early times.

The word *yoga* is defined as "to yoke," which means union of soul and body. There are many yoga systems and many asanas, or postures, one of which is shavasana—lying flat on the back with arms along the side of the body, palms turned upward. It is a natural position to assume when one has been physically challenged, is tired, or is ill. Shavasana is also referred to as the corpse position, because the supine position is often the final posture in life. It is the posture most used in comeditation.

According to the English translation by Evans-Wentz of *The Tibetan Book of the Dead,* this is the thrust of basic spiritual teachings in the Orient: "Buddhists and Hindu alike believe that the last thought at the moment of death determines the character of the next incarnation."[3] The belief that the last thoughts at the time of death will determine the direction that person will take after death pervades this work. Practicing the purest thought state that one can attain is a means of preparation for that all-important day. Daily, assuming the position that one will take when laid out at death allows the meditator to become familiar with that final posture and well focused on it. Recognizing constant change in everything reminds us that death is continuous with change and need not be feared.

Tibetan Buddhist practices especially emphasize releasing the consciousness to bathe in the "clear light of the void," or the universal source. This ability to contemplate with a deep mind is the culminating eighth step in the path to righteousness, or the cure of unhappiness. (The Buddha's eight steps to enlightenment are these: right views, right purpose, right speech, right conduct, right means of livelihood, right effort, right thoughts, and right concentration, or meditation.) The importance of meditation was taught by the Buddha and his long line of followers as a way to overcome suffering by directing consciousness and experience in life and after death. Lama Govinda's introductory foreword to Evans-Wentz's *The Tibetan Book of the Dead* quotes from the *Lankavatara Sutra:*

> May I undistractedly enter the path of listening, reflecting, and meditating,
> So that, . . . once having attained human embodiment,
> No time may be squandered through useless distractions.

To perfect the art of living by practicing the art of dying is to lay aside ambitions and aggravations derived from one's pride. The control of passions insulates one from evil in life and after death. The discovery that one cannot be separated from the source because the knowledge of oneself is but a small part of the many aspects of "all that is" is the beginning of attaining inner peace.

It is believed that the Tibetans further developed their ideas about the state between life and new life so well through the ages because of their isolation. They had little contact with the outside world for two reasons: they lived in the virtually inaccessible Himalayan mountains, and they believed the old ways were sacred and had no desire to mix with outsiders who emphasized acquisitions and change rather than inner perfection. But the core of their success was the fact that the monks showed their respect for one another by being willing to sit with the one who was ill as a sacred duty and privilege without becoming impatient.

Comeditation was first described in Western literature in Richard's 1979 booklet, *Letting Go: A Holistic and Meditative Approach to Living and Dying.* The booklet was revised in 1982 following our work with clients and joint lectures to college classes, hospices and other caregiving institutions, churches and other organizations, and national conferences. We did a pilot study during this early period at the New England Medical Center in Boston, confirming numerous published studies by responsible researchers who had determined the effects of meditation on physiological behavior. Our adaptation allows the body to release tensions while the mind is freed to let go. The recipient selects the phrase that becomes the focus, and this repetition serves as contact between the two while the recipient becomes entirely liberated from sources of stress.

We believe that we have been very privileged to have learned this method. While we have adapted it to patient care in various, practical ways, we have also taught it to a multitude of people with general and professional interests. Tibetan lamas intended the practice to be used only by those disciples who had advanced through years of spiritual training. We respect this tradition of careful selection but also are in awe of the method's potentials for extension into modern practice.

The Comeditation Process

Any two people who share a few quiet moments together, calmed by each other's company, are in a state from which comeditation can develop. When two people are in close proximity to each other, without verbal exchange but sharing some common interest, both will begin to adjust their breathing rates to the other's pattern as they view one another. By eliminating the busy gestures and anxious chatter that fill the spaces of most interchanges, the two simply relate on a physiological and emotional level.

We often set up a similar experiment in our workshops. Without any introduction, we will ask the participants to turn so that each faces another participant and simply watches the other breathe for three minutes. When questioned about the experience afterwards, most answer that they found themselves breathing at the same time as their partners. Many remark about how calming those brief minutes seemed to them. A few may observe that they felt a new and special bond with their partners. This simple three-minute interlude demonstrates the strong influence of another's presence on one's physical, emotional, and social well-being even without instructions or an exchange of words.

By beginning with progressi c relaxation for complete body rest and adding the refinements of full lung use and reinforcing sounds, that simple exercise is extended into a deep meditative experience. So, while the comeditation method was refined by the Tibetans, we teach our adaptive technique as a natural means of sharing intimate moments with another to provide basic tranquility with the release of physical and emotional tensions.

Although any body-mind training is a learning process, dozens of people have reported remarkable effects when their first experiences with comeditation were as our workshop demonstration models, in the worst of circumstances—on a stage or table surrounded by observers, with unanticipated noises and bright lights. Nevertheless, most who have volunteered to relax in such a potentially anxiety-provoking atmosphere have been amazed by the profound relaxation they actually experienced with comeditation. Frequently, even long-time meditators say they have never achieved such a deep state.

Although the progressive muscle-relaxation procedure we recommend is a common initiation into hypnosis, the important difference between comeditation and hypnotherapy is that in comeditation no sound or suggestion is used unless the subject has agreed upon it entirely. The process may be given by a nonprofessional caregiver with no experience because there are no surprises. The subject is in complete control because the assistant is following the subject's breath.

A description of the comeditation procedure follows. A detailed guide in appendix A has been prepared for your personal use, and you may find it helpful to refer to it while reading these next few paragraphs. Appendix B provides worksheets for you to personalize and photocopy for easy referral.

The process of comeditation is adapted for the benefit of the recipient. First, the two participants should discuss the procedure to clarify it, and to determine whether changes should be made. Does the recipient want a visualization to be suggested? Does the recipient want the counting phase to be included? If certain words were used in a previous session the recipient should decide whether to continue using them or choose different words. The amount of time spent on the segments may be altered according to the recipient's wishes.

Second, the place selected to accommodate the recipient at rest must be quiet enough for the assistant's normal voice to be heard. The assistant's chair should be placed near the recipient's ear. If the recipient's physical condition makes lying flat difficult, the assistant should help in repositioning with pillows, bed adjustments, or other such measures. It is important that the recipient be positioned with the spine as straight as possible. It is also appropriate for the weight of the body to be supported. A bed or lounge chair may be supplemented with pillows or folded blankets or towels so that no dangling or flopping of extremities occurs.

When both participants are comfortable, the routine progressive muscle relaxation is begun. We recommend first suggesting that the recipient wiggle or contract each body part and then relax it as it is mentioned. When the assistant says "Think to yourself" or "If you wish, copy in your mind 'the toes and feet are relaxing,'" the recipient hears the words as suggestions that may be followed as he or she is comfortable with the progression. Begin at the toes and feet and continue up the body, specifying each part, progressing to the head and then relaxing the arms and hands. Then, if tension continues, return to the head, scan down the body to break up clusters of focused energy (muscle spasm or pain), and end at the feet. The suggestion "All tension is leaving the toes of the right foot" followed by "All tension is leaving the toes of the left foot" allows additional time for the recipient to mentally break up and push out distracting clusters of discomfort.

The concept that pain is a concentration of energies may be useful when the recipient is acutely uncomfortable. By visualizing a flow away from the pain focus (such as healing energies washing over and breaking up the noxious cluster, or the aching knot being loosened and untangled), the recipient may alter his or her perception of the discomfort. When pain is met with total relaxation as tensions are envisioned leaving the body, the pain may seem to disperse. The cause has not been corrected, but the body does not have to give it full attention. Now, the recipient is freer to move into conscious awareness.

After the subject is completely relaxed, the assistant then makes a sound corresponding to each of the recipient's exhalations. First, the sound of *ahhh* is made by both the recipient and the assistant together. The recipient expresses all the used air from the depths of both lungs by making the sound of *ahhh,* just as one does at the end of an exhausting day. (It may be helpful to remind the subject of the good feeling experienced when one comes home, pulling off the coat while eyeing a favorite chair, and says *ahhh* spontaneously while settling down.) The recipient should make the sound out loud, three to five or more times; then only the assistant makes the sound while the subject listens.

The assistant should always present suggestions so the recipient has a choice, by saying "If you wish" (for instance, "If you wish you may just listen; I will make the sound of *ahhh* for you, nothing else is necessary"). This rule of choice should continue through the entire session. If a visualization is offered, even if the recipient has requested it in the planning, the option "If you wish" should accompany the suggestion. "When you are ready" may also be included in the instructions (for example, "When you are ready to conclude, make a fist with your right hand"). This deference to the recipient's choices means that the recipient is not complying with another's command. If a vision does not come easily, or an action does not occur as the assistant suggests it, the recipient has not "failed." The recipient does not feel rushed, or pulled from a preferred state, but continues to hear the assistant and understands the time frame already agreed to.

In the second sound sequence, the assistant counts from one to ten and repeats the series, depending upon the subject's responses and preferences. The recipient may visualize during this phase if desired. We commonly say, "If you wish, you may visualize the numbers going from above your head, over your body, and disappearing in the horizon beyond your feet." We do not recommend describing the numbers or the horizon. All images should occur spontaneously within the recipient's mind. At different times there will be different impressions. A person who finds that no thought at all occurs has reached the meditator's goal: pure consciousness.

The third phase of sounds, synchronized to the recipient's exhalations, is the repetition of special words previously chosen by him or her. This is sometimes called a *mantra* (a sacred sound). The words are selected to reinforce personal beliefs, strengths, or desires or to provide comfort. Commonly, our clients request a part of a psalm, a prayer, or a poem. Many prefer single words (such as "love," or "peace"), and some ask for a continuation of either the *ahhh* or the numbers. Some students of various meditation teachers (such as Transcendental Meditation) have been told to keep certain word-sounds only to themselves. Those who do not choose to share their secret sound may think of it privately while an agreed-upon substitute sound signals the recipient that an exhalation is occurring. The recipient then says the personal word-sound inwardly. More suggestions for sounds, words, poems, and prayers are found in appendix C.

When the session is closing (about twenty minutes is common), the assistant suggests to the recipient that the comfort and peace of the present moment can be carried into the day's activities. The recipient should be told that the session is ending. Allow a few moments of quiet. The assistant then invites the recipient to feel the head, body, and legs against the mat or bed, and to try making a fist with the hand nearest the assistant when he or she is ready. At this time only, the assistant may touch that hand. This touch at the session's conclusion enables the assistant to determine how much strength has returned and whether the person has become cold. Extra time will be needed before the recipient moves about alone if the hand is either very weak or extremely cold. Neither, however, is cause for alarm.

The recipient is then advised to open his or her eyes when ready to return to the surroundings, to lie quietly for a moment before moving slowly to a sitting position, and to be sure normal circulation has returned before rising, as a precaution to avoid dizziness. Slowing of the body functions creates a condition similar to deep sleep. Just as a person feels unsteady if springing up from a deep sleep because of a sudden disturbance, a person who has been resting in a deep meditative state is likely to have the same lightheadedness, because the blood pressure has accommodated to the lying position. It will return to normal quickly, but if it is forced, the release from tension resulting from the meditation may not last.

This concludes the meditation. We advise the assistant to sit with the recipient awhile to allow him or her to discuss how the session felt, what the resulting impressions were, and what effect they have had. Are there any issues the recipient wishes to pursue? If so, a plan should be made, and if the recipient is unable to get about, the assistant should arrange for some help in obtaining the appropriate support. When comeditation is practiced two or more times a day, there is usually less need for discussion, but the opportunity should be available in case the recipient desires it.

Modifications of the Standard Comeditation Plan

Adaptation is the key to our comeditation approach. One potential area of variation is the position. If the subject is able to lie flat, a reclining position is best. The spine should be as straight as possible. Most people in average health have more effective results when no pillow is used, their arms are at their sides, and the hands are rotated with palms facing upward. This is the yoga shavasana position, which we referred to earlier.

Supports, such as pillows, should be used to provide comfort and stabilization if the subject is not able to recline fully. A subject with spinal curvature may require a small pillow under the head and neck. If a substantial lift is required, an additional pillow under the shoulders will help prevent strain. Someone with leg pain may find that a pillow under the knees is helpful. Lower back pain may be helped by having pillows that extend from under the buttocks, become higher under the knees, and become lower from the calves to the feet. A person with a swollen abdomen, as in advanced pregnancy or fluid distension from cirrhosis, may find it necessary to turn sideways. Then, the upper limbs should be supported away from the body.

A person who cannot lean back because of shortness of breath may lean forward on pillows piled high on a table to allow both full chest expansion and total support for relaxation. A person who has developed limb contractures should be helped to lie as straight as possible with supports to prevent the limbs from resting heavily upon the body or from flopping when relaxation is achieved. If contractured limbs are extended as much as possible, they will often stretch more with total relaxation. This may provide an opportunity for rehabilitation.

~

Beverly was developing contractures because of inactivity and withdrawal as her multiple sclerosis advanced. Her brother saw a half-hour interview featuring Richard and Hulen on TV, and he began to use comeditation with his sister, trying to relieve her pain and help her sleep better. When he propped her so that she could rest her stiffened limbs, the tension lessened. Soon he found that she not only extended her arms and legs a little better but also began to try feeding herself when the session was scheduled before mealtime. They had not expected to ever begin rehabilitation again. Their enthusiasm was inspiring, because each improvement reinforced Beverly's trust in her brother's eagerness to try a little more. Every day seemed to present a reason for them to delight in shared pleasures.

For many months Beverly did much better, and her brother and she were happy enjoying the freedom they both felt as the result of her smoother muscle use and the decrease in pain. He even arranged for her to spend time in the outside air, looking at her beloved yard. As with any advancing illness, however, onslaughts of the disease were inevitable, so even their triumphs were gradually eroded again.

But Beverly and her brother now had a method of coping. They had discovered that comeditation dealt with acceptance and inner strengthening as well as relaxation. This special communion, in which they shared their mutual devotion and their belief in a higher power, affirmed them both even as she was dying.

~

In the care of chronically ill patients, dignity is demonstrated by the spirit of those who persevere. Because developing handicaps impede smooth muscle function and limit range and flexibility, the afflicted person tends to stop trying. Also, others are inclined to perform tasks for the patient in order to avoid watching the struggle, to avoid the embarrassment of clumsy motions and spills, and to avoid having to clean up after a mess has been created. The patients and families who keep trying, and who are able to treat such incidents with humor and affection, are the heroes of their own personal wars. Each little success is worthy of celebration because every motion regained symbolizes triumph over challenge.

A variety of progressive muscle-relaxation methods may be used. Because we are concerned with letting go as a practice that may eventually lead to the acceptance of natural, imminent death, we recommend using the progression that may be experienced when the body begins to shut down. This relaxation process begins with the toes and feet and proceeds upward; then the guide suggests reviewing the body from head to toes, sending the tensions outward. We adapt the procedure for the individual subject's needs. If the person has back or leg pain, for instance, extra time will be spent on specifically allowing that part to relax.

If the person has done the process many times and has no actual pain, the directions for muscle relaxation may be directed to general areas rather than to the specific body structures. As an example, when working with patients who have pain because of any spinal involvement, we say, "The pelvis and spine are relaxing, and allow your back to fall into the surface"; but many guides go from the legs to the abdomen (omitting the pelvis and spine) because the spine will relax if the muscles associated with the organ structures really do relax. With experience, the subject and assistant can develop their own clues to deal with specific needs.

Likewise, the sounds may vary according to the subject's preferences or moods. The *ahhh* may be comforting. When it is sounded jointly, the subject may enjoy an opportunity to get rid of retained carbon dioxide, or of emotional build-up. Expressing the sound many times may help the subject breathe more deeply and slowly. However, a person who feels exhausted may want to begin listening as soon as possible, rather than continuing the sound, to save on personal effort.

The choice of sounds may vary according to patterns that are developed or according to the mood of each session. A person with increased pain may want a longer period of visualization, or the special (or sacred) words may be so comforting that nothing else is desired. Words that seemed precious at one time may seem inadequate at another time, so the subject should always be given the opportunity to suggest another choice.

To achieve a full meditative experience usually takes about twenty minutes. Twenty minutes, two to four times a day, for any relaxation technique is a recommended therapeutic prescription by leading pain-management specialists.[4] It may not be possible, however, for busy caregivers to spend so much time at the patient's bedside. Also, the patient may want the comedititation most in the middle of the night but be reluctant to ask resting caregivers who have been exhausted from a full day of chores. Or, the patient's hearing difficulties may require amplified sound through earphones.

In such situations, a tape recording may be made to be used by the patient independently, although the special reinforcement created to direct attention to each exhalation is not possible with a recording. When the subject's breathing pattern is not directly observed in order to have each sound timed to the moment of exhalation, the effect is irregular because the specific respiratory cycle of the patient will vary from time to time. The use of a taped session is occasionally desirable, however, because it provides a sense of independence. Being able to help himself or herself is especially important when the patient becomes concerned about being a burden to others.

To avoid distractions, we generally advise against touching the meditating person, but if the subject is deaf or the helper is blind, exceptions must be made. The deaf subject may be signaled in the dominant hand with a light squeeze or ASL signed with the chosen words. The blind assistant may lightly touch the recipient's blanket near the diaphragm to determine the chest movements. The reason to avoid extraneous touching is that the consciousness of the subject must be freed from all distractions. Later, when the activities of the day are resumed, touching may be a comforting way to express care and to provide skin stimulation—unless the patient is extremely sensitive to touch.

If the person is actually dying or is in a state of extremis he or she may want to have the comeditation continue for several hours. In such a situation, compromises must be attempted. Dying often takes a long time, and no one actually knows when death will come. Even in coma, a patient will need certain medications on schedule to avoid pain and greater confusion. The body needs to be moved frequently, soiling must be cleaned away, and the skin should be massaged lightly to avoid rapid skin breakdown. A helper may be able to make the sound while the caregiver continues the essential tasks.

One family lightly sang or hummed the father's favorite hymn as he died from a massive stroke. The hospital staff were told to maintain their schedule but to let the family members remain at the bedside to keep this vigil. The staff performed their duties quietly while respecting the family's attendance. The daughter who told us this story believed that her father's breathing became less labored during their "meditation" period. She said he died peacefully although he had seemed restless before she suggested using this variation of comeditation.

Even a comatose patient has periods of sleep that are distinct from more wakeful periods. While people have emerged from coma to tell of feeling more secure and comforted by hearing their special words, they are not sufficiently aware during the sleep period to justify exhausting the caregivers further. Playing a prerecorded tape that has been looped may allow the patient to come in and out of awareness with the contact provided by the meditation, while giving the caregivers a well-deserved break.

Although a reduction in the respiratory rate is expected in well and active people, when respiration is compromised, the rate may slow but still be considered more rapid than normal. We do not have a goal for the patient's breathing rate. However, if the person has been hyperventilating (twenty-four to fifty or more breaths a minute) and the breathing drops to within the rate for a normal person with that physical condition (such as from forty-six to twenty-eight breaths a minute), the process can be considered successful in reducing anxiety.

When we teach health-care professionals, we emphasize the appropriateness of instructing a patient with lung involvement by using the principles of "good chest P.T." That is, a respiratory physical therapist teaches such a patient to clear the tiny lung sacs (alveoli)—the air exchange units—by consciously expelling the old air (well over 3 percent carbon dioxide, and less than 16 percent oxygen), so fresh air (at least 21 percent oxygen and only traces of carbon dioxide) can come in to provide oxygen to the blood. As stated in chapter 2, because nature abhors a vacuum we know that good air will be inhaled automatically if there is space in the lung.

If a lung area is filling up with fluid because of a pathologic condition such as heart failure or infection, that happens regardless of air exchange. Even in those situations it is better to let the lungs work as deeply as possible to take advantage of the entire lung capacity. Anyone with respiratory compromise will demonstrate an effective response if the breathing rate is reduced from frank hyperventilation (more than thirty breaths a minute) to a slightly accelerated rate (more than twenty breaths a minute).

A person who is able to breathe normally will possibly breathe as slowly as two to eight breaths a minute when fully relaxed and waiting for inhalation to occur. Do not be alarmed. With deep inhalation, proper oxygenation is occurring (the patient is getting enough air), and the fingers and lips remain their normal color.

This slower breathing rate indicates a deep meditative level, which will allow the person to experience that special point between self-consciousness and universal consciousness. This is the point at which the person realizes that the true inner self is transcendent. We often hear reactions similar to that expressed by Jeannine, a minister, who wished to be able to share our technique with her parishioners. While she had used meditation as a form of prayer in the past, Jeannine was amazed by the depth of her experience. She said, "I was enfolded by this warm, clear light. I realized that I wasn't breathing for a while, but I knew that I was safe, and that everything was just as it should be." To her, this was the reassurance of God's love that she tried to convey to the members of her congregation in relating the stories she had heard of near-death experiences.

Some studies suggest that apnea (a period of not breathing) may reduce the urgency to breathe because of "complacent accommodation"—the willingness to accept whatever occurs because the body becomes accustomed to the feeling. For instance, it is suspected that an asthma patient may not seek medical care quickly enough because the reduced oxygen (which occurs when airways are compromised) becomes a nonthreatening part of that person's life when that same feeling is experienced frequently over a long time. It must be remembered, however, that the disease does provide symptoms that are clear warning signs to the asthmatic. Relaxation should be used to complement the patient's treatment program, not delay it. By separating from activity; taking deep, even breaths while beginning the home emergency medical response; and then trying to reduce anxiety by a relaxation process (such as comeditation, engaging the careful attention of another), the patient is able to control anxiety until professional emergency care is obtained. Because the physical reflections of emotion are prominent in respiratory function, the underlying thoughts of the person having a respiratory crisis are probably as important as the outward behavior.

Automatic control of respiration, which is centered in the brain stem (the only part of the body that must fail for death to be legally established), stimulates deep and rapid breathing when there is insufficient oxygen. The signals to breathe stimulate the chest muscles and diaphragm to rise and fall to aid the lungs' air exchange until the body's needs are met. This automatic response always overrides apnea unless there is pathological injury to the brain stem (as in a stroke), airway obstruction (as occurs with asthma secretions), or other structural blockage. As comeditation is calming and allows more complete use of lung capacity, it will not contribute to the problem, even in patients who have those conditions.

We have introduced the comeditation method to patients who experienced acute angina pectoris (pain radiating from the heart). We first instructed them to breathe deeply and calmly while taking out a nitroglycerine tablet and placing it under the tongue as prescribed, then resting in a comfortable position for a meditation session while the medicine dissolved and had a chance to work. If the pain was no better after five minutes (about the time of the shared *ahhh* sounds) the patient could signal with a nod of the head for the assistant to place a second tablet under his or her tongue. If no assistant were available, the patient could place two tablets within easy reach for self-administration without altering position.

The third tablet could be taken, if needed, following the next five-minute segment. A visualization of the pain dispersing and going to the horizon may help the patient tolerate the discomfort until the medicine and the calming effect of the meditation combine to correct the heart-muscle spasms. If an emergency rescue is necessary, the call can be appropriately made following the twenty-minute session, as most doctors advise their angina pectoris patients to take one nitroglycerine tablet at a time, taking three if necessary, and evaluating their condition every five minutes. The patient should rest quietly, in the meditative state if possible, until the rescue squad arrives. If a cardiac crisis is taking place, damage should be lessened when physical and emotional stresses are controlled, thereby minimizing the heart's workload.

A transpersonal experience, such as the event of perfect light described by Jeannine, is a realization of transcendence. Some people have interpreted it as life and death blossoming in radiance. It is not a method for speeding oneself into death. Every death occurs biologically. If the body is not ready to die, there is no mental exercise that will literally propel one into the hereafter. The experience simply expands conscious awareness beyond pettiness and narrow fears.

As a link between shared lives and a peaceful transition, comeditation becomes part of the survivors' treasured memories after their loved one dies. In addition, however, the qualities of gentle care and emotional fulfillment derived from comeditation can ease the grief process.

A group of young professionals had been concerned about their friend who was dying of AIDS as his loving wife attended to his confused behavior, his many sores and rashes, his aggressive pneumonia, and his diarrhea. Then they realized that she, rather than the patient, was in need of emotional help as well as rest. They contacted the local AIDS Action Committee to gain more assistance, and they learned to do comeditation so they could help her relax when they visited. The man died after more than three weeks of disoriented delirium. But instead of being relieved, his wife was despondent because her own future seemed so uncertain and because her frantic activity was now replaced with vacant grief. In addition to offering her their loving support, the friends again gave her regular sessions of comeditation to help her find emotional calm. Gradually she was able to regain her self-control and confidence as an independent woman. She said that those personal sessions brought her from withdrawal to self-realization.

We have presented the comeditation technique to AIDS support groups, hospice staff, and stroke and arthritis support groups to teach someone who is in the patient's home frequently a method to help ease discomfort and despair. As one of the many spokes in the wheel of total caregiving, comeditation is useful. As the most adaptable therapy in addressing the many aspects of the individual body, mind, and spirit, it is unifying.

Comeditation and Children

Many pediatric specialists have found that stress-reduction techniques are as important with anxious children as with adults. The authors' lecture audiences frequently includes parents and child-care nurses. An Australian pediatric unit supervisor has made comeditation a part of the routine nursing-care plan. When speaking with the pediatric social work staff of a leading Boston, Massachusetts, cancer hospital, we found that they all used some form of relaxation with their clients and wanted to learn comeditation because of our adaptive instructions. Although touching may distract an adult, picking up a very small child serves as an immediate chest-to-chest breathing contact.

Even when the child cannot be removed from bed, a caregiver can make a sound at the rate of the child's crying and thus begin the calming process by distracting the child and providing the security of another's response. Gradual relaxation follows. Numbers can be used in counting with a child. They are familiar sounds to most children, they stimulate interest as the sequence is anticipated, and they cause sensory dulling because of repetition. Numbers may be used to encourage imaginative visualization. Although a distressed child may need a little more guidance, the child's creative mind can be allowed to expand. Older children enjoy choosing or creating a song or poem as a special, personal refrain. Hearing these words gives the effect of a quieting bedtime story—the parent's voice provides security, while the special attention assures the child of another's care. If the child has a role in planning the words or the song, the affirmation of worth is personal. Sometimes children begin writing creatively as a result of this inspiration.

Adapting Comeditation to Modern Life

We work in efficiently engineered industries and homes, use computers to complete transactions and store information, and worry about being the people we want to be. We experience anxiety because of our choices, our fears about insecurity in the midst of plenty, and our relationships. Underneath these features of modern life, we share the same basic drives and fears as everyone who has ever lived. When we are about to die we want to be separated from pain, we want people who care nearby, and we are concerned about "passing on." Both during active life and during the period of approaching death, we want to be able to feel at ease and to slow the racing of our hearts and minds. But learning to settle into a quieting mode is difficult because it is contrary to the habits we have learned throughout our lives.

Through the 1970s, studies in the field of body-mind function were reported by the popular press. New-age workshops, pain-management clinics, and stress-reduction programs were beginning to be accepted in many areas of the United States. Thus, some of the Buddhists' principles were being taught already by these innovators. In spite of those early programs, the heart of the Tibetans' transitional process was not being used. Specifically, two aspects were neglected: one person working directly with another, and the helper making a sound at the precise moment of the other's exhalation to heighten the consciousness of the other.

When a sound is made directly as the listener is breathing out, there is a feeling of interconnection. The sound triggers a comforting awareness of another who cares in a very intimate way. Positive reinforcement occurs through a social communication. Likewise, the synchronicity of exhalation and sound provides a direct connection with the listener's physical action, allowing the body to relax, as defenses are not needed. The feeling of being cared for and of physical security leads to psychological comfort. As physical, psychological, and social concerns are satisfied the listener is free to recognize the spirituality within, or to realize inner clarity and serenity.

~

Gus, a hospice patient who was dying at home, had an episode of acute congestive heart failure a couple of hours before we visited. He and his family had fought fiercely because they could not face his death, even though they all knew it was inevitable. He was moaning continually, but he denied that he needed more pain medication, although he admitted that pain was constant. As his moan was a common expression, we offered to use his sound as the sound of *ahhh* (expressed as *ouaahhh* from the back of the throat, then echoing inside the mouth for the length of the recipient's exhalation) in a relaxation process. He responded quickly, saying, "At last someone understands." Noting evidence within the room of his Roman Catholic background, we included a brief explanation of the procedure a suggestion that Amen is similar in verbal quality, but he asked to use only *ahhh* throughout the session. He experienced a deep meditation while staying in contact with the comeditation assistant during the entire period.

At the conclusion, with tears in his eyes, he reached out and said, "Thank you so much." On being asked how the session affected him, he said all pain was gone and he felt totally at peace, but he didn't want to talk. He indicated that he wanted to remain in that state of tranquility as long as possible, yet he accepted his family's noisy return with a faint smile. (We will return to Gus's story in chapter 8.)

~

In working with many people, most of whom we have not known previously, we have discovered that physical, psychological, and social comfort are expressed following comeditation. Our workshops have included health-care professionals and lay persons of many educational levels and degrees of physical fitness. When there is sufficient time, participants divide into groups of twos and threes so each person may both experience and give a session of comeditation. When working with a client, rather than acting strictly as therapists we make it a practice to teach the method to someone who is close to that person. Thus we are able to assess the effects of comeditation on both recipients and assistants.

It is not unusual for the assistant to find that the process has been beneficial to him or her as well as to the patient if the assistant has maintained a comfortable body position during the session. While there have been varying degrees of responses, virtually everyone who has experienced comeditation has been impressed by the degree of relaxation and the physical and emotional renewal felt at the end of the sessions. We have concluded, therefore, that any responsible person can do the process with any other person, under most circumstances in which relaxation is desired.

A teacher can instruct the client's personal friends or family members, other caregivers, or volunteers. When there is a close tie between the two participants, and the sounds or words used are particularly meaningful to the listener, the effect may be even more profound. Both facilitator and recipient must, however, be willing to repeat the process regularly and to exchange their observations in order to work out the most helpful pattern for the listener.

Each session will be different. Some will seem dramatically effective. Some will seem filled with distractions. And many will ease the participants into comfort and well-being, as expected, while the acute issues become less disturbing. The subtle effects of this practice should not be underestimated. The reduction of tension, the lessened muscle spasms, the calmer thinking, and the improved resolve combined with other aspects of balanced daily living will lead to improvement of many disturbing issues. Problems associated with pain, anxiety, and inactivity may become workable simply because the body is less tense and anxiety is less overpowering.

This is the result of body-mind coordination. Through learning to relax deeply in comeditation, and then becoming aware of how certain areas feel when tension varies, the subject can learn to make small, effective adjustments during normal activity. When the assistant is able to share observations and to provide encouragement for timely responses (such as relaxing tense muscles when confronting stress) the benefits are multiplied.

~

Doris had developed a mysterious neurological illness, which affected her limbs and caused her to choke when she attempted to swallow. Her weight went from her normal "over 100 pounds" to 83 and then to 77 pounds. She was so frightened to swallow that she sometimes spit out her own saliva after it pooled in her mouth. Therefore she was not only very thin but was unable to take the nutrients she needed, and she was dehydrated.

We suggested that she use a relaxation method because her body seemed so tense. Although we could not address the biological cause of her problem, it seemed that one aspect that we could affect was overreactive guarding. She would need a lot of coaching to overcome such intense fear, but help was available through a very supportive husband. Also, she and her husband had built their religious faith into their lives; their prayers were a daily routine, and their church membership made them part of a warm society. The special words that Doris chose gave thanks to God's goodness. Characteristically of her, she worked hard at positive thinking although she was inwardly terrified. This was both an advantage and an obstacle in her recovery.

Because she required herself to be optimistic, she geared herself into a hopeful attitude and a willingness to continually try. But she got her encouragement from increasingly tinier efforts that did not lead to disaster but still caused her to go downhill. Our work with her, therefore, had to become multifaceted. First, she had to learn how to fully relax. Second, she had to learn to account for her foods and liquids accurately in order to understand exactly what she was taking in and how it was affecting her body. Then, she had to learn how to apply the relaxation principles to her activities of daily living. She had to be willing to adjust her foods and her actions to her actual needs. After she began practicing comeditation with her husband as assistant, we coached them both to recognize how her neck muscles engorged and tightened when she became anxious. She had to be willing to relax as fully as if she were going to sleep when she thought she was choking to death. By applying the relaxation principles she used in comeditation to the feeling of choking, she was able to let pureed foods slide down her throat. Gradually, she transferred these lessons to chewing and then to swallowing soft solid food. She also applied these principles to walking and performing household tasks.

Doris no longer needed home visits when she weighed 97 pounds, and she was able to go to a restaurant without fear. She and her husband gave special thanks to God before eating their meal, because they believed that the prayer they had used as their special words in comeditation and their attitude of thankfulness and trust had provided a very special connection with God's help.

~

This couple used comeditation as a way of understanding how true relaxation felt and how extreme tension could affect swallowing. Anyone can lie down to think about relaxing the bones, muscles, and tendons alone. Commonly, sleep will follow, but when anxiety is high, both mind and muscles tighten during sleep. Sometimes awakening is less strenuous than trying to sleep. Irritated nerve fibers transmit new stimulation as increased irritation, especially if there is pain.[5] Therefore, as long as a person's body is experiencing elements of irritation, whatever the cause, this "on-edge" quality is always present unless the person's conscious attention is changed.

Doris needed to have a more effective means of cellular retraining if she were to actually be able to release the automatic guarding that had become integrated in her continual, lifelong efforts to try harder. Therefore, comeditation, with her loving husband coaching while also praising God's blessings, permitted Doris to relinquish her tension more completely than she had ever done before. Alone, comeditation is helpful in allowing the person to fully relax because it provides total acceptance and relieves the person from the effort of trying. The primary meditator just listens and lets go. By learning to actually relax, Doris was able to relearn control of her neck responses even when she felt that she was choking to death.

By adapting the experiences of the relaxation process when at rest to her movements and reactions when moving (swallowing, walking, doing household chores) and interacting (thinking of herself in relation to her husband, her church, and her family), Doris and her husband used a biobehavioral approach. When this approach is integrated with self-understanding, it becomes a valuable tool rather than simply a restful interlude. Through certain actions such as posture, exercise variations, thoughts, responses (both emotional and functional), and relaxation periods, an individual's behavior can control the effects of the nervous system on the body and the mind.

Biobehavioral training is a legitimate caregiving process. It is a treatment method that many health-insurance companies now recognize as a necessary approach to patient rehabilitation or care in progressive illness. With third-party-payer sanction, a caregiver can provide holistic support for the patient on an emotional level while helping the patient learn a means of physical relief by letting go. That is, the person is enabled to discover the subtle effects of fleeting thoughts, and the power of simple responses to maintain control within one's own self.

Personal Challenges

Of course, at first we must remind ourselves throughout each day to apply the new lessons. Being creatures of habit, we must monitor ourselves constantly when trying to reinforce and to improve our self-management techniques. Learning relaxation principles with the help of another can be carried into auditory memory, but being up and about, without the assistant's guidance, requires a person to act independently.

Because, for many people, it is not possible to have another's assistance frequently, an electrical biofeedback unit may act as a guide to help the subject know when the relaxation response is biologically effective. But even with such a machine, an instructor is required in the learning and developing phases. Although some people seem to understand these techniques quite naturally, many require more intense instruction. The comeditation method is used by many biofeedback specialists during the early training phase, especially with their more anxious clients.

It is, of course, appropriate to recognize that any one-on-one relaxation instruction is a form of comeditation. The instructor works with the student by watching the student's body and facial reactions, adjusting the timing and suggestions as he or she senses the student's readiness. Respiration provides an important clue to the instructor. The teacher's voice is a reassuring reinforcement to the pupil. The process will allow them to share a closer relationship than they would have if the instructor had merely told the client what to do and then disappeared into another room. Later, the learner will mentally hear the instructor's voice whenever the directions are remembered.

In comeditation it is absolutely necessary that the process be understood and accepted by both the recipient and the guide before the session begins. The power of comeditation is due to the nurturing effect of hearing preestablished words and sounds that are synchronized with the recipient's out-breaths. Both recipient and assistant are focused only on their mutual endeavor. There must be no hurried urgings, no surprises, no contrary thoughts. If either person is reluctant for any reason, the session should be postponed until the problem is explored or until another partner is available. An attempt at meditating alone would be more meaningful than sharing such a precious experience with an antagonistic or unsympathetic person.

～

Ellen had severe back and leg pain caused by pressure from a spinal tumor. Her husband wanted to help her by giving comeditation. The times he was most eager to please her, however, were when he had been to a bar drinking and bemoaning their troubles to his alcoholic friends.

Although she found that a comeditation session could transform leg pain that she called "about 9" to "under 2" (on a scale from zero [no pain] to 10 [the worst pain imaginable]), she did not want her husband to be near her when he was drunk. In fact, the sound of his voice made her so angry that her additional muscle tightening seemed to make the pain go beyond her worst imagining. We prepared for Ellen an audio-tape of progressive muscle relaxation followed by the suggestion that she visualize her favorite scene. The recording was synchronized to her breath at an average rate when she was emotionally upset, then to the slower rate she used as she relaxed. Next we recorded soothing music of her choice, to run to the end, because we could not make a sound timed specifically to her exhalations if we were not present. She found that the tape helped her pain and her anger toward her husband while allowing her to avoid his attention when he upset her.

Later, when she required more care and her respirations became irregular, her sister and her daughter learned the comeditation method, scheduling their sessions to potentiate her pain medication. Also, on becoming her primary caregivers, they required her husband to go to AA as a condition of remaining in the home. Ellen's anger lessened, as did her depression and helpless anxiety.

~

To achieve the most profound effect, both the recipient and the assistant need to recognize that this sharing is a sacred trust. The subject's breath is symbolic of that person's life essence. The guidance offered is a bridge between rational thought and inner consciousness. When deep relaxation occurs, respiration, heart rate, and blood pressure, as well as the glandular functions associated with the autonomic nervous system, are calmed. In this way, the mind controls the body. The process is therapeutic because the mind and body together learn how to overcome stress. Many medical benefits, therefore, may be gained simply because tension is not present to stimulate irritating neurotransmitters or cause an overproduction of waste chemicals within the tissues.

However, we do not claim that the comeditation method can be used to cure a seriously progressive disease. Sickness of any sort must be managed one hour and one day at a time. But all illnesses can be tolerated better when anxiety, pain, and fears are reduced. Likewise, it is appropriate for a person with a healthy body but a troubled mind to use an approach that is effective.

Later, when death is actually near, the methods for calming and inner strengthening that have already been learned will provide automatic comfort as metabolic imbalances interfere with rational thought. Dying, itself, becomes a subtle change of focus toward inner peace. Fear has no purpose when the spirit is at ease inside and outside of life.

4
A HOLISTIC APPROACH TO HEALTH CARE

~

Life is short, art is long, opportunity fleeting, experiment deceptive, and judgment difficult. Hence, not only the physician, but also the patient, and everyone else who is involved in the situation, must cooperate.

—Hippocrates (approx. 400 B.C.)

Holistic Means Integrating the Whole

The wholeness of life is realized when every part of one's being is integrated into a harmonious pattern. As a person works through life's challenges and satisfactions, each episode plays a role in the individual's whole development. Character and inner quality develop through trials and periods of personal growth. The whole is more than the sum of the parts; the unique blend of genetic inheritances and life experiences produces the total identity of any one of us.

Being holistically oriented means recognizing the influences of every action or inaction upon the whole person that each of us is now and is becoming. The foods we eat, the movements made by our bodies, the thoughts we entertain, and the waste and projections we disperse in the outside world are parts of our holistic behavior that affects ourselves and our society. Our holistic natures are held within a balance that is maintained throughout our lives, whether we apply conscious effort or not. This nature does not change regardless of health or disease, or whether we are newborn, in the prime of life, or dying.

When any problem disturbs the body, the mind, or both, the whole person is affected. When the body is dysfunctional, the individual becomes anxious. If the person is emotionally distraught, neuroendocrine stressors may lead to changes in normal function in addition to whatever illness is present. When a person becomes sick for a period of time, social relationships are affected. As life tries to accommodate different rules and unstable circumstances, the person may begin to question an earlier philosophic perspective. Thus, disturbances can easily mount into broad threats to wellness, which relate only indirectly to a disease process. Holistic health care is based on the ideal of addressing the many aspects of the body-mind and balancing the whole. Like all health-care approaches, comeditation is an effective tool when used as an adjunct of a total program. Like most other nonmedical approaches, it is considered an alternative therapy. *Alternative* implies a practice that is a choice rather than part of a standard protocol. This does not mean that the technique has low value but rather that it has not yet become widely utilized in standard medical programs.

As a part of a holistic approach, comeditation has a fourfold effect, with positive influences on each aspect of the experiencer: physical, mental, emotional, and spiritual. As the body is relaxed the mind is allowed to become peaceful; conversely, as the emotions are tempered the body is soothed as well. The assistant's presence serves as a protective link between the inner self and outer reality. In the process of deep meditation, a transcendent or spiritual awareness may be realized.

Past and Present Approaches to Health Care

Many health-care techniques that are now designated "holistic" and "alternative" have evolved from practices of long ago, just as have many basic medical treatments. Holistic health care began when the earliest humans reacted to each others' illness or injury. Applying astringent herbs to reduce a swelling bruise, rubbing sore muscles after a strenuous trek, or assisting a difficult childbirth are examples of humans using materials at hand and their own bodies to ease and heal themselves and one another. The vast array of caregiving efforts developed by our ancestors were perpetuated through the ages by every family into our own twentieth century. The families' limitations were supplemented by special members of each society who learned and practiced healing techniques, but these healers and their patients acknowledged the mystery between recovery and failed health as a spiritual power.

Even today, our most skilled physicians know that some patients have apparently miraculous recoveries when a condition seems to be beyond help, and other patients die in spite of the most dramatically new, laboratory-perfect management of a well-understood disease process. Just as in ancient times, modern health care requires a blend of physical competence, psychological well-being, social concern, and spiritual vitality.

As discussed earlier, holistic health encompasses the whole person. Each aspect of the patient contributes to the integrity of the other aspects of that person, and each member of a group affects the others within that family, their society, and therefore the world. This concept grew during the "back to basics" period of the 1960s because many people, especially in the United States, became aware that "medicine" had become an unquestionable authority.

In the days of the American frontier, men and women were strengthened by an attitude of responsibility for themselves. This self-reliance was gradually undermined in urban society, with its distinct divisions between jobs and status levels. A paternalistic medical system developed a hierarchy, with the physician and surgeon at the top, the ancillary health-care services as adjuncts to filling the doctors' orders, and the patient (the object of the orders) at the bottom. The doctor-neighbor-friend who had once shared the townspeople's personal struggles became an apparently remote and intellectually superior being. In a system that honored scientific objectivity along with industrial and commercial predominance, medical knowledge and skills began to erode the individual's role in self-determination.

In the 1950s, patients were expected to be hospitalized through long periods of illness and recovery. While the family physician (usually male) continued to think of himself as an educated friend with whom his patients could share their complaints and anxieties, he functioned as an unquestioned figure within a hospital that supported his control. Staff members were not allowed to tell the patient what medicine was being given, what his or her vital signs were, and, often, even what diagnosis was being treated. These secrecies were believed to be "for the patient's own good," as the practice of medicine was considered too complicated and mysterious for lay people to understand. Draining wounds were considered too offensive and too needful of expert care to be dealt with at home. Anyone who was sick "belonged in a hospital."

When Hulen was an eighteen-year-old student nurse in 1950, she found herself trying to understand the attitudes and practices that prevailed in the hospital world. Professionalism was synonymous with efficiency. If the doctor wanted the patient to have information, it was his role—but not his obligation—to provide it. Decision making was believed to be too complex for the patient to face, because lack of knowledge might cause irresponsible choices, and a prognosis of handicap or death might provoke depression and hopelessness.

At that time, the medical statistics provided little expectation of cure for cancer or any chronic disease, and less proof of divine intervention. Surgeons removed lesions and performed treatments to make the patient more comfortable and to lengthen the period of survival. An elderly woman who was relieved of severe pain following a nerve block became ecstatic, saying, "Oh thank God, thank God, Doctor!" The surgeon replied, "God gave you the pain, you should thank me for relieving it. When it comes back, I'll treat you again." This was not an unusual comment for that doctor. This surgeon's philosophy was revealed in his disdain for the beliefs held by others. Although his skills established his limitations, they allowed him to claim his successes as well. While this patient–doctor exchange did not reflect the medical profession as a whole, it was typical of the time. Science was factual, devoid of illusion, and potentially empowering.

A decade later, in the 1960s, the hippie lifestyle combined inspiration from self-sufficient rural societies with the intellectual knowledge and questioning of college-educated youth. Many young adults formed communities where they provided for themselves with naturally grown food, used herbal and body conditioning therapies, and helped one another with childbirth and child rearing. Members of this emerging society began to consider that individuals could and should have responsibility for their own bodies. In health care, medical experts became viewed as advisors and skilled technicians rather than as all-powerful authorities. Patients made an effort to become informed, make judgments, and work out their own health-care program.

This new attitude was also embraced by the early hospice advocates, even those of us who were health-care workers ourselves. Throughout the late 1970s and early 1980s, older adults in cities throughout the upper American continent and Europe organized to develop hospice programs to provide home support for those who were terminally ill. Their goal was to give compassionate, personal care to individuals whose lives could not be saved by invasive measures. By emphasizing home care, hospices enabled people to die surrounded by the love and comfort that their own homes symbolized. Both groups—the folk communities and hospices—proved how capable and courageous the average family could be in health care.

Although public-health nurses began teaching basic caregiving techniques to families in their own homes as early as the 1890s, procedures became more complex and home and hospital care became correspondingly more complicated. By the 1960s, nurses' roles became broadened to include teaching clients self-care, which included understanding disease processes and performing appropriate treatments. The further development of this combination—adaptive professional guidance and support, and patient-family self-responsibility—has allowed insurers in the early 1990s to restrict hospital care to the most technologically needful clients.

Now, with such limited admission and discharge policies, however, thousands of patients are required to function mostly on their own. Whether they are eager to do so or not, responsibility for self-care (even complex treatments) and decision making is not only a person's right but a condition of today's economy. While informed client responsibility is the only way to contain spiraling health-care costs, the medical changes that have occurred during the twentieth century have been overwhelming.

The Modern Hospice Concept

The ideals of holistic care are defined best in our modern hospice programs. Those ideals should serve as a guide for any patient-care plan, regardless of the disease status or whether the patient alone or agents within an organization are overseeing the care. Incorporating in 1978, the National Hospice Organization (NHO) established twenty-two standards to direct patient care, recognize family needs, and assure responsibility to the overall community.[1] These standards, appropriate for all health-care programs, can be grouped into five basic principles: symptom management, the patient-family unit, patient autonomy, caregiving team coordination, and community responsibility.

Symptom Management
Symptom management includes pain control and use of other appropriate therapies to prevent or treat distress. This principle is designed not only to address the physical effects of a disease but to consider all related problems within a disease process, including side effects resulting from compensatory

actions and treatments. Discomfort in a certain area may prompt a person to go to a doctor to determine a diagnosis and treatment; but as the condition continues problems are not restricted to that specific area.

~

Bill's original problem was cancer of the lung. Early surgery and chemotherapy had cleared the lung site. But as he recovered from the surgery and the tissues healed, he had to overcome soreness from traumatized muscles and bones and he needed to exercise to expand his remaining lung capacity. In a few months he had intolerable lower back pain, although x-rays did not show a spinal lesion. His doctor ordered morphine for the pain and also ordered a home-care nurse.

Bill became a hospice patient because laboratory tests indicated that the cancer was developing in the liver and bladder, thus predicting widespread metastasis. While he complained of "less wind," when we first met him, he did not have to struggle to breathe, and he knew that oxygen could be available to him at home if he needed it. The patient was satisfied that he had "put up a fight" even though he knew the cancer would kill him. It was his decision to request hospice to be his home-care team because he did not want to prolong dying, but he did want to stay at home and receive help there.

The physician asked the nurse to evaluate Bill's response to the medicine, to help determine the right dosage of the narcotic, and to advise if other care was appropriate. While the medicine was prescribed to control pain, it was important to see that Bill's mind remained alert, that he not have nausea that would prevent him from enjoying food or taking liquids, and that constipation be avoided. These are all common side effects of narcotics, and they are the reason many people suffer rather than take the prescribed medicine. (For a dying patient, addiction is of little concern.) Bill and his family would require assistance and support while carrying out the details of his care.

It was necessary to evaluate the effects of the medicines and various symptoms frequently. By giving the family a notebook of flow sheets, the nurse taught the family to keep a running record so corrections could be made as changes in treatment occurred. Bill's diet had to be designed around his altered taste sensations and his increased need for hydration. Bill and his family were taught appropriate management of his bowel activity, his pain level, his alertness, body care, and exercise needs.

Position changes, walking, and body alignment and strengthening exercises, combined with total relaxation (lying straight in comeditation or using meditative recall) several times a day, helped to reduce the amount of medicine Bill needed, and helped him maintain function and feel that he was the primary decision maker in spite of the disease progress. Nevertheless, both counseling and diversionary activities were needed because of the hopelessness and depression that Bill and his family sometimes felt.

While it was appropriate for them to learn comeditation to help relieve Bill's symptoms and to give them periods of quiet communion together, it was also necessary to limit that time. Each member needed the opportunity to pursue personal interests and to relate to the world outside the sick room. Each person needed to deal privately with the results of this more complicated life.

~

Depression is a normal reaction for many people when they feel they cannot escape the reality of physical and emotional pain and have lost control over their destiny. They all grieve for themselves and their loved ones. They crave their own community support and validation, yet are tied down as part of the home team with redefined roles and undefinable expectations. While the patient is the primary focus, the family members sometimes experience pain and hardship with little consideration of the changes they have had to make or of the problems they face when they must function alone. When hospice was being planned, these issues were taken into account. Now they are part of basic hospice policy and are addressed by all staff members.

The Patient-Family Unit
The family is included with the patient as a total unit. Before health personnel enter their lives, the family members are focused on caring for and about one another. Their interactions provide the basic harmonic chord that symbolizes their lives. Not only does the illness of one of the group affect the family members emotionally, but if the patient needs assistance in physical care it will probably become a family responsibility. Even when caregivers are hired, the patient and the family must decide how to use financial and physical-energy resources, and deal with changes in each person's role. Therefore, hospice programs recognize that both the patient and the individual family members must cope with the illness and the many changes required by each of them. By engaging the family when planning schedules and enlisting vol-

unteers and counselors to provide support, the hospice system attempts to address the needs of everyone within the patient-family unit. Bereavement support for the family members after the patient's death simply verifies the pledge to this primary unit.

Patient Autonomy

Patient autonomy means that the patient makes the decisions regarding treatment. But, the patient should be encouraged to share with those who are closest to him or her, so they are able to understand the reasons behind difficult choices. Similarly, those who have the patient's best interests in mind owe the patient the respect of allowing him or her to express concerns and determine the way that care will go. When there is conflict, dialogue is the only way to allow each to understand the other. In order to resolve difficult situations it is often necessary to experience tears and confront undesirable truths.

During these times, those who are experiencing emotional pain enrich their relationships and obtain comfort through sharing their thoughts and feelings. A person who has a terminal illness knows that his or her body is in trouble, and the loved ones know as well. When family members are silent in the effort to protect the others from an awareness that is already gnawing inside, they distance themselves from one another when they are most needful of support. They need to express their sorrows and their admiration of one another, to give one another solace, and supplement one another's courage. Such interaction reflects mutual respect as the patient is encouraged to make as many choices as possible.

Caregiving-Team Coordination

The caregiving-team approach was devised to address the many physical and emotional problems that come into play when serious illness requires multiple responses and interventions. Communication and coordination are the cornerstones of such caregiving. The goals are always to help the patient manage the pain, to maintain as much physical function as possible for as long as the patient lives, and to enable each day to be as fulfilling as possible. As physical changes occur, the patient's needs and goals change too. Team coordination (including the patient-family unit) allows everyone to work together toward the same goals. When team members share their insights, maintaining strict confidentiality within the team, each team member is able to respond more effectively in providing the appropriate care.

A well-staffed hospice will engage a physician, several registered nurses, a pharmacist advisor, nursing aides, one or more physical therapists, a dietetic consultant, a social worker adept at psychological counseling, a pastoral counselor, and coordinating administrative staff. If the hospice is large or if the client's condition or demonstrated needs warrant other ancillary personnel, an occupational therapist and a recreational or expressive therapist might be engaged. Often, the nurse will fill many of these roles to reduce traffic in and out of the home. A massage therapist, a chiropractor (trained especially to work gently with cancer patients), or an acupuncturist can be recommended for private consultation if the patient believes such treatment would be helpful.

In addition, the hospice staff includes a volunteer coordinator, who trains and supervises an unpaid group of lay and professional caregivers. When assigned to a client the volunteer may serve as a good family friend, provide help in many ways (such as moments of respite for the family to do errands), and act as a patient advocate when medical or family opinions differ. As a form of community support, the volunteer may, on the request of the patient, act as a liaison with the patient's church to encourage "good Samaritan" deeds, spiritual counseling, and/or funeral planning.

Community Responsibility

Public responsibility includes accountability and community education. The educational responsibility of hospice has four components. Teaching the patient-family unit is the first. The goals are to improve factual knowledge of the physical and psychological processes that occur during caregiving and to address the many tasks that must be performed by the patient and family to maintain appropriate care. For instance, learning to give and to take medicines at specified times and in response to certain symptoms results in self-sufficient home care. Modifying the diet to adjust to taste aversions, while assuring that the patient gets the necessary minerals to prevent muscle spasms, and learning to give massage or apply heat or cold to tender areas are other examples of the array of tasks that can be performed by responsive family members. If they understand the reasons why a certain activity is appropriate, they are more willing to make the effort to achieve the benefit.

Presenting programs to the community at large, training organizational volunteers, and training professional caregivers are the other components of the educational commitment. In this context, health-care education has three goals: (1) to understand the principles of caregiving relative to the physical processes and needs of the patient, (2) to understand that changes (including death) are a part of life but that appropriate interventions may be weighed according to their total effect and the client's desires, and (3) to understand that all those who provide care must also take care of themselves.

The next responsibility is to the community as a whole. That is, each professional caregiver and the sponsoring organization must be accountable to the individuals within their care, to the insurers or agency paying for this work, and to the greater community that is dependent on competent services. Record keeping and protocols serve to explain the status of the patient and the actions of the caregivers as well. While much time and a burdensome portion of the basic charges go into the documentation effort, quality assurance is needed both for consumer protection and for improvement of care.

The larger community is also affected by changes in a person's health. Valuable skills may be lost, both within the work force and within the family's social and functional structure. For example, a parent who participated in a child's financial security as well as in school and group activities may suddenly withdraw completely. Not only is the mother unable to support others economically and as a valuable participant, but now both she and her child need support, financially and functionally. And long after the patient dies, the child and all those remaining bear the scars of their loss, which further impacts upon the community. Unresolved experiences of fear, trauma, and alienation affect each one individually. The effects may be seen in schoolroom behavior and job performance. Prolonged grief affects the ability of the spouse to provide family support, and of the children to develop emotionally. Family members may find it hard to care for themselves physically, emotionally, and financially. These are all community health concerns.

All those who work with the patient constitute a team. They will be more effective and understand the patient's total situation better if each recognizes the others' role, and communicates (at least through a liaison, such as a nurse or the patient) when appropriate. In the present Medicare system, for instance, the doctor is responsible for signing a form that describes the orders: the functions each member of a home health care team will perform. These must be reexamined at least every eight weeks. However, the case manager (usually the nurse) prepares the form and confirms that these tasks are being carried out throughout the commitment period. This method assures responsibility as well as the necessity for the treatment.

In the development of a care plan, the patient's attitude is as central to the overall picture as are the symptoms. His or her desires, hopes, and fears influence a predetermined plan of action that must be respected at the moment of crisis if the patient is not able to weigh the facts and express a choice. The caregivers and family are obligated to try to honor the patient's requests, and they depend upon community support (such as ambulance transport to the hospital and funeral rituals) to verify their public connection.

The History of Hospice

The word *hospice* is derived from the Latin *hospes,* which refers to both host and guest—literally, a place of shelter. The Hospitaler Knights of the Crusades maintained welfare stations called "hospices" for the weary, wounded, and dying. One of Florence Nightingale's first nurses, Mary Aikenhead, founded a shelter for the incurably ill in Dublin after the Crimean War. Aikenhead's hospice served as a model for the Irish Sisters of Charity.

Working in the Sisters of Charity Hospice of St. Joseph in London, in the 1960s, Dr. Cicely Saunders had developed the theories and caregiving skills of pain and symptom relief that led to the modern hospice concept. In 1967, Dr. Saunders opened St. Christopher's Hospice on Sydenham Hill, near London, as the first facility established to provide adequate, quickly responsive symptom management while nurturing the clients and their families with dignity and compassion through physical decline and death.[2] There, she established a pain-management rehabilitation policy to help patients cope with physical changes as they occurred. In addition, she developed the practice of patient-family support to encourage all family members to communicate and interact with the dying patient.[3]

Her theories included expecting that the patient might improve so the patient could go home, especially if family and visiting caregivers provided support. She allowed controlled-substance pain medication to remain at the patient's bedside so the patient could take the medicine in the early stages of pain return and thus forestall extreme suffering. This allowed many patients to actually use less narcotic, thereby becoming more alert and more functional.

She also opened the unit for families to bring their children to visit. She established the staff's children's nursery, which had regular interaction with the patients. Later, she determined that one day a week no visitors would be allowed; this provided respite for the family and private time for the patients during a very exhausting period.

Rehabilitative therapies were used to maintain and improve function, for in spite of most patient's declining potential, they would experience less pain if circulation were maintained and bed position was good. The patients' spirits improved when they were able to do things for themselves. In addition, psychological and spiritual counseling was addressed by social services and pastoral care according to the client's needs and choices.[4]

Dr. Saunders visited to the Boston, Massachusetts, area in December 1970, and immediately Hulen joined a small staff dedicated to implementing her ideals, under the guidance of Dr. John Noble at Middlesex County Hospital. Whatever was judged as appropriate to help a patient manage discomfort and enhance his or her quality of life was ordered. Therapists, a nutritionist, social-service staff, pastoral counselors, and even housekeeping staff were involved in addressing every patient's needs. When an artist patient had a difficult period, Hulen brought in paint supplies and encouraged her to express her feelings. When a patient feared he would never see his dog again, his family was allowed to "sneak" his dog onto the unit. Special family events were arranged. People began to live longer than expected, possibly because their needs were fully supported while they felt they were living within their own extended family.

While the European community embraced Dr. Saunders's principles, it was the Americans who effected a revolution from impersonal hospital technology to gentle home support. In valuing the right to life, American health care had taken the authoritative stance that whatever *can* be done *must* be done to sustain life in any form. The great community-sponsored hospice movement across America insisted that these hospital policies be modified. By acknowledging that life will eventually end, those who understood the hospice ideals found that the right to liberty and the pursuit of happiness became more precious. Complementing these basic caregiving principles, the landmark work of Dr. Elisabeth Kübler-Ross, *On Death and Dying* (1969), became an important reference for professionals who worked with the dying. The psychiatrist's attempts to boldly talk with the terminally ill and understand their viewpoints balanced the hospice approach, which changed caregiving itself.

Hospice Development

The hospice movement developed as a response of families and caregivers to the medical approach that considered any death to be "100 percent noncompliant to outcome auditing standards." Perhaps that last phrase sounds like a humorous exaggeration, but it has never been amusing to be involved in resuscitative efforts based on a hospital policy designed to protect the hospital rather than account for the patient's best interests. Before hospice standards were recognized, an institution with a high death rate would be judged as providing lower-quality care. That is, in reviews of the record, if the patient died the care was evaluated as a total failure, no matter how sick the patient or how impeccable the care. The basis of these standards was that any condition, even old age or aggressive cancer, might be considered a combination of signs and symptoms that could be managed almost indefinitely with measures to adjust chemical imbalances and overcome invading disease processes. No one wanted to take the responsibility for death. Medical personnel often viewed the death of a patient as a symbol of their own personal failure to meet the medical challenges. Lacking the appreciation of the positive aspects of letting the patient go—the end of physical suffering, the application of family and community resources to more resolvable problems, releasing the spirit for its next phase—medical protocol demanded the restoration of life followed by progression within the system's options.

As treatment technologies multiplied, people began to resent the attention given to medical issues rather than to the suffering person. Many people wanted control over their own and their loved ones' experiences when death was known to be near. If the person was dying in spite of the most aggressive medical care available, the only controllable factor was the environment. They disagreed with the notion that any treatment that might possibly halt each threat of death should be undertaken, if that meant the patient's pain, pride, and history of being human were virtually ignored.

∿

Henry, one of our earliest patients with terminal-stage cancer of the lung, was in a hospital not served by a hospice. We were called by Henry's wife when he had suggested that his old friend Richard might help. His respiration was very rapid, but he was receiving intravenous fluid that contained a medicine to control the accumulation of fluid in his lungs. An oxygen mask augmented the amount of oxygen available to him. Gathered around the bed, his brothers tried to make small talk with him to engage his wisecracking wit without speaking frankly of their feelings, although they all knew he was dying. Henry's wife told us that his request to call us as thanatologists was his coded way of admitting that he was ready for death to happen that day.

We were eager to help Henry relax and breathe more deeply so he would not have to strain so much. His whole countenance suggested tension and extreme effort. But when we helped him let go of guarding efforts, and when he let his mind float with the sounds of a voice cued to letting his breath move outward toward the horizon, his respirations slowed, his face and body softened, and he nodded "yes" when his wife asked him if he felt more comfortable.

We took a break to talk with his wife about doing the comeditation process with him. He had asked her to choose "something simple" for their special words. She decided to use the word *love*. Knowing the patient to be an open and warm person, we thought it was a most appropriate choice. The single word *love* signified their love for each other and love of family, friends, and God. We returned to give another demonstration, offering the word *love,* and again watched Henry become more restful and breathe more fully. His wife took over the refrain, encouraging him to relax in her soft, even voice.

We left confident that she would be able to use the comeditation method whenever she felt it would be helpful. She called us the next day to say that Henry had gone into a light coma a few hours after we left. Rather than sit helplessly at his side, she said the word *love* over and over as she watched each exhalation. She was certain that he was comforted as he heard her voice, taking it as a reminder that she was there. He gently let go of his last breath just before dawn as she was saying their special word, *love,* on his exhalations.

She sat beside him quietly for a moment, grateful that the last moment had been so peaceful. Then she went to the hospital nurses' station and said, "He's gone now; I'm going to call the family." When she returned, she discovered that the hospital staff had called a "code" to attempt resuscitation. They worked with Henry's dead body for more than hour before they would allow her to go into his room.

She was told it was hospital policy to attempt resuscitation unless the primary doctor authorized a do-not-resuscitate order. Because it was still nighttime, the resident on call did not wish to disturb the patient's doctor until he had done everything possible to "bring the patient back." Also, the resident said, he had worked with her husband quite a lot in the past week and didn't want to let him go.

Henry's wife was profoundly distressed by this violation of her loved one's body and the fact that she could not return to her beloved husband to face her own grief. She had felt comfort as she halted the comeditation after his last breath, but she was robbed of resolution because of the hospital staff's inability to accept an inevitable death.

~

The word *nurture* is derived from the same root as the word *nurse*. While both may mean giving another nutrients, they have both also evolved to imply helping another develop and be comforted. In a good hospice program, people are nurtured because they were helped in their living, which goes on during their bodies' decline, and they are nurtured with supportive attendance through their dying by being given gentle, compassionate care. As the title of Elisabeth Kübler-Ross' book *Death: The Final Stage of Growth* makes clear, hospice care helps the patient and family to develop themselves as well as face death.

The *1994–1995 Guide to the Nation's Hospices* listed more than 1,850 affiliated programs.[5] The fact that almost every community in the United States now has a functioning hospice program is a testament to the grassroots enthusiasm to reclaim the process of dying as a personal challenge. Pain management (palliative care) for the seriously ill has set the pace for pain care overall. Scheduled analgesic administration, as originated by modern hospice practice, has been recognized as the preferred course in treating post-surgical patients and those with intractable pain. In many respects the hospice principles have become state-of-the-art caregiving standards for the 1990s.

Making Choices in Holistic Care

Choosing a Treatment

Many patients and families are confused by the profusion of health-care choices available. After they evaluate the side effects of medication, they may prefer alternatives that seem more within their concept of normal activity. For instance, diet and dietary supplements, exercise and movement therapies, and relaxation and autohypnosis techniques are refinements of the earliest rural practices that used home-grown foods, physical work, and rest in natural surroundings.

Meanwhile, some medical investigators acknowledge that many of these practices not only help maintain good health but also slow and arrest the progress of many diseases. Hypertension, heart disease, diabetes, arthritis, multiple sclerosis, gastrointestinal conditions, and chronic pain originating from spine and muscle tension have especially been found to be very responsive to behavioral and emotional factors. Science is proving what the common folk have known for ages: a sick condition becomes more acute when stress is high; remission may be sustained when the person is peaceful.

It is the whole person that must be considered and treated. For instance, it is necessary for the physician not only to evaluate the patient's blood-chemical profile but also to know if the person is emotionally depressed and to know how the factors in that person's life impact on such simple self-care activities as maintaining a recommended diet, taking prescribed medicines on time, and coping with disturbed sleep. The patient will not comply with a program that seems to override his or her personal priorities. It is common, for example, for a patient to pleasantly agree with the doctor about purchasing and taking an expensive medicine, but not to carry out the plan at home because of real or perceived poverty. This is a danger when the doctor treats only within the limits of a medical speciality.

As medical care has become more specialized, many single-focused services have evolved under the holistic umbrella as well. A specialist may provide theories and information to support a particular approach, but no caregiver is functioning holistically if the whole patient and the complexities of his or her life and disease processes are not well understood. No treatment method should stand independently as a cure-all, regardless of the claims made for it. Even an oncologist administering chemotherapy to a cancer patient must consider the patient's dietary intake and retention, general activity level, emotional status, and many other factors, for instance. If the many related body-mind issues are ignored, while the medicine is effectively ridding the body of cancer cells the patient may die of another cause. In the same way, alternative health-care practices such as chiropractic, acupuncture, and special diets must not stand alone.

~

We were once asked to teach comeditation to a woman with severe lymphedema of the arm due to breast cancer. She was profoundly depressed and functionally incapacitated because of her arm's extraordinary size. Although Carole was not inclined to eat, she followed a very restrictive holistic diet as dictated by an advisor following standard, rigid rules for cancer treatment. We taught her and her husband the principles of relaxation, and we were open to philosophic discussions about death and letting go, but we knew these efforts were mostly stop-gaps. Carole and her husband would apply comeditation when her edema caused distress, and when they sought peaceful moments of spiritual communion, but we knew the physical problems would persist. In order to obtain even moderate relief for both the edema and the depression, she needed to improve her protein and mineral balances.

Under the circumstances, death was not a threat to her because her religious background assured her of a welcoming transition. Carole's biggest task was to feel more comfortable with her body. We believed that could happen only if she resolved the dietary deficits. However, she preferred adhering to her rigid diet. While scores of people swear they have been helped by this diet, we believed that the nonadaptive nature of her instructions made the diet unsuitable for her at that time.

However, a diet change would not reverse her condition. The choices she made, therefore, should have been on what would give her the most satisfaction during her few remaining weeks. If she felt that the food in her diet was about the only thing that would stay down, the introduction of new food theories would have simply pitted one dietary authority against another, leaving the patient uncertain. To Carole and her husband, her time was more valuable than that.

~

The scientific community demands that treatment methods, to be acceptable, undergo a process of "blind-study" trials, with publication of the results so that others can duplicate the experiment. It does not accept anecdotal case histories. If this routine is not followed, many holistic methods, such as "unscientific" diets, are declared worthless by conventional physicians. A medical practitioner cannot advocate an unfamiliar process, or a system that uses approaches and guidelines that are different from those in his or her training, unless personal or professional experiences have provoked a thoughtful investigation. Although the medical-oriented peer review helps to assure standards of safety regarding state-of-the-art protocols, scientific scrutiny merely provides information of successes and failures; it does not give a 100-percent guarantee. In a holistic approach, the patient is the ultimate researcher. In considering treatment combinations, the public must be selective, for it is our bodies, our futures, and our money that are at stake.

Success and failure are qualitative. In group comparison studies, one-third of patients receiving any sort of treatment—or believing themselves to be receiving it—will have some improvement, even when they are unknowingly in the group not actually being treated. This "placebo effect" apparently occurs because attention is paid to the person's complaints, and some changes in behavior (such as reduction in tension) take place, providing some relief. The fact that a useless substance can have a positive effect on a known condition is linked with studies of natural neurotransmitter production and actions. Many noninvasive treatments—for instance, massage, exercise, relaxation, and other techniques performed without medicines—stimulate the production of soothing neurotransmitters (such as serotonin and the endorphins) so that the patient's body becomes its own pharmacist.

Hippocrates, regarded as the father of modern medicine, taught that the physician merely treats the symptoms with the skills he develops, whereas the knowledge inherent within the patient's own body returns it to its normal healthy balance and effects the healing. This innate intelligence of the body is part of each cell, and the caregiver simply provides the opportunity for correction to occur.

Modern chiropractors learn that the basis of chiropractic is this principle of innate intelligence. It is the foundation of their successes. The body's cells will maintain the correction if the balance of the whole body is intact. Problems develop in related areas of the body that indicate the internal linkage of bones, nerves, and organs.[6] These associated responses provide guidelines for treatments such as chiropractic adjustment, acupuncture, physical therapy, massage, biofeedback, and pain-control techniques. Thus, many different treatment systems are now based on shared principles.

So, since the time of ancient Greece (probably prior to 400 B.C.), when Hippocrates inspired his students with the principles of responsible caregiving, the integrity and interactions of the human body have been recognized. The wholeness of the individual (body/mind/spirit) is a reflection of harmonies maintained by the individual cells, by the overall person, and by the skills of talented caregivers. It also reflects the support or withdrawal of society.

The treatment histories of leprosy in bibical times, of tuberculosis in the 1930s, and of the HIV-AIDS complex in our present era are examples of society's impact on caregiving and the effects on patients and their networks. Those who were shunned have had to deal with pain, infections, squalid living conditions, and emotional degradation. Often, they have welcomed death as an end to the unreasonable suffering imposed by the attitudes of others. Those who have had emotional and physical support have astounded statisticians by their productivity and their ability to overcome physical setbacks. These exceptional patients have extended their futures—in both time and quality of living—for themselves and their communities.

Choosing a Medical Practitioner

Numerous factors still continue to limit our caregiving potential. Investigations of drugs and treatments are extraordinarily costly. The cost of the treatment to the patient and family, in both time and money, may determine whether the patient will live a little longer, thus preserving the family, or the family break up because of financial and emotional strain even before the unavoidable death occurs. The patient and family must consider what kind of treatment to seek, whether medical insurance will cover the cost, and whether the treatment will make the patient sicker even though the disease process slows.

An all-knowing guide or personal advocate—like the intimate family doctor who carried the wondrous black bag (containing only a few medicines) to help every situation—is still desirable. However, to excel and to stay up to date in their fields of interest, most physicians have become specialists. Our present dilemma is likely to expand. There is so much to know about the human body and mind and so many complex healing techniques that no one can embrace it all. In spite of incentives that encourage young physicians to become general practitioners, the old country doctor is obsolete.

It is necessary for each of us to select the specialists appropriate for our individual needs. The primary physician, who may have passed several specialty board exams, may think of himself or herself as a generalist or as an expert in a certain area. One who accepts the role of primary physician accepts the task of dealing with multiple problems while understanding both medical and behavioral interactions. This role bears a commitment to maintain a long-term relationship with each client in health and in various phases of illness. The primary doctor is expected to refer the client to other specialists or therapists when symptoms indicate that more specialized knowledge or treatment is needed. But sometimes the client may choose alternative care that the primary doctor considers inappropriate because, by the doctor's standards, the explanations for treatment are based on unorthodox precepts. Nowhere in health care has there been more such conflict than in the treatment of breast cancer.

~

Bobbi learned of her breast tumor when lumpectomy, as an alternative to total radical mastectomy, was first being studied. Because she had just entered a new relationship, she was determined to save her breast and to avoid medicines that would make her ill. After her lumpectomy, she embarked on a complex program that entailed coffee enemas, multiple vitamins, and a diet of freshly extracted juices and specially purchased items. Her physician became upset with her because she was spending money she could not afford to spend, she was feeling sicker because of this self-determined course, and she was refusing medically investigated treatments that might have saved her life. She lived a little more than three years after her initial medical treatments. However, when one considers the size of her tumor when it was removed and the survival rates of similar patients who underwent chemotherapy, her life may not have lasted much longer with her conventional doctor's therapies. During her holistic treatment she thrived on the control she believed she was exerting. Each bit of nourishment was treated like a sacrament. She also secured and was supported by the commitment of her new lover. While her early death may suggest failure of treatment, she believed her life was enriched during those last three years. Ultimately, it is the sense of inner enrichment and personal satisfaction experienced during the treatment period or later that determines quality of life.

Bobbi and her lover learned comeditation before her biopsy. They practiced it as an adjunct to their relationship. When they were upset they found that a comeditation session helped them calm down and discuss their situation more objectively. They felt an intimate sharing through this special relaxation process, and as she became weaker it was an alternative to physical lovemaking. He reported to friends that she died peacefully, aware of his loving presence.

~

Bobbi determined her own course after reading extensively about many alternatives. We did not advocate the choices she made, but we did let her know that we would be available to help her whenever she wished. Because of our own medical background, however, we found it difficult to understand the foundation for the many unusual therapies she wove into her life. The greatest conflict between standard medical caregivers and holistic practitioners is conceptual.

To most medically trained professionals, truth must be determined by cadaver studies, surgical examination, or microscopic inspection. But many holistically trained practitioners follow a system that is based, at least in part, on the ancient Chinese concept of "meridians," or invisible pathways that join organs and parts of the body. This system recognizes an invisible flow of energy, *chi,* as the essential element in health and life. The Chinese meridians are still recognized throughout the world today. Principles of balance, such as heat and cold, weakness and stimulation, are applied to concepts of disease. Diets, herbal treatments, and bodywork (such as exercise, massage, and acupuncture) are intended to return the body to its natural balance. Sickness is often considered to be the result of the body's overreacting in its efforts to maintain wellness, thus causing imbalances that need correction.

Many of these time-honored classical principles have been used effectively in medically sponsored programs for both analysis and treatment. Modern pain management is an example of this marriage of East and West. Numerous physical-therapy, exercise, massage, and body-mind awareness disciplines have been developed by specialists who have combined ancient knowledge with recent investigations in the attempt to learn how best to manage physical pain. For instance, it has been determined that the myofascia (the skeletal muscles and associated fibrous membranes) is primarily responsible for the symptoms of one-third of those who consult a doctor in general medical practice because of pain.

When myofascial symptoms are present, trigger points, or tiny hyperirritable spots, radiate acute sensations of pain when compressed. These trigger points are associated with "referred pain"; that is, sensitivity at a given point is associated with the sensation of pain at another specific area. Once established, trigger points may be reactivated with little provocation, such as sleeping in a strained position. Many aggravating symptoms occur because of inactivity or poor body position rather than the underlying disease. Long-term patients and their families would do well to approach new muscular pain as if it were temporary and treatable, and try to address it as a separate problem before worrying about the underlying disease becoming worse.

Dr. Janet Travell, the White House physician for President Kennedy and President Johnson, identified and became the world authority on trigger-point patterns as collaborative studies throughout the United States and the United Kingdom developed and defined this field. Dr. Travell has stated that associated areas of pain and treatment responses have been determined to correspond with the Chinese meridian charts by about 60 percent.[7] The theories regarding trigger points and meridians are applicable to any pain that might develop from posture or pressure, tumor invasion, chronic recurrence (such as headache, leg pain, and tendinitis), and long hours in a sitting or lying position. We believe that any therapist treating pain needs to understand trigger-point principles when applying exercise, relaxation techniques, or counseling (according to his or her training) in order to provide the client with effective relief.

The adaptation of ancient health practices to modern living and disease treatment has also been applied through the use of stress management to treat many patients with cardiovascular disease, diabetes, arthritis, and cancer. Mind-body interaction, once confused by the medical community with imagination and fakery, has gradually become accepted within the last twenty years by those same skeptics. Today, exercise and relaxation techniques are regularly combined with counseling as important elements of most hospital-based wellness programs.

While many medical caregivers are willing to give credence to many holistic practices, most cannot relate to the terminology used, just as many lay people have difficulty understanding "medical-speak." It is necessary for the client to explain to the physician the reasons for selecting a certain holistic method, the treatment received, and the results experienced. And it is necessary for the physician to make an effort to understand the client, evaluate the results objectively, and invite updating. Only through mutual communication can the doctor-patient relationship be viable and a safeguard for the client's health.

Often, the physician's disapproval of holistic practitioners is due to fear that treatment outside of medical supervision will weaken the doctor's control. Also, if the treatment seems nonthreatening but the patient is known to have no money for luxuries, the doctor may discourage what he or she considers a nonessential expense, knowing that few holistic treatments are covered by insurance programs. The patient must decide. For the most appropriate resources to be used for best advantage, it is necessary to create a team in which the central figure, the client, is the team leader, communicating with the various caregivers individually for continuity and understanding. Gradually over time, therapies that truly help in recovery and maintenance may well become approved and eligible for insurance.

Focused Thought-Energies

Healers have been controversial throughout history. Jesus of Nazareth was a healer whose practices were questioned by authorities. Many church communities practice the laying on of hands to unite the power of prayer with physical influences. Therapeutic touch brushes the aura (the energy envelope surrounding the skin) to improve body integrity. This Native American practice was introduced to Western medicine by Dr. Dolores Krieger and is now an option in the University of New York postgraduate nursing program and is taught in many other nursing courses throughout the United States. The therapist's sensitized hands pass over the patient and detect variations in depth and temperature. By sweeping the patient's energy field to smooth this subtle surface, therapeutic touch relaxes, relieves pain, and supports the body's inclination to rebalance. The practitioner must focus, as in full meditative awareness, to enhance the subject's sensitive energies; thus, therapeutic touch is a form of healing prayer.[8]

Dr. Larry Dossey, former director of the Office of Alternative Medicine at the National Institutes of Health, refers to many projects researching the power of prayer in his book *Healing Words*.[9] Dr. Dossey specifically discusses a study by Randolph Byrd to evaluate the effect of intercessory prayer. Half of the patients who came to a hospital because of chest pains and/or heart attack had their first names given to one of several prayer groups. The other half of these patients served as the control group; that is, their names were not sent out. The medical or surgical care for all of the patients followed normal procedures, and neither the staff nor the patients knew who was or was not being prayed for.[10] Dr. Dossey says, "When the data was analyzed it looked like the 'prayed-for group' had been given some sort of special medication." None of the prayed-for group required mechanical ventilation, the group required fewer potent medications, and very few died. Twelve of those in the control group who did not have prayers on their behalf required mechanical ventilation; four more of them died; and their medication management was more complex.

Comeditation involves two people joining in a prayerful attitude to affect body energies, whether these energies are thought of as an irritable nervous system, physical afflictions, common anxieties, or some form of imbalance. The process can be used throughout an illness to provide comfort, relief, and communion with a higher power, whether that power is thought of as an inner light, cellular consciousness, or God in heaven. In the process of letting go, the comeditators allow peace to enter. The physical improvement that results is due to the calming of mind, spirit, and body. The will to accept the wisdom of the higher power allows relief to occur; it also leads to an understanding that the transition from life to death is but another station in the continuum.

The common factor in holistic practices is the inclusion of a recognized energy complex that infuses all life. Whether the words used suggest a spiritual quality such as "God within," "life force," or prayer "to the all powerful God," or simply recognize the mystery that divides the narrow line between life and death, the caregiver knows that his or her actions are not the only factor in the client's improvement or decline. Most medical practitioners with years of experience in watching patients improve and watching patients die appreciate this magic of life energy as much as do most sensitive holistic healers. In fact, in death the mysteries of life are most apparent.

Through careful observation, treatment, documentation, review, and the transmission and exchange of knowledge, formerly fatal diseases are now conditions that can be addressed by medical intervention and changes in living practices. Attention to diet, exercise, emotional strains, and the ways in which we seek comfort constitutes a gift to ourselves of not only more days but also a better quality of life. But knowing that the extra time is but a reprieve, and that all existence has periods of coming together and of separating, we must also make room in our overall plan for that period when death should not be refused.

Dr. Sherwin Nuland of Yale University has written a popular book, *How We Die,* in which he portrays death as an ugly and demeaning process.[11] But it is the changes in the body that inevitably occur with disease with which the patients and caregivers must contend. Given the alternative, most people would rather live in some modified manner, at least for a while. These assaults cause the body to suffer, the mind to despair, social identity to be eroded, and spiritual security to be questioned. But a person's last days can be a period of evolution in which unexplainable beauty fills the room. Often the patient's true self becomes apparent for the first time since early childhood. The patient and those associated with him or her have the opportunity to focus on more clearly shared values. Each day allows them to renew their dedication, to realize short-term goals, and to speculate on purposes greater than immediate distractions. Life within the next few moments can hold promises of hope: hope for a restful nap, hope for a grandchild's future, hope for the judgment of a life well spent. Hope is the ability to look forward to a desired outcome, whatever that might be.

5
WHAT IS HELP?
WHAT IS HOPE?

~

I sent my soul through the Invisible
Some letter of the after-life to spell;
And by and by my soul returned to me
And answered, "I Myself am Heav'n and Hell."

—The Rubaiyat of Omar Khayyam

Home Care

A comforted death is a positive, obtainable goal that does not represent giving up, but the admission that eventually there must be a final resolution. Reaching that final destination may involve a circuitous route. Symptoms must be managed, and a multitude of issues must be dealt with every day: bathing, exercise, mouth care, food cravings, irregularities of digestion and elimination, temperature changes, and skin problems will require extra effort and attention. Pain from the disease, pain from bad posture or lack of movement, and discomforts associated with daily maintenance must be evaluated, treated appropriately, and worked into a plan to prevent recurrence. Scheduled care for certain conditions, bed changing, doing laundry, shopping for unplanned needs, answering phone calls and mail, and assuring vigils must be worked into the routine. Yet, with sufficient help and guidance, almost any lay person can keep a loved one at home even through the most difficult illness.

There are three requirements for successful home care: abundant support, both professional and personal; the resolve to deal with unpleasant issues; and the understanding that changes will occur in spite of the best of care. Self-reproach is never appropriate when natural processes overtake conscientious caregiving.

Each person who is closely involved with the patient will experience emotions and face conflicts that each would prefer to avoid. There will be grief before as well as after the death occurs. Caregiving problems will be of utmost importance and, once resolved, will require consideration again and again. The myriad emotions that each caregiver must confront will not be exactly like those anyone else experiences, but there will be a common bond. Sharing concerns and working together will provide confidence for the less sure, assistance and backup for the skilled, and assurance for the patient.

Some caregivers overextend themselves in order to minimize the effects of the illness on others. This causes the primary person to suffer from burnout—work exhaustion. The problems of caring for someone who is very ill for a long time are compounded if the primary caregivers also become sick. Each person in the network is responsible for self-care as well as for individual commitments to the patient. If everyone is feeling a strain, additional help must be obtained. Respite periods need to be arranged. The sick person is aware of the efforts being made on his or her behalf. At this stage of life, most patients would rather compromise than have another person make undue sacrifices.

The ultimate objective—to allow the patient to be himself or herself as much as possible—will still be obtainable. Nurturing is a natural consequence of time spent together without pressure. These relaxed exchanges will become significant to the patient regardless of the setting or the physical condition.

Comeditation can provide moments of sharing while reinforcing the hopes and ideals of the person who is ill. As the process allows relaxation to alleviate discomfort, both the caregiver and the patient evolve. The words used are selected by the patient. The rate is determined by the patient's breath. Scheduling is according to the patient's needs and preferences, but the assistant must be willing to take the time to sit patiently by the bedside without being distracted by tasks or unresolved issues. By just being together, listening, both let go of anxieties separately but as one, experiencing a special peace.

It is not my task to give specific directions to you as you approach death, but I can help you sing the song that is within you.

—Anonymous

Holistic care addresses where in the body the patient is uncomfortable, what the patient's mental attitudes are, how social support is supplied, and what effect spiritual unrest may be having on the person's sense of well-being. The process of illness reflects the elements of one's life. Even minor illnesses may require the body to take a necessary rest, and provide the opportunity to review, replan, and reconnect to the needs of the present as well the hopes for the future. On the other hand, during long periods of wellness, our day-to-day experiences reinforce our strengths, our firm expectations, and our self-complacency. But we often fail to realize how character and judgment are being tested until we are in the midst of crisis.

Each of us has basic, unique qualities that change little throughout a lifetime. But attitudes, preferences, and manners of coping and expression are the result of inherited traits, habits that have been developed, and structural or chemical variations within the brain. The process of disease affects the ability to think, and may also influence a person's self-perception and general desires.

As a dying person attempts to bring closure to his or her own affairs, other people are affected. Decisions made near the end of a person's life may be trying for those who are emotionally related. The compulsion to help a dear one is often as strong as the requirements of the one to be helped. Even in the most ideal situations, it is difficult to define what can be done, what is necessary, what the results of assistance and intervention might be, and how to deal with ordinary issues that take on symbolic significance. At times the task is formidable, especially when the body chemistry is affected and when anxieties interfere with reasoning. But a person who is slightly confused or feeling despondent is more secure surrounded by familiar people and objects. Help at home sometimes represents the only hope that the dying person can admit is a realistic goal.

~

Kathy was nineteen when she was diagnosed with ovarian cancer. She was terrified that the disease might be fatal, but she was even more disturbed that her life would be devoid of love, children, and the many events that she associated with becoming an adult. When surgery revealed that only one ovary was cancerous, with metastasis to the nearby pelvic tissue, her doctors complied with her presurgical request to remove only the ovary and tissue involved. A regimen of radiation and chemotherapy was planned to arrest the cancer's further spread and development. The outpatient cancer clinic monitoring her progress was managed by a nurse who was immediately charmed by Kathy's bouncy walk and ready wit. At first Kathy joked about becoming nauseated as she began to walk into the clinic. Then she said her vomiting began while her mother was driving her as soon as the hospital came into view. Knowing that soon Kathy would feel sick the moment she and her mother began to prepare to go for her treatment, the clinic's nurse-manager recommended that Kathy take medication for nausea early in the morning of her clinic appointment. She was scheduled for an early appointment because her mother worked an evening shift. The nurse offered to teach both mother and daughter a relaxation method that could help control Kathy's nausea.

Kathy and her mother found that comeditation did help her whenever her stomach felt upset and that she felt more settled emotionally after having comeditation. To ease the trip to the clinic, they asked a good friend to drive them so her mother could help Kathy in the back seat. Soon the friend was providing other diversions and encouraging Kathy to plan her future. The treatment was completed, with good results, and Kathy resumed her life at college.

Within two years Kathy was making plans for marriage to a college classmate she had dated before her surgery. But gastrointestinal symptoms, attributed at first to the emotional excitement over getting married and taking exams, were found to be caused by metastasic cancer of the colon. Treatment was delayed because Kathy was pregnant, and she refused to do or take anything that might affect the baby. After the baby was born, Kathy was scheduled to undergo colostomy and begin another course of cancer treatment. Next to bearing a healthy baby, her greatest desire was to see her child grow and to know Kathy as her mom.

Soon Kathy's mother had the new family living with her. She was doing comeditation with Kathy daily, helping to care for the new baby, and integrating treatments (which made Kathy sick and weak) with new diets, health-food supplements, and body-maintenance appointments. Her neighbor gave Kathy a massage twice a week. Kathy found that her greatest problem was coping with the new abdominal colostomy appliance. Because of the side effects of the cancer treatments, her overactive gastrointestinal tract, which discharged into the abdominal pouch, made her feel totally unsuitable as a wife. Fortunately, her husband truly did love her. He began to do comeditation in the evening to help her settle down, and it became part of their loving ritual together.

For a year after treatment was completed they delighted in the baby's growth and were grateful for their happy, almost normal life together. Kathy reported enthusiastically to her clinic friends that she and her husband were saving up to move to their own apartment. But the tests that monitored her disease revealed suspect lesions in her liver, and her doctors were concerned about other findings as well. When she went through another course of radiation and chemotherapy, her energy waned and she didn't recover as quickly as she had previously.

Her mother was grateful when the clinic nurse offered to send in a home-care nurse and an aide to help with Kathy's routine. Each day, when Kathy's child had her nap, Kathy's mother sat beside Kathy's bed and did a comeditation session with her. Both mother and daughter felt those moments as a special time of sharing and rest for both of them. As Kathy's symptoms became more severe they used comeditation as an adjunct to the medicines the doctor ordered to ease her distress.

Within a few months they were advised to invite the local hospice team to replace the home-care staff. They considered the differences between the two services. Kathy and her family wanted to continue keeping her at home. They were determined to make whatever adjustments might be necessary to let her have as much time with her little girl as possible, and to make sure her mother and husband could be with Kathy as she died. Agreeing with hospice principles, they did not deny that death was approaching, but they wanted to chose their own day-to-day goals. Comeditation helped them get through those trying days and restless nights. Comeditation also helped Kathy's mother and husband let go when her labored breathing became shallow. Her final exhalation was so faint that they were not sure when it occurred. They felt assured that all Kathy wished for herself had been done and they would continue her legacy with her daughter. They were strengthened by Kathy's spirit. Their grief was mixed with peaceful memories, as when they had done comeditation with her. After her death they felt her spirit inside themselves, especially during moments of joy as they watched Kathy's child develop her bouncy walk, and during their own quiet meditations.

～

When a patient is expected to require extensive home care for a long time, patient and caregivers alike must make many compromises. Sentimental attachments must be examined from the point of view of practicality and consideration of others. For example; very sick hospitalized patients are often overheard saying, "I just want to go home to die in my own bed." Usually, going home can be accommodated if there are family and community resources to provide care, and changes in the home layout can make the spaces appropriate for caregiving.

Home care provides the opportunity for loved ones to fulfill the patient's needs. It demonstrates that in spite of changes, the person who is ill is still a part of his or her home. Modifications will be made to accommodate this person in almost any manner necessary for his or her comfort and security. Because it is home, schedules will be lax and people will behave naturally. But the bulk of the caring work will fall on those at home. The value of a home caregiver should never be underestimated.

An amateur caregiver may tearfully express frustration about not being able to achieve hospital standards. The hypersensitive patient may fuss about everything, not because the care is so poor but because he or she yearns for everything to be as it was at an earlier time. Home care, however, should not be abandoned because it does not meet clinical expectations or because the old atmosphere has changed. Everyone involved must remember that together they can create a collage combining old memories with new requirements. While there may be unanswerable questions, it is only through sharing that mutual anxieties can be understood and made to serve an effective purpose. Everyone must remember to take one day at a time, rest when they can, forgive themselves as well as others, and allow small pleasures to inspire them.

Kathy and her family faced problems common to most families with an ill or dying family member. For instance, they had to plan for her to spend time alone. Although her husband worked days and her mother worked evenings, there were many gaps because of overlapping work schedules, childcare delivery and pickup, and shopping and other errands. In addition, both caregivers required essential personal time. When Kathy was feeling very sick she dreaded solitude, but being responsible for herself was a matter of self-respect. Most people value their independence. Young people, especially, are eager to prove themselves capable of self-management, even when family ties are tight. Ill people are likely to question their self-esteem as they confront their limitations and find it strengthened when they overcome difficulties. Support groups can be a great help in modifying daily activities for patient safety and also giving consideration to the caregiver.

It is important for the family to obtain professional guidance and to share the various caregiving tasks among many people. If the patient has been living alone, other family members must commit themselves to a definite schedule to provide assistance, hire someone to help, or apply for community resources to supplement their needs. Visiting-nurse organizations, hospital-referral services, specific disease-support programs, church and charitable groups, local aging councils, and elder-affairs programs are good resources. Friends and neighbors often would like to be helpful but don't want to intrude upon a family for fear of embarrassing them. Now is the time to ask for their help.

Normal tasks need to be modified. For instance, meal preparation for the family seems to take unavailable time when energies are low and preparing the patient's food takes priority. Medication and treatment schedules may include rather complicated procedures that can be easily learned but require confidence and commitment. Patient care involves bathing; bedding changes; exercise; position changes; attention to basics such as skin condition, urine output, bowel activity, liquid intake; and help with eating and mobility. Laundry seems to multiply mysteriously. The presence of a willing other person will allow the primary caregiver a chance to get out of the house, lest the patient have a problem and not be able to obtain help.

If the patient is able to function for essential needs and is mentally alert, a "life-line" system linked to an emergency-response service allows more independence. This is a patient-service agreement, not a hospice provision. Although emergency service may be questioned if a contract has been signed with a hospice for terminal care, an understanding with a hospice does not preclude the setting of a fracture from a fall or other treatment for injuries that might beset an average person at risk. If the patient must be left alone, be sure that a note giving time of the caregiver's return and listing emergency telephone numbers is at hand. Consider the patient's needs and preferences and the time of day the person will be alone, in relation to convenience, safety, anticipated moods, and health requirements. Thoughtful gestures, such as having tissues within reach and a disposal bag to drop them in, as well as moving needed items close to the bedside, can allay anxious concerns and may avert a fall. Every family has its own pattern. Share ideas with friends and support-group members to broaden choices and improve coping options.

The following practical measures can aid the homebound patient's independence:

- When a caregiver leaves the house, establish the time of expected return, and post time and emergency numbers on a bulletin board within the patient's range of sight.

- Have an easily readable clock within the patient's line of sight.
- Place medicines that are scheduled to be taken during the alone period within reach. Also, have "as needed" medicines within reach, but if the patient is forgetful, determine and leave only the amount likely to be needed. This limitation will avoid overdosage, and allow the caregiver to know what the patient's needs have been.
- Set a clock alarm or a medicine box with a time signal to alert the patient for dosage time, if the patient is not confused by having to turn the sound off.
- Have fresh liquids and snacks easily available. Use insulated containers, plastic wraps, and lunch boxes to keep the food fresh. Tell callers that small holding single-serving food items make welcome gifts.
- Attach a refuse bag to the bed.
- Have disposable utensils, such as plastic spoons and knives, handy.
- Use plastic knives to open mail, cut serving sizes, and clip magazines or newspapers.
- Provide several means of distraction (such as TV with remote control, radio, favorite audiotapes, magazines and books, writing materials, and a telephone) near at hand. Telephones are for safety, also!
- Include moist disposable towels and a deodorant spray with the toileting supplies.
- Obtain a "fracture" style bedpan, which is low and is easy for a person to use alone. A beside commode should sit on nonskid floor covering or against a wall. Cover it with plastic to confine odors; use deodorizing cleaners.
- Set a timer on a lamp to go on just before dusk, as a safety precaution.
- Keep the light on to help reduce fear and confusion (such as after napping).
- Store treatment supplies, such as hot or could packs, in large-mouthed thermal units that can be reached easily by the sick person.
- Hang a reaching tool for easy grasping, to extend the patient's access to the surroundings. Provide long-handled shoe horns.
- If the patient is bedridden, hang a trapeze over the bed to aid posi-

tion changes and save the patient's elbows and back from abrasion when he or she is trying to move toward the head of the bed. A board or box at the foot of the bed will help prevent sliding down.

- Copy keys for trusted health-care workers and expected visitors so the patient will not have to answer the door.
- Have a visitor's expected time of arrival posted on the bulletin board so that hearing someone at the door at that time will not alarm the patient.
- Schedule phone calls from yourself or others, to give the patient contact with someone at least every two hours. This assures safety, reminds the sick person that he or she has not been forgotten, stimulates orientation, and prevents daytime sleeping, which would interfere with nighttime rest.
- Discourage smoking! If smoking cannot be prohibited, place giant metal trays on the floor and tables at the bedside, and maintain smoke detectors.

This may seem like a long list, but these items are relatively simple when made part of a routine. Each one is related to the normal activities of daily living that people modify all their lives. All suggestions are offered to address the patient's needs, but each situation must be adapted to specific, individual preferences. Any nursing guidance is to help you through difficult times. Alter, reject, and add to the suggestions as you see fit. If the patient has always liked to have the covers loose around the feet, for instance, making the bed the way you have for years is better than trying to satisfy a bedmaking instructor.

Attendants need to be able to reach the patient from all sides of the bed. A family who lives in a multistoried home with a main floor bathroom can accommodate the patient and provide seating for visitors better in a dining room, parlor, or den than in an upstairs bedroom. Use of the main floor also assures that the family activity is nearby with easy kitchen access, and the caregivers do not have to run up and down stairs all day. If there are strong assistants who can help the patient with stairs, the patient may choose to sleep in an upstairs bedroom at night and spend the day on the main floor.

Of equal importance to patient care is caregiver protection. No caregiver should be required to risk a back injury from stooping over a low bed. Hospital-style beds were designed not only to raise the patient's head and lift the legs but also to adjust for height: low, so the patient can get in and out of bed easily, and high, so bed-making and patient care can be carried out without strain. If the patient is going to require a great deal of bed care, even for a short time, most of that care should be at a comfortable height for the caregiver. Hospital-style beds are easily rented through hospital home-supply outlets and are covered by most insurance policies. Side rails should also be ordered because they are handy aids when the patient changes position in bed, and they provide safety.

Using disposable gloves when cleaning excrement and soiled linen, and frequent handwashing (such as before and after caregiving, before handling any food, and after coughing) are other health-care precautions that may seem like unnatural interferences but are actually good habits of daily living. These measures protect both patient and caregivers. Antibiotics are not advised for a person who is dying; also, antibiotics in general are becoming less effective as organisms become more resistant. Avoid the discomfort of infection in both the patient and the assistants by prevention. On the other hand, demonstrations of affection are needed, and most forms of contact are safe. Don't be afraid to cuddle.

The most important thing any caregiver can do is avoid back strain and pulled muscles. Taking risks when trying to hurry, and lowering self-protection priorities under urgency, are dangerous compromises. Good body mechanics must be considered in every action for both the patient and all those who do the various chores. Painful backs can turn helpers into invalids themselves. Patients who "twist wrong" may cause damage that results in more pain than is caused by the disease itself. Yet, the simplest precautions will avoid injury. The following are good habits to establish whether providing patient care or just living in the day-to-day world:

- Keep your back as straight as possible.
- Keep your feet firmly on the floor, under your center of balance, spreading your legs comfortably apart to increase stability.
- Bend your knees and shift your weight onto your legs when lifting or moving.
- Always balance evenly when changing positions.
- Never twist your body while lifting.
- Be sure the patient is stabilized before changing his or her position. When two or more people are repositioning the patient, move together, caregivers facing the direction in which the move is intended.

- Keep the weight you are moving as close to the body as possible.
- Keep the working area between your waist and chest levels when possible.

Another issue that often causes anxiety to a family is the patient's food. To the sick person, someone's willingness to prepare favorite dishes or to go across town for a tempting cake symbolizes love. The wife or mother who has long nourished others as an expression of herself may feel compelled to offer nourishment as a way of connecting with her loved ones and of trying to "make it better," if only for a while. But when a person is very ill, the actual consumption of nourishing foods may not be possible because of organic problems. Unfortunately, as the person becomes sicker, even the most restrained urgings to eat are less appreciated because of nausea and total disinterest.

If the person is in a terminal stage, intake of food becomes much less important, and it is more appropriate to apply gently lubricating lotions to the skin and provide frequent mouth care. Patient comfort is the goal. Skin care prevents rapid tissue breakdown, which might be felt as sores. The tissues are very fragile and extraordinarily sensitive, however, so keep the massaging hands broad, actions gentle. Mouth care prevents drying of the membranes and reduces thirst. If the patient is unable to swallow, or vomits more than he or she takes in, urging fluids is counterproductive and stressful. Tiny ice chips on the tongue, cleansing the oral cavity with a peppermint-flavored swab ("Toothettes"), and coating the mouth with a light swab of oil is all that is needed. Take time to sit with the person, reminiscing, comeditating, or just enjoying each other's company.

The dying process produces toxins that affect mental function and give the patient a different perspective than those of the observers. The following list suggests some small comfort measures that will let the patient know someone cares and that might relieve potential irritations before they cause distress:

- When a dying person cannot swallow, thirst signals the lack of fluid within the body. Comfort is obtained by a tiny bit of crushed ice, which may be absorbed or swallowed when it melts.
- As mentioned above, a dry mouth is relieved by frequent mouth care, especially if a touch of oil is used on the cleansing swab to maintain a feeling of moisture.

- The so-called death rattle can be quieted by positioning the patient so the mucus in the throat does not cause a vibrating resonance, and so substances (such as mucus, saliva, and moisture given for dryness) that can no longer be swallowed can drain out of the mouth.
- Cooling sponges and anti-inflammatory suppositories can help keep the patient comfortable even during a high fever.
- Warmed blankets can seem to the patient like being enveloped with love when circulation to the extremities slows as the heart conserves its energy.
- Position the patient's limbs so there is no surface-to-surface pressure by placing a pillow or rolled soft towel under the upper part. For instance, if an arm, hand, or leg is against any part of the body, prop it slightly to the side and support the entire undersurface with a smooth, perspiration absorbent material.
- Lift the patient who had difficulty moving alone with a "pull sheet." Place the longest side of a folded sheet across the center of the bed. If the patient is restless, tuck the sides under the mattress when the sheet is not being used to lift. If the patient rarely moves, roll or fanfold the excess at the side of the bed so it is always ready. Place an incontinent pad between the pull sheet and the patient. The softer pull sheet surface is against the skin but the absorbent qualities of the pad protect the undersheet and mattress. Two people lift on the count of three.
- Keep the bedding smooth and unwrinkled to help prevent bedsores.
- Use protective coverings for elbows, heels, and ankles before bedsores occur. Adapt heavy socks, or purchase protectors from a surgical supply outlet. Wearing high-topped tennis shoes in bed will maintain the angle of the ankle and protect the foot.
- Prevent and treat early pressure sores with "egg crate" mattress and chair toppers, an air mattress or cushion (which may be covered by insurance), or water-filled mattress toppers (which are better but often are not covered by insurance).
- As an economical substitute for a water mattress if a bedsore persists, fill a plastic Ziplock freezer bag with water, reinforce the closure with glue, insert that bag in another bag and seal firmly, and cut a hole in a foam mattress topper to hold the bag where the patient's sore normally touches the bed. After placing the filled bag in the mattress-

topper space, make the bed as usual, avoiding heavy layers over the water bag. Be sure the mattress has a protective plastic cover before trying this measure.

- When tender feet are irritated by the bedding, fill a well-sealed plastic bag or examining glove with water so it can be worn inside a loose sock to protect an early heel or ankle sore. Don't let the patient walk on it!

The biggest advantage of home care is that sensitive family members provide immediate responses to signs of discomfort without tiresome questioning or delay. Touching and moments of privacy come easily at home. Periods of relaxation and activity may be worked in according to the patient's choices rather than a hospital schedule. Memories evoked during the course of a day at home satisfy the sense of safety and stir an appreciation of what the people who live and have lived in that home have accomplished. As the home has been the location for gathering together one's resources before engaging the world, it is equally the preferred place to gather one's resources before entering into death.

~

Yvonne will be remembered as an inspiring example to her family and caregivers because she made the home as much of a place of warmth and love as she was dying as it had been throughout her very active married life. She learned that she was terminally ill on the same day her daughter told her she was planning to be married. Determined not to ruin her daughter's wedding, she coordinated hospitalizations with home-care services to keep herself functioning as well as possible during her daughter's bridal showers and through the wedding and reception.

After the bride and groom went on their honeymoon, she allowed herself full home-care support and a time of closeness with her husband. She had developed the practice of saying "Peace be with you" when acknowledging the trials of her loved ones, so it was a natural refrain for her comeditation guides to use. She died the day the newlyweds returned from their honeymoon, comforted by the loving vigil of her entire family. The refrain "Peace be with you" was the natural inward response of everyone in attendance.

~

In the home, with loved ones gathered, the comeditation procedure that has been used for relaxation, pain reduction, and inner growth can become part of the vigil.

The practice we have advocated throughout our work is the total acceptance of the person who is doing the best he or she can to get through one moment at a time. By adapting to physical and emotional variations as they occur, the helpers enable the person to discover the affirmations and inner strengths he or she needs for the final passage. This acceptance allows a release from pain into light.

> Spirit is not in the I but between I and You. It is not like the blood that circulates in you but like the air in which you breathe. Man lives in the spirit when he is able to respond to [a] You. . . . It is solely by virtue of his power to relate that man is able to live in spirit.[1]

Coping with Progressive Illness and Serious Loss

The stages of death, as described by Elisabeth Kübler-Ross in *On Death and Dying,* are recognized as issues with which the client and family must continually cope. Dr. Kübler-Ross studied how people who were dying felt about what was happening.[2] Theirs were emotions that anyone who faces loss or change might encounter. People who lose their jobs or go through divorce or a natural disaster experience these same feelings. Initially, they are confused and uncertain or may deny the loss or change.

Anger is an automatic response to threat and raises our defenses. Often, this irritation is directed toward another as a way of absolving oneself from blame. This is why ordinarily loving people may lash out unexpectedly. As we begin to contemplate a threat we use our intellect to ponder the possibilities. Bargaining, or mentally playing with alternative solutions, gives us a chance to imagine choices and to think that we might be able to exercise more personal control. But when a person cannot find consolation, depression is a natural response to a futile situation. Finally, when adjustment to reality reveals that many fears were more threatening than the actual experience, acceptance follows. Threading through all these emotions is hope for a gentle resolution or for fulfillment within a particular person's goals and expectations. Every hospice worker knows that these feelings come and go in varying orders, times, and intensities, affecting everyone in the family.

Because it is fear that causes the anguish, the hospice solution is to reduce the fear of dying by supporting patients and their families to address symptoms effectively, confront and resolve difficult issues, and show love for the dying and for the living by giving care while preparing to let go. These lessons are valuable at every stage of life. When a person is accepted totally, physical and personal problems can be approached objectively as well as tenderly, and that person can rediscover feelings of affirmation and inner strength.

The patient is the central focus. To be accepted by a hospice the patient must have been given a life expectancy of six months or less by a physician; however, the issues that prevail in hospice caregiving are applicable to most emotionally traumatic experiences. Whether the person is critically ill, is physically well but emotionally troubled, or feels both physically and emotionally at risk, the emotions accompanying awareness of loss are ever present.

Our own working strategy has been to help the patient work through the multiple layers of fear and pain even when there is little hope of physical recovery. Our approach encompasses behavior modification to manage the symptoms, and encouraging the patient to reflect on emotions, thoughts, and spiritual concepts in the search for comfort. Certain principles that are usually associated with rehabilitation and improvement are just as applicable to terminal care: frequent assessment, adaptation, support.[3]

Assessment. Not only do we advocate the use of professional observation skills, we expect the patient to do self-evaluation as well. Only the patient can determine just how today's discomfort differs from yesterday's. We all need to develop objectivity regarding ourselves, whatever our circumstances, if we are to attend responsibly to life's challenges.

Adaptation. Actions to modify discomfort can make the difference between an intolerable, overwhelming existence and a bearable—even occasionally rewarding—day. As problems arise, concessions are made to maintain priorities and compensate for perfect function. Most situations can be made better by finding some response that suggests, at least, modified hope.

Support. Strengthening applies not only to physical balance but to emotional needs as well, whether the patient is recovering from a stroke, is coming home after radical cancer surgery expecting to gradually resume normal activities, has had a recent mental crisis, or is at the end of life and needs physical and emotional reinforcement. Sometimes it is the person who feels threatened by physical decline but does not have clinical evidence of advanced disease who may be most in need of special support.

The person whose illness has progressed and is actually dying is likely to have been preparing over a period of time with a sympathetic, responsive, support system. Therefore, as anticipated death draws nearer, all concerned (including the patient) find themselves gradually gliding into the acceptance stage while adjusting to the patient's body changes. Both the patient, who can feel emotional changes resulting from physical deficits, and those close by are aware that the body is shutting down. While they do not welcome parting, they are preparing themselves for the resolution. Both patients and loved ones hope to come to the end of this undeniable suffering and to find peace with completion. They may each be satisfied that the best efforts have been made, devotion has been expressed, and regrets are absolved. These thoughts provide comfort.

In our counseling and caregiving we take a holistic approach. When people inquire about comeditation, we want them to tell us why they think comeditation may be helpful. What physical symptoms do they expect to address with deep relaxation? How has emotional upheaval affected personal interaction and basic day-to-day routines? Are support people available? Has a spiritual search provided any sort of satisfaction, comfort, or certainty? How can we help them balance their lives in spite of the illness? How can we help them to manage their responses to pain and disability while interacting with others and their own inner selves?

It is one's perception of oneself that determines how one suffers. We have had our own points of view affected by close association with people who endured incredible odds while trying to maintain their balance. We remember well one person who helped us understand that dignity is a matter of character regardless of bodily changes.

~

Lydia lost the use of all of her limbs through a series of strokes just before she was able to complete a degree in nursing. Married to a doctor who fell in love with her soon after her illness began, she became blind following the birth of their only child. Within a few months she was unable to function alone, but she never lowered her standards or her expectation of having a rewarding life. The ability to think, to engage others in conversation, and to require others to treat her with dignity were to her essential to being a full human being. This modified life, being all that was left to her, grew more precious as the years went by.

Full emergency care became mandatory when she experienced a near-fatal wheelchair accident. Only her strong self-esteem provided her with the power to insist that her standards be met consistently. She challenged others as she challenged herself. She also demonstrated friendship and joy, eagerness to learn and to teach, a desire to exchange ideas, and earnest concern over worldly issues. She returned respect with equal recognition.

Yet, even she, after more than thirty years of increasing handicaps and inward assaults, directed that a do-not-resuscitate order be placed on her chart. The hours she spent alone had provided her with natural periods of meditation. As she accepted herself over the years she began to become ready to let go, feeling that her purpose in life had been resolved.

She had never been afraid of death, but she did not believe in God, an afterlife, or a second chance. She simply saw herself as working out her life in the only way possible for her, with strength of personality. Her strong sense of self provided her with the necessary stamina to experience joys and affection as well as disappointments and afflictions. Her life was valuable because it happened. She was a splendid teacher because of her example. She did not need a world beyond her caregivers to be an effective human being.

Depression and Comeditation

Depression is a natural reaction to loss. In the emotions of the dying, it is the second stage described by Kübler-Ross. Most of us have bouts of depression throughout our lives as loves change and study or work disappointments occur. At any time on the path of growing older, a period of depression may be experienced as we look back and see that we have not achieved the happiness or success anticipated in our youth. But as long as we can direct our attention to goals that are important to us, most of us can bounce back with renewed dedication.

When physical disabilities limit activity, however, and the future seems to promise only more disappointments, suffering, and the end of life, a person can feel immersed in an inescapable fog. Unexpected defensive anger and certain classic symptoms of depression such as insomnia, refusing food, and low energy may be unfairly attributed to the disease process. Whether or not these signs have a pathological basis, they warrant both counseling and a trial with antidepressant medication. The integration of the total person is too important during the last stages of life to allow depression—even if it is understandable—to overwhelm his or her self-identity.

Most authorities recommend helping the person through the depressive phase by providing tender companionship and encouraging the review of lifelong values. It is helpful, also, to understand how the body's self-defense reactions respond to the extreme emotional and physical overload associated with actual or threatened loss. As first recognized by Dr. Hans Selye, the hormonal reactions to stress occur in stages: after alarm comes the stage of resistance.[4] The body cuts off the outpouring of the chemicals that provide energy, pain reduction, and confidence. Like injured animals, humans under stress seek shelter and seclusion. Withdrawal provides a period of rest and natural rebalancing.

Therefore, depression after any serious loss or devastation is not considered pathological. That is, a desire to withdraw is not a dysfunction of the mind requiring psychiatric intervention. But it is a condition that affects the whole person with actual physical symptoms. Among the symptoms of depression are gastrointestinal upset and other complaints of "feeling sick." Functionally, the person may feel weak and have little desire to do anything; emotionally, he or she may react more slowly and have no sense of humor; and spiritually, the person is likely to feel separated from all, both human and divine. Uninterrupted, such changes contribute to self-doubt and self-loathing and reinforce the depression pattern. If no intervention occurs, the dangerous stage of suicidal thoughts may develop, and a normal mood variation is then officially transformed into a psychiatric problem.

Any depression warrants attention from loved ones and may benefit from professional guidance. A sympathetic listener, capable of objective counsel, can turn an episode of despair into an opportunity for reinforcement of self-esteem. On the positive side, as a normal reaction to grief, depression provides one with private time to reevaluate, to seek comfort measures, and to determine a new strategy.

During any period of depression, comeditation can be a valuable adjunctive aid to counseling. In using comeditation to combat depression, all aspects of the person are nurtured. The person who is depressed chooses the sounds to be made and sets the pace with his or her own breathing, and the helper follows this established pattern. The distressed person is urged to let go and release bodily tension. With the body completely relaxed the person may also be able to let go of intense emotions. Even if the person only seeks a few moments of peace of mind, the profound feeling of letting go can be carried through for some time after the session. With the security of a concerned companion sharing those moments, the person may break through repressed feelings. Healing may occur as the person is encouraged to define fears and realistic hopes and set attainable goals. Thus, the sense of failure is given a lesser place, and attention is turned toward positive expectations.

~

Hilda was a ninety-year-old widow who had focused her anxiety on her poor health all her life. She thought her depression was due to the loss of everyone close to her. She had outlived her family, friends, and everyone of her generation she knew. As she increasingly required more assistance with all aspects of her life, this formerly independent woman was also outliving her money and her security. When we met, her chief complaint was angina, which responded to nitroglycerine placed under her tongue several times a day. While her medication program averted new damage to the heart, the terror that she felt with each acute episode left her exhausted and fearful of engaging in any activity, and it further contributed to her depression. Nevertheless, in order to achieve her will, she challenged and manipulated everyone who came to work with her; then, being upset, she developed the angina—a vicious cycle. Unable to eat, she had lost twenty pounds in less than a year.

We invited her to try a comeditation session so she could see how relaxation would defuse the pain syndrome. Our goal was to help her learn a behavioral modification of her pathological problem: relaxation to offset the heart spasm that resulted from her being upset. She not only learned to reduce the frequency and intensity of her angina episodes but she also began to use our visits to review her past, not as senile reminiscing but as a way of defining who she was and how she wanted to be identified. As she developed these thoughts, her approach to her companions began to mellow, and without realizing that it was her attitude that made the difference, she reduced the incidents of acute pain. Although her appetite was quickly satisfied, she began to enjoy the taste of food again when she could think of mealtime as a way of sharing with her companions.

~

What is meaningful for you? If you were stripped of everything, what single thought could sustain you? For Lydia, it was life's nobility; for Dr. Viktor Frankl in a Nazi concentration camp, it was his devotion to his wife that inspired him to find meaning in simple incidents; for Job in the Bible, it was love of God. The existential uplifting of the spirit need not be verbalized; it may simply be realized. Often it comes when one is at the brink of despair. But those who know nothing but a void are sometimes not able to make the jump into philosophic resolution. When time and energy seem to be waning, depression may nullify every instant of normal thought. Despair occurs when a person believes that no one can ease the suffering and nothing can change the dreaded outcome. Sometimes it is death with the anticipation of purgatory or hell that provokes anxiety. More often it is the fear of increased pain, emotional abandonment, or loss of body functions that creates depression in people who are ill.

In working with clients our strategy begins with getting acquainted. Whether you are a patient or a caregiver, we hope to stimulate your thoughts, helping you understand yourself and your situation better. We encourage you to raise questions and try to understand the nature of your problems with those who can provide options. How do you deal with the diagnosis, the doctors' advice, the resources you have available? Become conscious of your behaviors when you experience pain or stress so you can modify them for better control of your problems. How have your coping patterns helped you, and how have they interfered with your adjustment to your present situation?

Control

Control of ourselves and of others' actions that affect us is a goal of maturation in our society. When life changes occur, however, personal control can become very limited. While causes and effects may be traceable, each choice along the way presents only a shift in the direction determined by our genetic heritage.

~

Kyle developed bladder cancer after years of working in a chemical plant. He did not knowingly risk exposure to caustic materials; his body was simply more susceptible than some of his fellow workmen, and his company—which should have been responsible for protective measures—did not recognize the risks until several employees had similar problems. Kyle's anger toward the company led to demands by workers for stricter handling of supplies and more generous medical benefits. His will to control a situation that he believed had victimized him strengthened the union's effectiveness. But as a patient, Kyle found that his ability to control his destiny was limited. He could only report symptoms and choose a treatment when offered and recommended by his doctor: radical surgery, radiation, and chemotherapy. His judgment was based on the little knowledge he could obtain from his advisors, articles he found at the library, and his own expectations for future. Inadvertent side effects, such as hair loss, dealing with a leaking urinary drainage appliance, and sexual impotence, had to be considered from his point of view as well as from his medical advisors' perspectives.

While medical personnel thought of those physical changes as minor inconveniences, he thought of them as threats to his identity. In the effort to continue living a few more years or perhaps only a few months, he had to know what his actual priorities were. This meant challenging his own courage and determining whether to fight or simply accept fate. He recognized that he had to fight, because accepting fate would be too difficult for him. When the clinic nurse suggested that he might learn a relaxation method, he rejected it because he believed he had to be constantly on guard to maintain control. Then he realized he was using time in his garden as his meditation time.

Going for kidney dialysis for two years, he had to regularly spend several hours at the treatment center watching others have periods of improvement that seemed greater than his own, and knowing also that some of these new friends died. Although he was inwardly frightened by the routine visits because the need for dialysis underscored the severity of his illness, talking with fellow patients and teasing the nurses gave him pleasure. His active participation helped him feel in control of himself and of the changes that were happening to his body.

When a nurse asked him how he seemed so calm session after session he replied that he thought of the peace he felt on turning the soil, planting and weeding his seedlings, and watching his plants grow. He thought of his sore veins as representing his roots that God was helping him to tend. Sometimes he thought of his breath as a gentle wind and just watched it caress the plants; sometimes he saw the intravenous drip as nourishing rain. At night his wife said a prayer for him as he just breathed and listened, letting go of all awareness except "peace." Without realizing it, he gained control by letting go.

~

If control and image have been the defining elements of a person's self-perception, any form of disaster might be handled from that viewpoint. After a biological catastrophe or a violation of self or property, the person's priority will be to regain some control. Desperate situations (such as the early diagnosis of a dangerous illness, the suspicion of a cheating spouse, or the news of a murdered child) are met initially with shock and anger rather than with a search for direction and information.

A person can provide direction for scattered energies by confronting the situation with the aid of documentation and by engaging experts who can give competent advice. Follow-through actions can also lend a feeling of control. Although it is extremely difficult to face an unpleasant issue, old habits do enable one to function. In the midst of emotional anguish, the person who has cultivated self-confidence will convey the impression of dignity, virtuosity, and courage. But this behavior may belie inner stress. For those who have a strong identity and personal pride, and are unwilling to compromise, the loss of absolute control may seem disastrous.

Hopeless-Helpless Syndrome

A psychological crisis ensues when a person realizes that a loss may lead directly to greater losses that will adversely affect function and independence and threaten the person's sense of identity. Obsession with this loss of control may result in withdrawal, abject feelings of loneliness, and disinterest in everything but the situation and its unwanted effects. The person has no hope and is unhelpable. This is not the normal detachment and withdrawal associated with the expected stages of death and dying. In normal withdrawal there is a sense of peace or at least a resolve to accept the inevitable.[5] When the person is in emotional peril, however, he or she has difficulty focusing on anything for long but keeps returning to expectations of disaster. In such a state of depression, the person may desire death because the emotional hurt is so acute. Anger becomes an automatic response to others, isolation is sought because solace cannot be received, and no positive thoughts can be considered. The phrase "hopeless-helpless syndrome" can be applied to this most extreme form of depression disorder, but it is not uncommon to find some of these symptoms emerging from time to time during any stage of depression.[6]

The terminally ill who are most severely hopeless and helpless may turn toward the wall, ignoring all contacts, all caregiving efforts, and every attempt at giving food or drink. The person has given up hope of ever being able to be helped. Little or no sharing of thoughts occurs. Visits from relatives, friends, social service workers, and pastoral counselors are met with more withdrawal or an occasional hostile stare. In this extreme behavioral pattern, if the patient does not share some formative thoughts, it cannot be certain whether the cause is brain damage, changes in the brain's chemical balances due to pathology or the side effects of treatment, a mental illness flare-up (in a patient with a history of manic depression or bipolar disorder), or a decision to withdraw from society in a monastic manner.

Differentiating Unhealthy from Healthy Motivation

While the individual remains the same person as always, influences on the brain are revealed in many subtle ways. Some disease processes, such as cancer and stroke, affect mental function through actual brain damage. Some conditions, such as liver and kidney disease, cause the buildup of toxins in the body that especially affect the ability to think. The buildup of Alzheimer's plaque may affect mental clarity, complicating the treatment of other medical problems. The side effects of many medicines, especially analgesics and antianxiety prescriptions, can alter perceptions or chemical balances. And symptoms such as nausea often make the person unable to take in or retain necessary foods and liquids. Any resulting chemical imbalances within the body, and therefore the brain, are all factors in determining whether the person's behavior is influenced by physiological conditions or free will. These signs of morbidity may be helped with treatment that combines medical rebalancing, personal interactions, and soothing measures such as body care, comeditation, and counseling.

On the other hand, various cultural and religious traditions have encouraged the dying to withdraw from the group, and for them the desire to do so seems natural. Buddhists teach that the preparation for the attainment of higher consciousness requires the disciple let go of all attachments. To the Buddhist who has spent a lifetime in training, a prolonged dying provides an opportunity to ready the mind by entering into a state in which few thoughts or distractions disturb the meditative, or focused, mind. This is the ultimate goal in preparing for transition through the stages of death. Sudden death or imposed distraction might rob the person of an entire life's purpose. While some interaction is permitted, the attendants are very careful to provide assistance and support only when the dying person indicates that it is appropriate or when a comeditation vigil has already been promised.

If the patient is concerned about the physical or mental changes and is willing to cooperate, many physiological effects may be addressed by careful medical management. But when all signs indicate that disease or mental distortions are causing emotional anguish, if the patient identifies with the suffering and refuses attempts to manage the problems, nothing can be done. Respect for the patient's right to choose is in conflict with others' desire to help. Less than twenty-five years ago, if a patient refused a medicine many hospital nurses were generally expected to give the dosage deemed essential for easing symptoms, either forcibly or by disguising it with foods. Today, federal law gives a patient the right to refuse medications or treatment even when their purpose is to relieve suffering. Although antidepressant drugs might treat self-destructive behavior, they cannot be given if the patient clearly forbids it, unless the person's actions are so extreme that a court order declaring the person to be legally incompetent mandates professional intervention. For a family or an institution to pursue such an effort, using both valuable time and money, is to demean the patient's personhood. Similarly, any caregiving actions or counseling efforts provided over protest are really invasions of privacy in spite of their good intentions.

What Help Can Be Given When All Help Is Refused?
When a patient is despondent, as much supportive assistance as possible should be obtained. Investigate the person's history to gain insight into the displayed bitterness. Arrange to make numerous, nonprovoking contacts for specific, unhurried periods of time every day. If background information provides clues to what the person is thinking, use that knowledge carefully while honoring the patient's right of confidentiality. Permit only exchanges that are likely to reinforce the positive aspects of the individual's personal struggle.

We have found that frequent attempts to claim the middle way have been the most successful caregiving responses to this kind of conflict. For instance, gestures that demonstrate respect and care may be tolerated because they address the person's need to receive concern and attention without needing to express feelings. Nursing chores, such as very gentle repositioning and cleansing, may be accepted in silence if an initial display of anger, such as overturning a basin, does not rebuff the caregiver. An explanation of intent must be offered, and the person's reactions or vague signals need to be interpreted sensitively and accurately. Refusal to be touched, for instance, may be due to intensely sharp, tingling pain and contacts must then be modified to give comfort but not stimulation.

A person who lies in uncontrollable excrement may feel humiliated, be fearful of others' reactions, and endure pain from irritation that becomes worse during movement. Such a person may want to avoid bathing, but the discovery that a bath can be achieved with giant towels dampened in a warm cleansing solution and spread across the body, and that the body needs to be turned only once, is likely to cause the patient to look forward to that refreshing change. One emaciated woman would drink only when her head was under the shower and initially refused bathing. But when two persons carefully lifted her with a taut sheet onto a litter to give her a shower, she seemed to welcome the warm water, the body cleansing, and the opportunity to satisfy her thirst. When the staff scheduled this routine twice a day, she moved more often and was less angry.

Comeditation is another caregiving gesture that provides comfort while respecting the patient's aversion to physical contact. If the person refuses comeditation, just spending time at the bedside in silence is an alternative. Focusing on the patient's exhalation while thinking words that take this particular person's situation into account may be helpful. We suggest thoughts such as *peace, compassion, forgiveness, comfort.* The person should be told that a certain word is being said inwardly as you sit beside the bed. Suggest a movement of the head if the word mentioned does not meet with the patient's approval; indicate that it is desirable for the patient to choose his or her own words instead. From time to time offer to say the word(s) aloud, teaching that it always be said when the person exhales, so you are following his or her direction. If the practice is to be kept up regularly it becomes a commitment that must be kept, because skipping the routine demonstrates to the patient that no one really cares, and previous gains are lost. When there is an actively thinking person inside the body on the bed, failure to communicate may indicate more-than-normal sensitivity rather than less.

If it is discovered that the person's fears of doom were provoked by a threatening church authority, offer to arrange for counsel, not from a representative of that church but from a social-service or a nonsectarian pastoral counselor. On the other hand, if deep personal guilt is the likely cause of the despair, a daily visit by a representative of the patient's church to give a prayer of forgiveness or absolution might be helpful. Remember to ask permission first by explaining what is intended. If no reaction follows, proceed only with the stated, non–guilt-evoking plan, then sit for a specified amount of time in silence unless the patient begins to talk. Follow through only as requested by the patient. Recognizing that the patient is highly vulnerable, the caregiver or friend must demonstrate respect and care for the patient without imposing undesired thoughts or gestures.

The object is to allow the person to die in peace if at all possible. This goal of relief from the cause of distress also may conflict with the knowledge that medication could help to alleviate pain and other disturbing symptoms. The person who refuses oral medication, injections, or suppositories, even when the purposes are explained, may accept skin patches. Although it is necessary to inform the patient about the medicines before administration, a positive statement and carry-through may relieve the patient from deciding whether to approve or disapprove. If the patch is not wanted, the patient should be able to remove it. The caregiver must carefully watch for side effects if the patient will not talk or move voluntarily. If medications are refused, other treatments such as bathing, massage, therapeutic touch, hot or cold applications, or Reiki healing may be able to provide some relief.

A severely depressed patient may be suffering from existential despair because of a conviction of worthlessness and powerlessness. In his book *Coping with Cancer*, Dr. Avery Weisman outlines a "vulnerability rating scale" based on the signals projected by a distressed person.[7] He states that vulnerability is the other side of coping well. A person with low self-esteem who is motivated by rigidly high expectations may have difficulty coping when physical or functional status is threatened. Variations in coping capacities have been studied in cancer patients by Weisman and others, who have consistently found that "happiness" is not essential to effective coping.

The existential despair that Weisman identifies as helpless uncertainty is the perception of vulnerability or powerlessness coupled with alienation from others, whether self-imposed or otherwise. Without personal validation, negative thoughts about oneself become magnified. Feelings of endangerment increase suspicion, alienation, and the fear of becoming a victim. We have observed through Richard's role as counselor to the HIV community that many AIDS patients are vulnerable to these feelings of lost hope and helplessness as their medical options decrease and one friend after another dies. One caregiver told us that in a patient census of forty, two-thirds had resumed drug or alcohol abuse as an expression of despair and the desire to escape the symptoms and debasement resulting from AIDS.

Alcohol and tranquilizing or analgesic medications are frequently overused in the effort to lessen the pain of anguish. In a patient who is less severely affected, exhaustion may prevent normal self-care efforts in spite of physical ability. Yet such a patient may have so much nervous energy as not to be able to rest, day or night. Although not dying, this person is also experiencing the hopeless-helpless phenomenon because he or she does not believe that anyone is able to help, and the situation seems inescapable. The worst possible outcome is an all-consuming fixation on despair. No medicine is able to relieve the pain, medication side effects are considered totally intolerable, and any effort by another person is likely to be considered inadequate.

This kind of reaction may also be associated with phobias or panic disorder. There may be no invasive illness, or the invasive illness may be slow moving and not actually require radical changes in activity. While death seems to offer peace, the person is obsessed with fear of the unknown and therefore becomes upset by the slightest physical symptom. Although suicide may be contemplated several times a day, the danger of self-harm is not as great as the suicidal thoughts may imply. The person may be so terrified by stories of hell or the prospect of being resuscitated after brain damage has occurred that extreme entrapment and total loss of control represent a greater threat than the actual pain. Psychotherapy is advised for anyone who experiences these symptoms. It is necessary to expose the roots of these feelings, because even though recent grief or stress may appear to be the stimulus for such acute suffering, these extreme reactions are tied to earlier concepts and traumas.

Most people do not have so much difficulty coping with adversity. A person who is able to integrate life events is able to adapt to new demands, obtain appropriate support, and modify expectations in order to maintain morale. But suffering and grief stimulate us all to recall previous periods of suffering, grief, and loss. Even when a person with few coping problems encounters some major trauma, every discomfort or challenge may be magnified, relationships can become strained, and resolution often seems evasive until that person is able to see the broader picture. The passage of time may help, but the steadfastness and reinforcement of others is the greatest boost to healthful coping. The use of comeditation with a caring person is a wonderful way for both to realize sharing, gain practice in letting go, and gain the perspective of finding peace in kairos (extended) time.

If mental anguish affects coping, help is available. We believe it should be in the form of a threefold approach, which includes counseling, medication, and the more holistic attitude-behavioral training. The physician may prescribe any of several very effective antidepressant medications. The patient must understand that several weeks are required for the medicine to be fully effective. Any side effects from the medicine will probably lessen within a short time, and the relief of such torturous hopeless-helpless feelings is worth the adjustment period. Chemical relief, however, does not change the situation or the person's automatic responses.

As in all symptom management, it is necessary to look at the various aspects of the problem objectively. In attitude adjustment the patient learns to let go of previously held resentments when they do not directly affect the immediate issues. Too often, patterns of behavior are begun in early life that are meant to hide the insecurity or fear the child harbors. A set of habits is developed to project to the world beyond the self the image of a strong and fully capable person. With maturity, a person's responses include maintaining the image of adult competency while indirectly still protecting himself or herself from the suffering experienced during childhood and from later hurts that have become sources of resentment. However, a very different, scared child may be lurking within a person's consciousness and emerge when anxieties are out of control. When a role change or an illness forces the loss of identity as a strong person, the griefs of the past may come cascading into the person's awareness as proof of frailty, causing an uncertain future to hold terror.

Counseling will help the person develop a new perspective. By seeing his or her situation at the time of the earlier occurrences, and admitting to recent vulnerability, the person is able to understand better the depth of the fear or insecurity. In defining each situation rationally, the person learns to recognize strengths that can be called upon in the present crisis. Releasing the grief associated with each aspect of the past and the anticipated future helps the person move into a new stage of acceptance.

So much feeling need not be dealt with alone. For most people who have to face major life changes, these are not abnormal reactions. Consulting a therapist (such as a hospice social worker) who is skilled in grief and loss counseling will provide an opportunity for the person to review the many aspects of the situation and to find workable solutions. Other support persons are needed as well. If the patient's family cannot be present, they should see that empathetic caregivers are part of the caregiving regime. In addition, it is essential that the person who is bound up in such intensive stress learn some form of relaxation.

If the person is able to recline or find a restful position in another person's presence, comeditation may offer the most effective treatment. The comeditation process becomes a therapy because the person listens (action) to another's voice (distraction). The selection of the elements composing his or her particular comeditation process are chosen (controlled) by the patient. As the helper watchfully makes each sound in coordination with the recipient's exhalation, the recipient can sense the comforting of another person's close attention without the violation of touch or manipulation. (If the person wants to abort the session midway, it is all right. This might mean the person cannot bear such a close interpersonal relationship at this time. The "how to do it" principles conveyed and the elementary relaxation experience may be all the person needs to be able to apply them privately.)

If the restless patient can just listen to an acceptable sound cued to his or her exhalation for a few minutes, the memory imprint will allow this, or another sound chosen as a substitute (possibly imagined), to be recalled when the person is alone but wants to calm down. As the sound is heard (actually or in the imagination) it serves as an emotional reinforcement because it verifies an expectation, serves as a distraction from agitation, and symbolizes caring attention and security. This combination helps the body let go. As the body releases bound-up tension, the psychological barriers soften as well. No one is intruding upon the person's privacy, but the feeling of comradeship provides trust and a sense of affirmation. If counseling is occurring at this time, the person is able to progress rapidly because it no longer seems necessary to project an embellished self-image. Rather, when the true nature of the person is present, both the subject and the helper become absorbed in the deeper qualities of that person's very special life. Hopelessness is reduced as the person perceives that help occurs through a compassionate and reinforcing relationship.

Habitual Responses

Certain habits are identified with the personality because they have been developed over a lifetime. They have become automatic socializing or coping devices because they worked. Wit, sarcasm, pouting, withdrawing, oversolicitation, anger transfer (example: an injured husband who has lost his job yells at his wife), taking reckless chances, restless energy or overcautious deliberation, and assuming falsely superior or submissive attitudes are a few examples of protective mannerisms. When these devices are incorporated into daily living they allow us to cope in familiar patterns. But when they are overdone, they misdirect everyone's attention from inner conflicts that need to be worked through. The goal is not to change the personality but to get under the affectations and communicate with the real person inside.

Anxieties produce tension. Tension is enacted psychologically and physically with fear, agitation, anger, and inner turmoil. Just as anger, fear, and anxiety can produce undesirable physical and emotional responses, the opposite reaction pattern—taking extra time to relax, breathe deeply, and clear the mind with calming thoughts—can holistically ease the tension and the anxieties as well. It is therefore even more necessary for the person who is unable to rest to learn to use a relaxation response that will allow the stress cycle to be broken.

Although comeditation is an appropriate technique for reversing tension, sometimes exercise is also necessary. Activity causes the mind to be distracted, allows the body to engage in full respirations, and helps the muscles feel tired and ready to relax after exertion. Therefore, we sometimes recommend scheduling some form of physical challenge, such as range-of-motion exercises, before comeditation.

When a person cannot lie down to relax in another's presence, then it becomes necessary to obtain tension reduction in any way possible. Sometimes, the basic teachings of the comeditation technique can be adapted so that the person can benefit by reviewing the process regularly alone. If the person is restless and requires some action to achieve a calmer mood, rubbing beads (such as a rosary) one at a time while counting or praying is often helpful. We taught one woman to crochet doily rounds for relaxation. The repetition of the movements directed her energy, and watching the crochet chain grow distracted her from her anxieties. She gained both a calming effect and a tangible reward for her efforts. Allowing water to play on the hands or body, drawing doodles, kneading clay or bread, and arranging flowers are other stress-reduction devices.

Many people feel that they are most relaxed and have a special sense of calm when they have exercised strenuously. But if illness will not permit a person to play a game of tennis or golf, or to run two miles, other forms of activity may be substituted. For instance, walking in the house while repeatedly counting from one to ten may help to release anger that cannot be resolved. During moments of extreme agitation, the trusted helper may walk behind the person, saying the numbers loudly to direct the person's attention to a neutral thought. Music or a comforting song may provide calm and distraction. One patient's daughter obtained a record of folk songs by a group from her mother's homeland, sung in the dialect of the old woman's childhood. This one effort, supplemented by the daughter's reminiscing, helped to balance a long life of struggles with past and present affections.

The point is not to ignore a problem but to discharge the harmful emotional energy that prevents rational evaluation. Whether the issue is immediate pain or discomfort that is intensified by emotional distress, the resulting strain needs to be addressed in a holistic manner. The body ought to be adjusted to reduce nerve pressure by position changes, pressure on trigger points, and massage. Changes in thoughts can also release tension. While comeditation is one of the most valuable tools in helping to relax body tension and simultaneously halt aggravating thoughts, it is not an end in itself but a means of creating a sense of harmony. But every factor that causes distraction or unrest needs to be considered in the search for the desired balance.

Medication should address the type and degree of discomfort. The person needs to be validated, and the mind and soul require an oasis of quiet communion. Then the issues can be brought into focus for problem solving. The person is able to make thoughtful choices based on personal values and to follow through with effective actions. These choices and actions may be as diverse as calling a doctor to explain unaddressed pain, confronting a former abuser, writing a letter of apology to the family of someone who died long ago, calling a rejected child to reconnect, writing a will, resolving to always take certain medicine on time, resolving to take no more food and only sips of water if the desire is not there, or arranging for one's own funeral. Sometimes, hopeless-helpless feelings are left behind and the feeling of despair changes to a sense of patient waiting. In any case, past and present incidents contribute to the identity of the individual. Wholeness of being is achieved by a unique series of action, reaction, development, and letting go. Thus, we create ourselves as unreplicable works of art, designing ourselves until the last moments of life.

But each one's value is influenced by every individual who shares a fraction of that life. Just as a sense of worth, feelings of care or abandonment, frustration, or depression are reflected in communication with others, gestures of care or neglect affect the patient's self-concept. The shopkeeper who saves a box of berries for a working daughter because her dying parent craves the taste demonstrates thoughtfulness. A devoted dog or a confused infant, coming to the bedside again and again in spite of being led away, further shows the concern of one living creature for another.

Those who help a person work through physical and emotional problems at the end of his or her life may seem to be thought of with greater significance than the amount of time spent together might justify. When we are reduced to a dependent state, we must rely on others to help us achieve our goals—completion of the present, compensations for the past, and projections into the future. Present comforting gestures may be more appreciated because the discomfort is so great. Past loyalties (such as the loyalty of the dog) are valued because they signify special commitments that verify who we are. Symbols of our future (like the infant) verify our existence and connect us to immortality.

Hope and the Afterlife

Emily Dickinson spoke of hope as "the thing with feathers that perches in the soul."[8] Our positive expectations may be as immediate as hope for the next few minutes or as distant as forever. Immortality is a broad concept and means different things to different people. Some may prefer to have little or no awareness of continuity and pass from life to death without regret or any expectation of reward. Some may trust that their genes will be carried through the generations, assuring continued life. Others may be content that an acclaimed project or achievement will preserve their names far into the future. Still others have given their lives for a political cause, believing that personal sacrifice was necessary for the betterment or protection of society.

The world's religions describe an afterlife that gives comfort because of the expectation of some form of continuation. If one has experienced the true warmth of love in this life, there seems to be little reason not to expect a more encompassing love when in the presence of the fullness of God's love. The message of a better afterlife and everlasting peace has been far more persuasive to many believers than have preachers who rant about eternal hell and damnation.

There are a number of books in the field of death and dying that discuss immortality. Michael Simpson notes that the quality of hope seems to be a way of being. There is always some possibility of improvement or anticipation, even if it is a condition that assumes that life does end: "Finite does not mean futile."[9] Some of the world's most beloved poetry speaks to the continuation of hope following death. To Emily Dickinson, hope nestles in the heart without trying to gain attention. Sometimes it seems not to be present, but when comfort is needed it is always available if the person will just reach for it. In meditation it has been found that hope can grow to fill one's entire being as one surrenders to the expansion within by letting go of fears and preconceptions of the ego. That is the fullness of "clear mind, peaceful heart."

Hope can be an anchor or a buoy adjusting to the changing turbulence its owner must endure. But it is merely speculation unless it is shared. When we let others know what is hoped for, we receive help in making the desire a reality. The only requirement hope makes is that it be allowed to exist.

6

THE PATIENT AND
THE FAMILY

~

Within me I find the strength to know you.
And now I am stronger, for we have shared.

—George Betts, 1972.

Caregiving

For the most part we have defined a caregiver as any person who provides care and support to another. Although we are essentially our own caregivers, we cope with our concerns by seeking information and guidance from others, hoping for gentle consolation and caring attention. As children, we run to a parent after a fall; we seem to know that certain things must be done to stop a hurt or provide comfort when we feel sick. As adults, we often prefer to take our complaints to our own primary doctor before consulting a specialist. Often, a kind touch and an understanding phrase gives us as much comfort as a painkiller.

Likewise, although some people assume a caregiving role more readily than others, each of us innately responds with a concerned attitude when confronted by someone who needs help. Even those of us who are repulsed by the sight of sickness are concerned that those we care about are helped, often being willing to pay for the assurance that another will do what we cannot. Thus, we are all caregivers. Similarly, we are all participants in the cycle of life, wellness, illness, and death. When a child, a spouse, or a parent needs assistance, we each respond in the best way possible for the time, circumstances, and individual personality. Each of us is different, so our commitments and personal reactions vary. But in the presence of vulnerability, we are affected by others quite differently than during normal interactions.

A devoted loved one, a person who visits periodically (a family member, a friend, or an organizational volunteer who becomes a friend), a live-in companion-nurse, a physician, or a staff member employed by any health-care facility—each will provide care within the limits of the skills and time pledged. Through this involvement, caregivers can form a unique bond with the person who is ill. By virtue of this intimacy they develop a kinship, which during the period of need makes them functionally members of an extended family. This concentrated attention on a sick person's well-being may distort evaluations of the caregiver's success or failure. It is very important that everyone's emotional expectations are kept within the limitations of realistic goals.

Coping Variations

Those who are closely associated with a dying person may also experience emotions similar to those of the "stages of dying" described by Elisabeth Kübler-Ross (see chapter 1), but they do not experience denial, anger, bargaining, depression, and acceptance on the same schedule as the patient; they vacillate in their own patterns. In crisis, people react with their own habitual coping styles. Acting out, emotional insulation, rationalization, and regression are patterns related to age, culture, personality, and habit. These patterns are intensified when a person is under stress. This variation in behaviors, while a family is facing serious illness and early losses, magnifies each person's loneliness.

When we are given a referral to work with a family, it is usually because nursing and/or counseling guidance is needed. While most of the physicians we work with know that we teach comeditation, they recognize that our broad approach to the multiple factors of caregiving produces the effects they are hoping to see. As long as their medical orders are supported and they are notified of changes appropriately, the methods we use are not as important to them as the results. We have found that most families feel the same way. While they recognize comeditation as beneficial, family members are so enveloped by the complexities of the progressing illness that they cannot separate one factor from another.

Many problems arise, are dealt with, and are worked around. Any action that helps family members through a crisis is praised and then allowed to fade into the next issue. The experience is like a ride on a rollercoaster: the important thing is to get through it without falling out and to stand without wobbling too much when it is over. For these reasons, our stories about the use of comeditation in working with people with serious illnesses are also examples of many other aspects of coping. The following case history shows how one family reacted to cancer.

~

Joe was the head of a large extended American family descended from Italian and Irish forebears. Interactions among family members had always been expressive. They fed off one another's suggestions and criticisms, but each was stubbornly independent. Visiting was frequent among the many cousins and their families, who all tried to project the image of success, knowledge, and generosity. After Joe learned that he had cancer of the lung, he discovered that his actual family was very small and frightened.

Joe and his wife shared a two-unit house with their son and their son's family. His two daughters both called to express their concerns weekly, but neither could leave family and job across the country unless Joe had an emergency. Although Joe had always tried to help out when any of the other relatives had crises, his wife and son felt that Joe was often used. Now the cousins' casual inquiries and conspicuous flourishes did not substitute for true support.

Joe's Aunt Josie was filled with fright when she thought of her nephew having cancer. She recalled social attitudes from her pre–World War I childhood, and insisted that the cancer diagnosis be kept secret. Yet, unable to shake her depression, she cried whenever she looked at Joe or his family. She curtailed her own activities because her sadness was so overwhelming. Incapable of suppressing her anxieties, she spoke to her friends of how she was suffering from worry, then became angry when they asked for details about Joe's sickness or questioned her faith in saintly intervention. Joe's wife went to church daily. She had always prayed for her needs to be met. Now, she offered God her own greater devotion and attendance as a bargaining strategy: "I'll attend Mass daily if you will only let Joe live." She spent her time at home trying to cook Joe's old favorites. As a form of denial, she repeatedly prepared the same quantities of food. Joe could force only a few tastes, leaving an abundance of leftovers for visitors. Always a good hostess, she cooked as if bribing the guests with meals would magnify their prayers for her husband. She believed she was successfully avoiding depression by constant activity, but she cried her exhausted body to sleep each night.

Angrily, Joe's son cursed loudly at everyone as his father's illness became more and more apparent. He blamed the doctors for not curing his father, his mother for not adapting, his wife for not anticipating everyone's unexplained moods, his children for being self-centered, and his father for "giving up too soon." He believed his was a realistic depression because he seemed to be the only one concerned about the greater expenses incurred in the face of his parent's meager income. He had always had trouble controlling his temper, but the whole situation was so frustrating that he could not withdraw as his father was inclined to do.

Joe turned his head from the noise to separate himself from his surroundings. This withdrawal removed him from the aches he felt when watching his family. Actually, Joe used this pattern to escape into fantasies. He could think of activities he enjoyed with his wife and grandchildren; he figured the odds on the World Series; he thought about how his obituary would read. He dealt with his pain by being quiet and by distracting himself.

His daughter-in-law, caught between denial and acceptance, immersed herself in doing her own household chores, caring for Joe, and helping her mother-in-law. She felt that she was struggling to maintain a secure home for her children. While she was grateful for the help and love received from her in-laws over the years, she resented her husband for being more preoccupied with his grief than with their own family's activities. While she tried to help her in-laws, she felt everyone was unreliable and left too much for her to do. Therefore, she was angry much of the time, but the more she expressed herself the less she felt that the others supported her. She yearned for normal life.

The twelve-year-old granddaughter wanted to spend time with her grandfather but was angry that his sickness occupied her parents, thus placing her middle-school activities in second place. When she was with her friends, she could forget how sad she felt thinking about her sick grandfather, but usually her school work seemed unimportant compared with her anxieties about her home life. Her grades slipped, and no one made an issue of it. This caused her to feel even less important.

The six-year-old grandson was trying to understand why someone as nice as his grandfather should become so sick. He wondered whether his refusal to go to a cousin's house with his grandparents had anything to do with the sickness. Grandpa had coughed blood and was taken to the hospital that same evening. Frightened that when his grandfather died a scary ghost might appear, the little boy tried to talk with others, but his sister teased him, his mother couldn't be bothered about ideas from cartoons, and his dad was too busy to talk with him privately.

Some older cousins described visions of threatening ghosts and told him about movies with vampires and the "living dead." He couldn't decide why such awful sickness happened to people or what death really meant, and he either cried or angrily acted out when he was scared. The strange smells in his grandfather's room, and the many sad faces, bothered him also, so now he hated to spend time with the others.

~

The individuals and the reactions in this account are typical of the many differences found in a multigenerational family. While everyone in Joe's family knew that he was dying, they initially rejected hospice care because they could not bring themselves to admit that he was not likely to live more than six months. They did admit that they needed nursing assistance, however. As we worked with them we referred to the hospice principles that were compatible with appropriate care for Joe. Family counseling helped them to work together, to include the children, and to strengthen their relationships. Soon they were telling callers that they couldn't get along without hospice.

In the early weeks of our working with them, the family welcomed comeditation as a means of pain relief when it was given by the nurse or home health aide. But each was so immersed in personal distress that none would settle down long enough to give a helpful session. Later, as they became accustomed to their own personal threats and were better able to focus upon the patient's needs, they were able to use comeditation in the form of a rosary recitation to help Joe with his pain and restlessness. Individually, then, each began to gain a sense of peace as each shared moments of communion with Joe. This peace was conveyed to the children as love and caring.

Joe himself began to think of death as a release from suffering, and he tried to help the others understand. He feared more for them and their future without him than for himself. He had tried to live a good life. Now, if his best was not enough for spiritual absolution, he was resigned to the consequences. He did not want to change who he was. The day he expressed that sentiment to his wife and son he felt relieved. Joe's death seemed to come too soon, but through deeper sharing, the family became more united by it.

Burnout and Issues Involved with Long-Term Caregiving

Anyone who becomes immersed intensively in caregiving is a potential candidate for burnout, especially one with some of these characteristics: idealism, dedication, high performance expectations of others and one's self, thoroughness, and a strong sense of responsibility and independence.[1] Personal changes and losses increase one's vulnerability to stress and the onset of some form of illness.[2] Anyone who cares for a person who might be slowly dying may become frustrated and under greater stress. By devoting increasingly greater portions of one's time and emotional energy to the highly stressful situation, the person—whether a committed family member or an overtaxed worker—is a subject for burnout.

If the family is experiencing prolonged strain, it is necessary for them to find help. The families used in the examples in this chapter did obtain assistance from other relatives and friends and from hospice or a visiting nursing organization; but they found they also had to pay privately for some additional hours to obtain periods of respite for themselves. When Joe's wife and daughter-in-law went to a movie, they were able to enjoy it and each other's company for a bit.

Changing scenes, getting outdoors for light and fresh air, and viewing nature are helpful. Directing energy into healthful exercise such as walking, in spite of physical fatigue, will encourage the body to stretch and improve its alignment. When the mind is cleared from repetitive anxieties, and the body's function is balanced, the cells in a person's body normalize. The principles that apply to the patient are equally appropriate for the helpers' well-being.

Proper nutrition, distractions, exercise, and rest are as important for caregivers as for patients. If snacks, coffee or other forms of caffeine, and cigarettes are used for a quick pick-me-up or to save time and effort, the self-sacrifice is self-imposed. Nobody can properly perform a difficult job of any sort when that body is malnourished or artificially keyed up. In the same way, the use of alcohol or illegal drugs as a temporary aid causes more harmful side effects to the user than benefits. If the stress continues for a long time, it is absolutely necessary for the person to incorporate a program aimed at maintaining his or her health during that entire period. Otherwise, the caregiver may become a patient also.

Anticipatory Grief

Regardless of how accepting a person may believe himself or herself to be, the losses and changes that inevitably take a toll when serious illness occurs are experienced as symptoms of grief. "Anticipatory grief" is the term used to describe the effects of grief that are experienced when there is awareness of loss before death. The losses may be actual events, such as a stroke that paralyzes the limbs; or they may be mere conjectures, such as terrifying visions of wasting and burial following a confirmed diagnosis of cancer. In either case, the person must deal emotionally with not only the facts of the disease but the many implications of disease progression.

Depression or agitation may result from functional and relationship changes. A dread of death may occur equally to the most theologically certain as to those who have been lifelong agnostics. Both the patient and those who are affected by that person may be expected to experience different forms of grief. For the family, the illness raises concern for the patient and creates changes within their own lives. Both the patient and family members may experience mental confusion, distractibility, poor appetite and nausea, listlessness with fatigue, and other unexplained problems and behaviors. These are symptoms of grief.

Marion Humphrey has defined the disequilibrium experienced with family shifting and role-assignment changes as the most devastating aspect of illness for the family member(s). She explains that it is compounded by the family's need to begin to perceive a future in which the loved one no longer exists.[3] Everyone involved must deal with multiple adaptive tasks. Humphrey cites Kalish and others who have described the many issues requiring the attention of the dying person and the people in that person's support system. Getting affairs in order, considering future medical care, integrating ongoing medical needs into daily life, adjusting to a changing identity, and confronting the fact of nonbeing (implying philosophical questions, doubts, and fears) are all difficult issues that must be considered when death may be imminent.[4]

Earlier medical practices forbade telling the client the facts of the illness, and the dying person had to deal with many anxieties and fears alone. Now, in spite of the fact that society recognizes the patient's right to know the truth and to make decisions about medical intervention, most people require time to hear, understand, and contemplate such weighty information. It is a natural response to block out incoming sounds when one is struck with news that is hurtful. Even a physician who tries to present evidence of a catastrophic illness with patience and tenderness is likely to be misunderstood. Doctors who are uncomfortable discussing the implications of their diagnosis and suggested treatment leave their clients emotionally wounded. This abruptness, coupled with the use of unfamiliar medical terms, can confuse the client and make him or her feel deserted and vulnerable. Then, the ancillary staff (particularly nurses and social workers) or someone the patient trusts must be able to clarify the doctor's message. The client may need assistance in sifting through the information and coming to terms with the choices. Eventually, as the person becomes more affected physically, assistance will be required while he or she is enduring the treatment process. Without support, the person's suspicion or anxiety may turn into anger followed by cynicism and despair. Assistance that could be beneficial may be rejected in bitterness.

Each family and each person within that family normally reacts uniquely to life's events. Issues that imply life or death, however, cause exaggerated behavior, whether silent withdrawal or hyperemotional behavior.

When in trouble, when in doubt, run in circles, scream and shout.

Old folk saying

Typically, the agitated person has the impression that no one else sees the true picture and that nothing effective will be done if he or she does not get upset. But the energy that is the result of excessive emotional reactions causes strained muscles, a disturbed digestive system, and a natural infusion of pain irritants. When the family is pressured by extraordinary circumstances, it is helpful for them to learn a calming technique that gives them time to assess the situation and gear their reactions to reality.

If a twenty-minute break for comeditation isn't feasible, a fifteen-second inner-body relaxation is a possible alternative. Take a deep breath and let your breath out fully while you move your shoulders and neck and loosen your jaw as your hands, arms and elbows become light. Become aware of straightening your spine as the relaxation works into your legs. While waiting for the next breath to come, feel every muscle relax further. Breathe fully with the diaphragm. Expel this breath fully also, while saying calming words internally. Designate special words of reinforcement to be used throughout each day. "Clear mind, peaceful heart," "I am calm, serene, and at peace," "Serenity, acceptance, wisdom," "Lord, abide with me," "Love is all," "God be with us," and "Eternally healing inner light" are a few choices that might be appropriate. See appendix C for other suggestions.

This technique is useful for everyone, because when one person is upset everyone is affected. The involved family members or caregivers have the difficult task of providing security while reinforcing the qualities that will help the out-of-control person to cope and remembering that the person who is acting out is making an effort to manage his or her behavior.

Ken Wilber, a leading transpersonal psychologist, writing about his experiences as he and his wife, Treya, dealt with her cancer of the breast, said that the most important function of a support person is to be an "emotional sponge." He noted that efforts to resist a threat actually point up the support person's own inability to cope.[5] The necessary response is empathy. The approach most hospice volunteers are taught is to "just be there." Simple presence conveys care.

The Wilbers believed they had cancer together. Like so many couples who relate closely to each another, through their trials they learned profound insights into each other, life, death, despair, joy, and their own spiritual values. Ken said he learned to "practice the wound of love." "Real love hurts; real love makes you totally vulnerable and open; real love will take you far beyond yourself; and, therefore, real love will devastate you. I kept thinking, if love does not shatter you, you do not know love." But the values that emerged were their rewards. He said that they directly served each other, "exchanging self for other, and in so doing, glimpsed that eternal spirit that transcends both self and other, both 'me' and 'mine.'" Treya, who remained an active participant in seminars through most of those five years, said that her experience became a beacon for self-understanding, both for herself and those around her. She considered herself fortunate to have been given advance warning. "Because I can no longer ignore death, I pay more attention to life."

One cannot be a sponge unless the excess can drain off elsewhere. Each support person must have some source of support as well. Respite care is the practice of providing a space for support persons to get a break from the bedside. Many hospices will arrange for a patient to be cared for in a nursing home or hospital inpatient unit when the family needs a rest, and to return home with the condition more stabilized after the family has had a chance to be restored. A relative, friend, professional caregiver, or trained volunteer may give the primary caregiver a precious break of a few hours on a regular basis.

A person who chooses to spend some personal time attending a support group receives the advantages of a changed visual focus from the few feet around the bed to a broader view of the outside world and the stimulation given by the participants in the group as they exchange ideas, techniques, and feelings. But even at home, each person can take a moment for refreshment at various times throughout each day by seeing details of design, remembering to look out the window, and taking a breath of air when getting the mail. For instance, before returning from taking out the trash, let the mind hear the birds; when listening to music, feel the sounds through the entire body while releasing the tension of other cares.

As each individual interacts through the processes of giving and taking, producing and procuring, sharing and expressing care, that person directly affects every other member of the family and community. When illness interferes with the normal pattern, everyone within that pattern is affected as well. The people who are close to that person often suffer from changes in routine and associations with others, reduction and redirection of resources, grief over loss, and anticipation of a sad future (often imaginary). They also experience a heightened awareness of the magic of life and the unique qualities that make up the person they are about to lose.

The Family Impact of Mid-Life Losses

For most of us, no time is a good time to have a life curtailed. Although we admire the spiritual comfort implied by John Fire Lame Deer's statement, "Today is a good day to die," generally we would prefer to be able to complete our commitments, see our loved ones safe, and influence our part of history for as long as possible. Yet accidents, war, and disease take many of us from our roles just when our presence should be most effective. All members of a family must accommodate themselves to serious losses, as did this family of a patient who required care for cancer of the brain.

~

Bebe was forty-one when she fell while carrying her baby, Lisa, and they were both rushed to the hospital. Her son, Billy, in the second grade, had expected his mother to be his Cub Scout den parent, but Bebe's hospitalization led to brain surgery and cancer treatment. When Bebe came home, her speech was slurred and she had trouble remembering. Sometimes she would become angry for reasons known only to her. Because of her dizziness and forgetfulness, Billy, his dad, and his grandparents had to help Bebe about the house and to the bathroom. Sometimes, she seemed to cry as much as the baby because of her headaches. Later, her shortness of breath during exertion restricted her activities even further. Her husband, Jim, tried to work from a home office so he could care for Bebe with the help of a health aide. But Jim had to ask Bebe's parents to care for Lisa, and he asked his family to help him care for Billy. Because he had already started free-lance work to supplement their income and help pay support for two children from a previous marriage, Jim was able to make the home-based transition fairly easily. But the setup now required interruptions, juggling schedules to accommodate caregivers as well as clients. He had to plan each day to include home-maintenance duties, care for both his wife and his children, and talk with people who called to express their concerns. Meeting with his clients helped Jim somewhat by enabling him to briefly forget his problems at home.

Formerly a very optimistic couple, Jim and Bebe were strained just to survive day to day. Jim's relationship with his first family collapsed because he couldn't meet the court-ordered payments, and he had trouble fitting the older children into his complicated life. Yet, in spite of her mental changes and his frequent exhaustion, Bebe and Jim were able to communicate their hopes and fears and to reaffirm their mutual devotion.

Bebe and her caregivers went from one medical crisis to another. She learned to manage episodes of shortness of breath and intense headaches with oxygen, medications, and meditation. Her caregivers learned to anticipate her changing moods, and they would act as comeditation guides when the pain, stress, or confusion was particularly difficult. With medicines and stress reduction they were able to keep her from having full seizures. She used a tape recorder with relaxing music during the night or when the children demanded the other adults' attention. The goal for the household was to maintain Bebe's interactive presence in the home with her children for as long as possible. Their success was their reward. Nevertheless, Bebe was distressed that she was missing so much of her children's lives. She wanted to continue to be their mother even though she thought, at times, that she would welcome death. She regretted the stresses her illness had placed on her husband's career and his relationship with her stepchildren. She regretted the burden that their families were having to assume as they compensated for her with her children. She regretted, most of all, the knowledge that the family would be better off without her, in spite of their grief and the effects of not having her there to fill her role as wife and mother.

But, in spite of recognizing all of this, she could not bear to relinquish her family, her lifelong dream, until the moment when she would have no choice. It had taken her many years to work out her life plan, but until recently her life had gone well. This early death had not been a part of her plan. She laughed at the irony when her younger sister showed her a cartoon Bebe had sent as encouragement when the younger woman had entered college. It was a *Peanuts* cartoon in which Lucy says to Linus "Someday I'll be rich and famous." Linus asks "How do you know?" Lucy responds, "It's only fair."

Children

A child, as with Bebe's son, Billy, not only experiences insecurity upon recognizing that a parent is disabled, but is compelled to take on tasks (such as taking his mother to the bathroom) with which others had helped him previously, and to question his own future capabilities. The child loses not only the parenting and supportive companionship but the means to pursue certain interests, such as scouting, sports, or music. Often, when the child needs the greatest amount of attention because of insecurity, concerned adults withdraw their time and energy. The child may act out anger by being aggressive toward other children, or the child may withdraw, being suspicious and reluctant to trust others. Billy's teachers reported that both withdrawal and aggressive acting-out interfered with his school activities; at home he was disobedient and sulky. His uncertainty about day-to-day life was more than he could handle, and his dreams of the future were frightening and lonely. He felt guilty when he had angry thoughts about his mother and she became sicker—almost as if his bad wishes had a magical effect. Psychological counseling for the child became another family necessity.

Three common issues of grief experienced by school-age children are fear, isolation, and guilt. Children use fear fantasies when struggling with issues of dependency, such as imagined shadowy figures ready to grab them when the parent leaves the bedroom. But sometimes fear is grounded on the actual possibility of suffering, separation, and loss. Then, the child must express and work through thoughts of real and imagined impressions in order to separate fact from fiction and to acquire comfortable solutions.

The practice of trying to protect the child from adult worries often causes a sensitive child to speculate privately. Is the secret too awful to be described? Are others blaming the child, so they don't like him or her any more? Children often believe that angry thoughts are so powerful that they themselves are the cause of a worsening illness or of an accident. Fear causes insecurity. Feelings of isolation may promote withdrawal or the inability to relate with others. Guilt may produce a sense of power confused by remorse. Yet, studies have shown that most children are able to deal with death in a matter-of-fact, realistic way. They simply need adults who can patiently help them talk through their ideas and help them reduce their exaggerated fears to facts that can be handled. They need to share their thoughts with an adult, leave to follow childhood pursuits, and return to share, again and again.

A child's understanding of death progresses relative to his or her developmental age. In the early stages of interaction, alert children grasp the concept that people and objects can disappear. Rabbi Earl Grollman, in *Explaining Death to Children,* acknowledges that games such as peek-a-boo, dropping things from a highchair then demanding retrieval, and hide-and-seek are examples of infant and toddler play that evoke fear on separation and elated giggles on rediscovery. But the very young child does not grasp the finality of death.[6] Bebe's daughter, Lisa, knew her mother only as a person who had limited periods of energy. She enjoyed her mother's affection, but she expected others to be active with her. Lisa's loss will be realized most acutely as she matures, and her adjustment will hinge primarily on the security or insecurity she feels as other people attempt to fill the role of mothering her. Nevertheless, she will always have a yearning for the woman she barely knew. If she becomes a parent herself someday, she may discover more issues that she needs to resolve, thereby awakening her greater sense of loss.

The Partner

The spouse of a sick and dying person, concerned about financial solvency, becomes responsible as well for all the chores that were previously shared. In addition, the spouse becomes obligated for all the new duties required in caregiving. Even when others do some tasks, accommodating the others' schedules and filling in at unexpected times is necessary. In long-term illness, the husband or wife must view the relationship with his or her partner in a new light—ever changing, nonrelenting, self-denying.

In seeking help from family, friends, and health professionals, the couple inadvertently expose their weaknesses to others. It is very difficult for any of us to admit our deficiencies in the best of times; when we are vulnerable because of illness, acknowledging our needs that are not likely to lessen soon is even harder. Bebe's husband, Jim, had to set aside his goals for his first family, and he had to ask for help from many other people. He felt completely overextended, needy himself, and angry with those who criticized him or made suggestions. He was also angry with Bebe for causing the mess, and with himself for not being the miracle worker he wanted to be.

When we set aside self-identifying goals, we often become resentful. Disappointments with ourselves surface. Simple gestures intended to express care cause unexpected emotional pain. Parents, siblings, aunts and uncles, employers, and friends who offer to help are often misunderstood. Or, in spite of extensive efforts, those same well-meaning people discover that their labors result in frustration because the need is so great. But most who work out their family's trials agree that they would not change their commitments to one another. The satisfaction from moments of sharing during the last few months far exceeds the personal pain or despair.

The experiences of the two families described in this chapter are not uncommon given the complexities of modern living. These two families are both exceptional, however, because there were numerous supportive members who could respond. The older parents felt the pain of the situation as much as the young; their concepts of their own maturity simply restrained their expressions. Concerns and anxieties were transformed into cooperative efforts to address perceived needs. But some obligations, such as those to the children, were neglected. Lost contact and security could never be recovered, and the loss would require a long period of adjustment. Still they all did the best they could do. Nothing else is necessary.

When we teach comeditation, we insert the phrase "Nothing else is necessary" when we are aware of distractions or the subject has difficulty settling down. The message we are trying to convey is that claiming a time for relaxation is a positive response to anxiety. When all that can be done (within a certain scope) has been done, letting go is appropriate, necessary, and beneficial. Family members sometimes find that letting go of their regrets is more difficult than grieving over the actual death. But when a task is finished, you can do no more; therefore, nothing else is necessary.

In *Facing Death,* Sandra Bertman notes, "Regardless of how one dies, death means separation not only from the flesh but also from the human community."[7] Ninety days, sixteen months, or several years of living with a debilitating disease means that the patient and his or her community must confront wasting, strain its resources, and deal with endlessly compounding consequences. But those precious months also provide all with the opportunity to bask in the experience of knowing one another. As a society, we must never forget the importance of a life as it winds down. Clarifying and questioning the issues of identity, remembering a personal legend, and demonstrating one's uniqueness are tasks that require time.

In spite of frustrations, the reality of vulnerability also demands a focus on values. A woman with a spreading brain tumor may have difficulty concentrating, but she may write letters of wisdom to her children, labeled for opening on certain occasions. She is able to marshall her waning energy to reach a difficult goal because she believes it is important to her legacy and to her loved ones' personal development. In accommodating the specter of death, the dying person must tie up life's issues as well as begin letting go.

Those who attend to the needs of the very ill learn not only the trials but the human richness of that person. Inner thoughts are expressed as the caregiver's touch becomes familiar, and personal habits are integrated into the caregiving routine. The patient shares a special intimacy with the helpers. When the helpers become the implements of the patient's every need, the expression of thoughts seems like speaking to oneself, for the other learns to interpret every gesture. It is this opportunity of sharing that intensifies the experiences of the final period of our lives.

There can be no more intimate sharing than the practice of comeditation during the waning days and hours. Each breath is held like a jewel between the comeditators. Imagery is suspended on a cord between this world and the space of pure consciousness. The words convey the deepest thoughts of the meditator, echoed again and again by the assistant, who is giving the dying person permission to float between the dimensions while preparing for death. If there had been conflict between the two, it may be resolved in spiritual communion without unnecessary, self-defensive attitudes. Brothers who would not speak for years may share nonjudgmental words through comeditation, and find the reunion of kinship. As it becomes too late to change the course of a life that is finishing, it is time to extend freedom to each other through togetherness. Such love unites and releases simultaneously.

The Professional Caregiver in the Home

Professional caregivers become part of this family network, not only because so many issues require attention but because they personally participate in one of the most traumatic events of the family's life. Medical advisors and helpers not only keep the patient as comfortable as possible but also reinforce the family. Each time the nurse demonstrates personal care, wound treatment, or a more sophisticated maintenance procedure, he or she is expressing confidence in the home caregivers and in the patient. The implication is that the patient, family, and nurses are sharing this problem together.

A caregiver experiences the greatest personal and professional satisfaction by being entrusted with the most intimate aspects of another's hopes, fears, joys, pains, and sorrows. It is a transpersonal experience; that is, all together form a unit that transcends ordinary conversation and creates a union through compassion.

At the same time, a professional participant will remain personally stabilized because training has provided objectivity. Thus, the client's trust is well placed. The patient's and family's needs are understood and often anticipated, so resources are accessed as promptly as possible. Clients know that the explanations and compromises offered by the professional person are reflections of genuine caring. Through such empathy the caregiver demonstrates that the difficult is possible to transcend. Even the acknowledgment of death is a recognition of spiritual qualities that might change but are not lost. At this time, the soul is not a dubious entity but a fact experienced in the relationship.

It is this spark, which communicates without words, that seems capable of existence beyond the material world. It is this transcendent quality that provides each personality with its unique energy. The setting is immaterial; caregivers who are willing to open themselves to the patient's transcendent personality in addition to a challenged physical condition are able to extend themselves whether they are practicing in the home, in the back of an ambulance, in a hospital, in an extended-care facility, or in a nursing home.

The choice of where each of us will receive care is important. A short stay in a hospital to address an acute condition, which we expect to return us to normal function, is met with anxiety but seldom resisted. Otherwise, most of us want to cling to our own homes until the last breath if at all possible. Unfortunately, however, many families are dispersed. Many sons and daughters live thousands of miles away from their parents' homes. Most older persons are separated from their siblings and their families as well. The clustered family support system of the past has become increasingly rare.

Regrettably, the adult children in some families have settled near their old neighborhoods but are so alienated emotionally that, rather than forming a support system, they become belligerent antagonists whenever they confront one another. Counseling should be used to help them resolve their problems before they are separated by death, but neither understanding nor forgiveness will erase old scars. Anyone who does not have several voluntary helpers able to commit their time for an extended period must consider nursing-home residence when decline occurs.

While most adults today develop their own group of friends, this networking takes place when they are active. They spend much of their free time together and are willing to act in some way as support while they have common bonds. But when illness removes a person from daily work and the shared social or sporting scene, friends continue with their own routine. While these acquaintances miss the other's companionship, and they may call or drop by occasionally, they often fill the void left by their sick friend with new acquaintances.

Fortunately, there are a range of options. Organizations such as local councils on aging, welfare social services, AIDS Action Committees, and the Medicaid system can help provide both volunteer and professional assistance. Some people are able to hire private companions in order to disrupt the normal living pattern as little as possible. When a widow or widower's dearest wish is to remain at home, some families choose to mortgage the house, expecting to pay for home-care expenses if the projected costs can be covered by the sale of the home after the person dies.

Finding a suitable nurse or companion to care for a patient at home is a challenge. Hiring a live-in caregiver privately can be much cheaper than contracting with a home-care agency, but references must be checked and the employer must exercise good judgment. The employee's time off must be arranged by the family, and the family will have to fill in when the employee is ill or requires unplannned personal time. Even arrangements with an agency to provide coverage may result in some unanticipated periods without a professional helper, and the agency's contract will specify the family's responsibility when lapses occur.

In spite of these and other problems, most matches work out quite well. Mutual respect, sincerity, and repeated admiration of the other's goodwill and competence are the hallmarks of healthy interaction. Caring relationships often develop through arrangements with both agency and private workers. But these involvements must always imply professional objectivity for both parties. The role exists because of the job to be done. If the job changes, the employee's position must be reevaluated. If the employee is not able to fulfill expectations, the employer must find another means of addressing the situation. Whatever the outcome, both must remember that they have had a very strong influence on each other's lives, and each is richer because of their experiences together.

When it is necessary to hire someone to live in the home in order for the patient to remain there, both parties must realize that there will be changes in the patient's condition as well as changes required by the caregiver in adjusting to a new atmosphere and lifestyle. We have worked with many families and caregivers whose declared devotion to one another turned sour before the patient died. This did not mean that their earlier empathy was false. Any emotional exchange must represent only the value of the moment. Misunderstandings often develop on both sides because of unanticipated developments that affect both parties.

To avoid a crisis that may be harmful to the patient and unfair to both family and employee, it is wise to monitor feelings and to be on guard for resentments that sneak in when certain ground rules are forgotten. For those who are hiring, the most important fact to keep in mind is this: The caregiver must be recognized as a complex person rather than a household efficiency item. The most important factor for the employee to keep in mind is this: The client must be expected to prefer the status quo. The caregiver will be hired on the basis of skills and expected competency in emergencies, but the job exists because the client wishes to change as little as possible. A contract detailing duties, sleeping arrangements, salary, personal time, and other privileges should be negotiated before either party makes a commitment.

Finding the right person to meet each unique situation requires diligence, insightfulness, and a great deal of luck. Yet, it is surprising how many seemingly unlikely matches work out well, filling work goals and companionship needs for both parties. The most common approach to beginning a search is that the family in need talks to friends, hoping that a network will lead them to a person who has proved to be trustworthy and competent.

Most families try a second approach if budget limitations require the employer to aim for extensive coverage while paying a minimum wage. The family places a want ad in a widely read newspaper and supplements this with notices in smaller papers and on bulletin boards. This is a risky approach. References must be checked, and the interview must determine character as well as competency. For positions requiring few chores and little interaction, a school resource counselor, such as a work-study or housing placement coordinator, might help the family find a suitable student assistant.

The most reliable and less time-consuming method of obtaining trained, bonded caregivers with the least risk is to go to a reputable home-health agency. While the charges will be greater, the caregiver will have a back-up team at the agency to provide support for changes in the patient's condition and to stand in as the caregiver requires time off. If the match is unsuitable the agency can be responsible for providing a replacement.

Employee and employer can work out their differences best if they avoid identifying each other with people from their respective pasts. The elderly patient is not the caregiver's grandparent; the younger woman is not the client's wayward daughter. By encouraging a dialogue, each will learn to appreciate the other's unique personalities and to find some common bonds. Client and caregiver must identify each other's responsibilities, abide by them, and guard against presuppositions. For instance, while some caregivers will keep a spotless kitchen because they cannot stand it otherwise, others will not think about the kitchen if it is not included in the job description.

Problems arise most often when mutual fondness has developed after a while. Without realizing their infractions as potential threats to the relationship, each begins to take the other for granted, and each gladly gives extra time or privileges to the other. For instance, a client may require much more care and physical assistance than was anticipated; an employee may require unexpected time off for personal reasons. Suddenly, a retrospective review of the situation causes one party or both to realize that the original agreement is being stretched. At this time, both parties often feel used. Even though a new contract may not be due, it is necessary to renegotiate.

Working out differences is much more advantageous for both than dissolving the arrangement completely because the bond that has been established has been valuable and still exists. The caregiver's familiar presence is a stabilizing factor for the patient. Having to "retrain" another stranger to the patient's special needs and preferences is traumatic for the person who is very ill. On the other hand, if the unsatisfactory caregiver is living in, that person may face not only unemployment with a poor reference but homelessness as well. Nevertheless, both parties must understand that sometimes a caregiver is not suitable for a task, and they should be prepared to dissolve the relationship if solutions cannot be found.

When conflict exists, an arbitrator may be useful. A social worker, a nurse, or an individual unrelated to either who has developed some insight into the problem may keep the discussion from becoming emotional. But the important aspects provided by a third party can be practiced in a one-on-one meeting if each participant is able to be open to the other's thoughts and to maintain objectivity.

When sitting down together, both parties should bring some documentation of grievances and be aware of their goals. Time and emotions must be controlled. Before beginning, take one minute to breathe deeply together, silently, while trying to release internal tensions. The one who requested the meeting should begin first, speaking calmly about how the problems that have arisen seem to affect the original understanding. No accusations, only specific facts, are to be presented for orderly evaluation. The goal is to determine what needs to be changed and what is a reasonable approach to making the change. Hiring other helpers or arranging for insurance-covered or community services to supplement the present caregiving are alternatives that might be considered. Each commits to an assignment to study the solutions to the problems. Plan a follow-up meeting with a similar format.

The worker must have scheduled time off regardless of the client's unanticipated circumstances. Although many caregivers prefer to alter plans if there are major concerns about the client's well-being, the caregiver's vulnerability to burnout is so great that such infractions of the agreement should be permitted only rarely. While the caregiver is being hired specifically to attend to the client's needs and is responsible for fulfilling this obligation, the client must deal with the unexpected.

Also, in spite of the most positive relationships, few individuals are without some difficulties; therefore, the client must be prepared when a worker chooses to give precedence to his or her own personal problems. Many who fill this necessary caregiving role accept these poorly paid positions as a means of survival while they work through other issues, such as settling in a new country.

After months of personal frustration in which his or her own life is seen as stagnating through increasingly sore muscles and never-ending routines, it is not uncommon for an employee to be unable to continue the commitment. If a specific period of time was accepted in the basic contract, provision for breaking the agreement should be included as a realistic consideration for both employer and employee. On parting, it is necessary for the employer to remember the dedication and the competence practiced daily throughout the previous months. Any feeling of affection was most assuredly genuine for both; it is better, if at all possible, to finish with good wishes.

The Nursing-Home Decision

Many individuals with a recognized serious diagnosis have a single beloved caregiver who may not be much healthier than they are. How, then, will that caregiver manage all of the tasks of daily living for two people? If the companion (spouse, friend, child, or parent) precedes the "patient" in death or nursing-home placement, without supportive back-up, what will happen? When does it become acceptable to go to a nursing home, forever leaving behind one's personal residence and the mementos collected over a lifetime? The fears many have of living in a nursing home are due primarily to reluctance to abandon their personal symbols of individuality. While it is true that no one will ever be able truly to appreciate the depth of any other individual's rich lifetime of productivity and multiple worries, joys, fears, creative expressions, and intellectual stirrings, the personality is never left behind. Even when mental deterioration changes the patient's behavior, qualities will shine through that invite sensitive staff members to relate to the patient.

The services that companions, aides, and practical nurses give are invaluable, and they choose caregiving because they genuinely think of themselves as being at their best when helping others. Most modern health-care facilities educate their staff continually to recognize the individual qualities of their residents. They encourage small items to be brought from home to personalize a resident's unit because they want them to have some familiar symbols for personal identification. They also know that these symbols can serve to stimulate both staff and other residents and visitors to talk with the patient. Once the new person is known as a complete individual, he or she is no longer a stranger. All those within the facility complete the new extended family, and the surroundings and routine begin to represent security. The fears, then, become reversed: life outside the institution seems threatening.

Family Grief

Most caregivers, whatever their roles, expect that their actions will make a difference. But we cannot demand more of ourselves than our own limitations will allow. For instance, for a wife to expect a husband to not die because she is there to jump at his every whim is an illusion of personal power as much as it is a bargaining device. Assuming the burden of the beloved's recovery upon oneself may be a way of making amends for past guilt, devotional drive, or an offering of oneself made at prayer. But the disease process must continue. Caring gestures and personal support will provide moments of value and may relieve certain symptoms, but love, devotion, and self-sacrifice will not wipe away the loved one's terminal illness.

When the other dies, pangs of remorse always remain in the survivors. Did we do enough? What else would have given just a moment of pleasure? If we could have provided a few more moments of life, would they have been filled with pain and suffering or would they have been meaningful? These are normal components of grief.

In the struggle to let go, those of us who care tend to challenge our own power. Even when God is recognized as a higher authority, we question ourselves first. Therese Rando, in *Grief, Dying, and Death,* explains that two emotions experienced in grief prove the most problematic because of their antisocial qualities: anger and guilt.[8] Anger is a natural consequence of being deprived of something desired. Guilt occurs when a person expects himself or herself to be capable of certain behavior but for some reason does not fill these expectations.

When an issue as fundamental as grief (both during serious illness and after death) heightens basic responses, our first reaction is childlike anger, followed by parent-like protectiveness, which may include self-reproach. Anyone who was associated with the loved one's illness—including the beloved—or anyone who might be thought of as having neglected the beloved is subject to review and blame. The grieving person experiences self-blame as the anger becomes guilt. The guilt may be about some slight oversight, about expressing "bad" feelings to the deceased, about surviving when the other did not, about not being able to protect the other from suffering or death, about losing self-control, or about any other subject either clearly or vaguely understood.

We have found that many who have difficulty dealing with their grief feel that the task is easier if they are assured that those awful feelings are normal.

Yes, it is normal to feel depressed, angry, and guilty; to experience waves of unexpected and uncontrollable sadness; or not be able to concentrate at times. Some people have periods of emotional regression when they can barely function, or hyperactive periods in which they must run from one task to another. Sometimes the sadness is interrupted with spurts of energy and obsessive activity. These behaviors are normal too.

When life seems out of kilter, the grieving person will find it useful to talk about the situation, explore disturbing fantasies, discuss options, plan new goals, and vent his or her sadness by crying. A professional grief counselor may be needed. Many psychotherapists are skilled in bereavement and serious-loss issues. Hospices sponsor bereavement programs, and there are independent groups with a trained leader that have open meetings to encourage anyone who has similar problems to receive and give support. Help is out there, but those who are in need must seek it. (See the section on "Grief" in the recommended readings.)

Grief occurs in three phases.[9] First the mourner must realize that the relationship with the departed has ended. The once very real connection with the deceased has become a collection of memories. The mourner's emotions may be erratic as the binding commitment to the person who is no longer able to be there is released. This is the acute phase of mourning. Modern society allows one to four weeks for it, but it may take as much as two years and sometimes more.

The second phase of mourning involves adjustment to life without the departed. It intertwines with the first stage. The bereaved becomes able to imagine functioning without the beloved. There is remorse, and often guilt on realizing that a period of time has passed without thinking of the one who has gone, but the self-confidence of accomplishing something alone is strengthening. Healing is taking place.

The third phase of mourning is working toward new commitments. New relationships may form during the early period of working things out without the beloved, but a new attachment to another person or interest simultaneously requires and provides emotional energy. Venturing into new areas is usually interrupted and postponed repeatedly; this erratic course allows the person time to think through many subtly related issues. When the deceased is recognized as a precious part of the past, feelings resurface but can be viewed and put away. When there is freedom to commit to a new life that is open to joy and love, the person becomes healed.

These three stages of grief work were first described by Dr. Eric

Lindemann in 1944 following the disastrous Coconut Grove nightclub fire in Boston, Massachusetts.[10] Many mental-health specialists have explored these concepts when responding to other tragedies and illnesses. Although different authors have discussed various aspects of the grief experience, all research has recognized Dr. Lindemann's initial schema. When the Massachusetts General Hospital (MGH) concluded its studies of the survivors and those who mourned the death of the hundreds who perished in that fire, the Lindemann grief-studies program continued in other areas. His associates counseled cancer patients, and this also confirmed the grief-work hypothesis and the issues of coping with loss. Dr. Avery Weisman, who connected "a good death" with the image of "safe conduct" mentioned earlier in this book, was a leading member of the MGH group.

Grief work involves mourning the present loss and the losses of the future that one had hoped to share with the dying or dead person. Sometimes the bitterest losses are not those of a reality experienced within a recent present but of the hopes that were anticipated in the past and now must be realized as impossible for the future. The loss of a child is considered the most painful of all because in addition to the precious life the parents have loved, the parents' expectations are gone, taking away part of their future as well. Slowly, the loss is confronted and incorporated into daily life, but it takes time, patience, and continual remotivation.

Many of the physical symptoms of grief are similar to those of panic (nausea, pressure in the chest, difficulty in thinking, unexpected terror, intense anxiety, difficulty in sleeping). The bereaved person may hallucinate—see the loved one in a favorite chair, or hear familiar sounds. If tales of ghosts have not tainted the imagination with automatic fear, most people feel comforted by these mysterious impressions. In a similar way, the presence of the loved one is felt in that person's favorite old sweater or tattered bathrobe.

If you have a friend who is mourning, being there and being willing to listen to the same reflections over and over again are your most important tasks. Encourage short breaks such as a walk in the park, a drive to view the changing foliage, or a humorous movie. By pointing out reasonable responses to issues of concern, you can encourage gradual changes. For instance, donating selected items to a Red Cross center for disaster victims could help others and be a worthy legacy for the deceased. Presenting a gift to a younger family member of a valued item, such as jewelry or furniture that belonged to the deceased, serves as a tangible way of stimulating pleasant memories of the person who died while honoring the receiver personally.

Sometimes the shadow of a deceased one seems persistently to supervise certain actions or jobs, as if the assignment continues in the mind of the bereaved. When the expectations of the deceased seem to hover over certain tasks, the family can learn from those guidelines, give the role to the one who most resembles the deceased, or let go and attempt to eliminate or modify the duty as much as possible.

For instance, a widower whose wife dominated the kitchen may insist that his daughters come to his house daily to cook his meals. With this attitude, he manipulates his children into visiting him or having him to their homes more often. He may resolve to eat only in a restaurant or only preprepared foods. He seems more independent, but the high salt content of his newly chosen diet is bad for his blood pressure. By going out, he may meet more people with whom he can pass the time of day, but if he is depressed or not feeling well he may not eat. On the other hand, by actually doing the chores he remembered his wife doing, he could learn to honor the memory of his deceased wife, improve his food selections, and become self-sufficient.

Often, the impulse to distance oneself from the life that was shared with the deceased is an attempt to heal. While some people feel driven to throw themselves into a different atmosphere, they usually discover that they cannot run away from themselves. They must complete their unresolved issues before they can fully commit to a new life.

~

Laura had been the sole caregiver of her husband until massive bleeding of his seeping hemorrhages from cancer convinced him that he must go to the hospital. Even when he was a hospice inpatient, his attitude and overall care were difficult. Laura accepted her daughter's support in her daily visits and was grateful to use the spare room in her daughter's home. After her husband's death, she resolved not to return for a single night to the apartment she had shared with her husband. The memories of those last months were just too painful.

However, she knew that she needed to be independent, both for her own well-being and for the sake of her daughter's marriage. Accompanied by other family members, she gradually went over every item in her apartment. Together, they decided on distribution, but her family always insisted that she consider each thing, and they gave her personal time whenever she needed it.

They encouraged her to keep her social contacts and to explore housing alternatives that fit her new income level. She decided to sell her former apartment and put her name on the waiting list at a new apartment complex where some of her friends were also moving. Gradually, she began to look forward to her new independence and she became accustomed to doing things alone. After she moved, she made friends with residents who had nothing in common with her former friends. Many of her new friends were recent widows like herself. Together they served as a support group for one another, because although Laura was adjusting to a new life, she could not dismiss the many memories of her husband.

She consciously increased her activities as a way to distract herself. In agreeing to go places with her new friends, she rediscovered the church she had gone to when her children were young. In returning to a faith in which she had found comfort in the past, and in remembering a happier time, she was able to see her married years in a gentler perspective. Identifying with her own active period, she was freer to expand her personality, becoming one of the most sought-after members of the new apartment complex.

~

Each person must reflect upon the events that led to the beloved's death in his or her own way. Just as no person dies exactly like anyone else; no person can grieve exactly like anyone else. The process of adjustment is uneven. If anxiety, erratic thoughts, or depression is paramount, comeditation will help the person to relax by freeing the mind while being comforted. By having another sit nearby with no goal other than patiently to provide a half hour of peace, the recipient feels nurtured and more completely whole. If a comeditation tape was made during the loved one's illness, playing it for oneself may be comforting during lonely moments. Such a tape would be for listening only; no one should try to pattern one's respiration after another's (as on the tape) for the purpose of comeditation.

Quiet, patiently shared moments are essential for family healing. Likewise, confidence building and separation, so necessary for reentering society, must occur gradually. These treasured moments of reflection, comfort, distress, reassessment, and renewal are uniquely personal, but working toward commitment to a different life is also a family affair.

7

THE ROLLERCOASTER EXPERIENCE OF LEUKEMIA, AIDS, AND OTHER DEVASTATING DISEASES

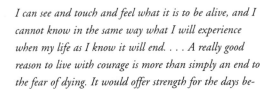

> *I can see and touch and feel what it is to be alive, and I*
> *cannot know in the same way what I will experience*
> *when my life as I know it will end. . . . A really good*
> *reason to live with courage is more than simply an end to*
> *the fear of dying. It would offer strength for the days be-*
> *fore the approach of the death.*

> **—Mark Mosher DeWolfe, 1988**
> **(a Unitarian minister who died of AIDS)**

Exacerbation and Remission

Since the 1940s the treatment of chronic disease has become a major focus in caregiving. Illnesses that would have meant undeniable death at the turn of the century, or even fifty years ago (such as various neurological conditions, cardiovascular and respiratory obstruction and deterioration, and serious infectious diseases), have become manageable conditions that require steady maintenance care and occasional emergency treatment.

Childhood leukemia was one of the first diseases to change dramatically our attitudes about devastating malignant illnesses. Acute lymphocytic leukemia (commonly first occurring in very young children) will result in death within a few months of discovery if untreated. But treatment (maybe equally life-threatening) offers the hope of remission and even cure. Today, hundreds of sick children who are brought to the brink of death (often by the treatment) gradually respond when given strong chemotherapeutic drugs, bone-marrow transplants, and/or radiation.

In leukemia, overproducing but underdeveloped white cells prevent the development of normal blood components (functioning white cells, red cells, and platelets). As a result, the patient is highly susceptible to infections, develops anemia with low energy and breathlessness, and bruises easily. These are all indications of a serious condition. A trip to the hospital for intensive treatment because of these symptoms is inevitably feared as painful and physically dangerous.

As is often the case in the progression of this disease health gradually returns, and the child goes home for recuperation, reenters school, and participates in activities just as eagerly as any other child. Of course, the medical staff expects the child to return after a while when his or her health deteriorates again. And again, these resilient youngsters hang on when all the signs indicate that they may not survive another round. Each return to normal activity, however, seems worth the pain and hardship to everyone involved.

This pendulum swing is the pattern for patients, regardless of age, who have any of the leukemias, many cancers, acquired immunodeficiency syndrome (AIDS), systemic lupus erythematosus (SLE), and more recently multiple sclerosis (MS), rheumatoid arthritis (RA), and many other diseases that have an autoimmune factor.

Stress has been found to be such a major factor in some diseases of dysfunctional autoimmune reactions that hypnotherapy with biobehavioral (body function/reaction) training has been accepted as a standard treatment protocol by several health insurance programs. While the incidences of cure are increasingly remarkable in some of the leukemias, success is measured by the length of remission periods in the other diseases. When disease complications severely affect the function of vital organs, recovery is less likely and recurrence with increasing devastation is expected.

The rollercoaster of profound illness, followed by recovery, climaxed by another incidence of severe illness, eventually does come to a halt. When the companion disorders finally overwhelm the body, the patient, the patient's loved ones, and the medical staff must admit that in spite of extraordinary courage and numerous medical triumphs, nature is designed to change us through disease and death.

At the top of a rollercoaster, the rider's view is expansive, inspiring confidence before preparing for the next plunge. An AIDS patient who overcomes a crisis has a new quality of courage; the fear of devastation is less alarming. While still shaking from weakened knees, he or she resolves to triumph over the next descent and may well deny the danger. Whatever one's philosophy, when death is the ever present alternative to life, most of us will try one more treatment even when we recognize that soon the medicines will work less and the symptoms will be more severe.

Fear of disease and debilitation prods us to try any medicine, any treatment. We have been enchanted by case histories of "exceptional patients" who are living years after the doctors declared their cases to be hopeless. Shouldn't we hope that we too can be exceptional? Why live through such an awful sickness? By close attention to self-care, by learning to relax during periods of stress, and by using available resources, many people have improved their health. It is this applied determination that has made AIDS, for example, a long-term disease rather than a terminal condition.

Hope

Hope is an innate human quality. It is one characteristic of mental wellness. Even when death becomes the accepted alternative, hope continues and is directed in different ways: toward successful completion of dying, toward a transition into an afterlife according to a particular belief, toward the family's continuation, or the survival of work in which one had a part. This drive stimulates action and provides us with the courage to seek solutions and to create.

As we have seen, one who becomes hopeless also becomes helpless, deeply depressed, and spiritually adrift. Antidepressant medicines have some effect on those who are depressed, and these, or the doctor's choices from an array of psychotropic drugs, should be prescribed conservatively when certain symptoms warrant them.

But the greatest influence on the exercise of hope is attitude. "One more try" is an attitude of hope. It represents confidence in one's self and in one's world. By learning to adjust one's attitude, one can reclaim hope even amid the most depressing events. Those who are able to integrate the practice of letting go discover that by accepting changes, they can be inspired by small gains. Reaching certain goals can propel the setting of new and higher goals. When a small success is enjoyed, such as awakening to a new day after a high fever the evening before, the person also is able to appreciate his or her power to heal and a sense of having control in spite of continued vulnerability.

This principle was fundamental to logotherapy, which Dr. Viktor Frankl developed after his concentration-camp experiences. In Greek *logos* means "word," "speech," or "reason," among other things, and is the root word of *logic*. Logotherapy, "therapy through meaning," was developed by Dr. Frankl as a psychotherapeutic method of helping those in despair find meaning in life and their personal vision of the universe. In the individual's search for meaning each person must identify what serves as his or her own foundation, what gives meaning to life.[1] Several young men with whom we have been acquainted found that they were strengthened by their AIDS because they chose to speak out on behalf of gay rights and health care. Once they acknowledged their vulnerability, their goals became larger than themselves.

Sometimes such vision comes spontaneously from within, occasionally it begins from the urgings of sensitive friends, and sometimes it evolves through months of counseling with a good behavioral or cognitive therapist or in the course of psychospiritual training. An important element in the development of courage is confidence inspired by support. Such motivating support can come from family or friends (including those who live in the mind as memories) and competent medical personnel. The medical team includes those encountered in a clinic or office, hospital, and nursing home, and at home. The person whose life's inspiration may be awakened during terminal illness might be a young child battling to get through one more treatment, a young man or woman who has been stricken at the time of greatest potential, or an aged grandparent whose triumph is to retain as much dignity as possible while the body is gradually failing.

Disinvestment and Reinvestment

Since the 1940s, counselors have recognized that one of the most difficult problems caused by the remission-exacerbation rollercoaster is the variation in commitment required by patients and their families. Family and close friends feel threatened themselves when a loved one is critically ill. Yet they all know that separation will one day be necessary. At some time, during repeated bouts of near-death, the patient and his or her significant others begin to anticipate death more than life. As the person adjusts to the idea of the expected death, he or she becomes emotionally disinvested in the present life. Some interpret the person's reactions at this time as depression, but true symptoms of depression may not be evident.

As the patient responds to treatment, or slight signs give hope that the person may survive, thoughts of recovery and dreams of a happy future loom. The person who is affected believes that anything that can be done must be done to protect this possibility. Enormous energy is spilled into obsessive efforts to protect the tenuous life. Enthusiastic affirmations may be voiced, as much to convince the speaker as to convince those who are listening. With this emotional reinvestment in that which had been feared lost, the commitment is deepened.

Disinvestment is actually a self-protective reaction in adjustment to an impending death. When a patient or loved one expects death realistically, we admire that person for courage and call it acceptance. Statistics show that those who realized before the death that the patient was not likely to survive were able to move through the grief period with fewer problems than those whose loved ones died suddenly. But when there is no certainty about whether the patient will die, even emotional preparation for death seems unfaithful. The conflict between self-protection and committed devotion to the patient's life arises when the illness is prolonged and the patient's condition varies extremely. In these situations, full recovery, invalidism, and death are impossible to predict.

Any action of separation is an act of disinvestment. One may be simultaneously obsessed with thoughts of the loved one lying in bed and attracted by advertisements in the newspaper travel section. As discussed earlier, brief snatches of time may be expanded in value by brief pleasurable diversions. These moments are necessary to clear the mind and maintain mental balance. But using distractions to actually remove oneself from painful reality may be a diversion that is extreme, premature, and selfish. Work may serve as such an escape. Developing new relationships may not be as much a matter of conscious disloyalty as a self-indulgent response to an unfillable void.

We also see disinvestment occurring when families reduce their nursing-home visits as their declining elder continues to degenerate. As grandpa's abilities to move and speak lessen, it is frequently assumed that along with his fading memory, his ability to comprehend and appreciate family overtures fades as well. In many cases this is accurate, because these sporadic visitors, although family, seem to the old man to be strangers whom he cannot recognize. He is familiar with the attendants who bathe him and help him in and out of bed daily, but his active memories of "family" date from long ago. Some disinvestment is appropriate.

But every relationship implies an emotional linkage. For the most part we humans are able to isolate our family and social involvement from our work and private escape habits. However, when a beloved child or lover or friend is clearly dying, we believe we cherish an inner pledge by attending solely to that person. In the meantime, work must be sustained, the other children require their share of attention, and ongoing problems must be solved.

Dedication to everything equally, at all times, is impossible under the best of circumstances. When a person is experiencing anxiety with anticipatory grief, life in general is an emotional overload. Reinvestment, whatever the stimulus, draws one deeper into the pathos. When something has to give, our minds allow us to have moments of forgetting our pain. As these moments increase, and energy is placed on other things, emotional investment becomes centered on escape. As strengthening through separation occurs, concern about whether the person lives or dies becomes secondary.

We do not imply that the person experiencing the withdrawal does not care whether the person lives or dies. Neither is it abandonment. Instead, it is an awareness of thought shifting. The patient may well be going through this emotional separation, just as the loved one is. Eugene Knott and Eugenia Wild discussed their personal experiences of the disinvestment–reinvestment phenomenon, as bereaved parents as well as professional grief counselors, in their chapter in *Loss and Anticipatory Grief.*[2] One author stated, "Several years [after my daughter's diagnosis] I was aware that while I was externally involved with her physical and medical care needs, I was not making an emotional connection with her." Although that realization was alarming, they both learned that the change was one of reintegration into a pattern that embraced the sick person along with more normal thoughts and concerns. Every relationship changes, especially that of a parent and growing child.

Both Wild and Knott found, however, that they were redrawn into their investment with their children as each new threat occurred and as each child's losses mounted. On the other hand, recovery required optimism, new anticipation, and enthusiastic rededication. Emotional reinvestment springs up spontaneously, sometimes when the person has begun to feel untouchable.

A person who experiences the rollercoaster over several years finds that the energy drain becomes part of everyday living. One cannot bounce back easily into the mainstream. Although the preparation time for accepting life without the beloved may be extensive, the hovering cloud of anxiety about the other's well-being becomes a fixture in one's life. This ever present angst does not vanish with the burial any more easily than it did during the fluctuations of dying and recovering.

Each person must anticipate a personal future, especially when the loss of another implies a threat to one's own identity. Detachment indicates freedom that is not yet desired, either by the patient who has not died or by the one who is awaiting the outcome. It is not unusual for parents to divorce when one of their children has a long-term illness. Neither is it rare for a lover to declare that the relationship is over when an AIDS patient has been hospitalized for acute secondary problems many times. Repeated vacillation is harmful to the emotional reserves of the participants and to their relationships. Often, the decision to part is attributed to uncontrollable factors, such as a change in job location, because the allure of escape cannot be admitted even to oneself.

This cycling between life and death is known as the "Lazarus syndrome." In the New Testament (John 11:1–55), on mourning Lazarus, Jesus raised him from the dead and subsequently had to prepare for his own death. But Lazarus was condemned to death again as well (John 12:10), for he could not be allowed to be an exception. As with Lazarus, the person who touches death and returns to life simultaneously inspires devotion and provides a warning of danger.

The Comatose Patient

A family or a society determined to sustain a patient in coma for many years, with the expectation that sometime the person will awaken, demonstrates the conviction of investment. The actual "sleeping beauty" scenario never happens because, in the rare instances when consciousness is regained, there must be long, painfully intensive retraining in an effort to achieve as much recovery as possible. Some "miracle people" recover much more mental and physical function than was believed possible, and these few examples of recovery from coma encourage many to never give up.

Those who have awakened from coma have benefited from intensive stimulation. Bedside vigil with nearly constant attention sometimes helps excite the resting brain. As hearing is the last sense to leave the body, it is believed that during waking periods, a comatose person does hear sounds. People who have used comeditation with patients in coma have reported that the patients later said, "I knew I was lying in bed, and I heard you say-ing my special words to me. Even though I could not respond to you, I knew you were helping me." There are two advantages to using comeditation in such a situation. First, it serves as a means of contact that can be compre-hended if the process is kept simple, and it serves as a reminder of something previously valued. Second, through transpersonal communication, when the patient is ready to let go, the one saying the comeditation may be able to sense it.

While it is important to give a patient every possible advantage when it is appropriate, it is equally important that the loved ones take care of them-selves. A comatose patient has sleep periods and seems to adjust somewhat to a hospital routine. Those who are keeping vigil must have a sleep and sep-aration routine as well. It is also wise for the loved ones to identify their own source of personal suffering and to see that the patient is going through a dif-ferent process.

In spite of every effort to be objective, and when there will not be any improvement, sometimes the task of letting go seems impossibly hard. When the patient's totally supported care is established, wounds heal, and it is dif-ficult to imagine that the person is not comfortable. Some people think that the doctor would be required to stop such expensive care if it was not in the patient's, the family's, and society's best interests. The family becomes deter-mined to stay beside the patient as long as the body seems to function, be-cause they are always hoping for their own special miracle.

But even these dedicated people have private periods of wavering and doubt. Nursing homes are filled with patients who have lingered in vegeta-tive comas for months and years. Their bodies become twisted. They recog-nize no one, not even close relatives. They may respond to noises, but they do not comprehend. If they were not artificially maintained, they would be dead. By whom, and how, is "God's will" being judged? Is this comatose life part of our worldly life, or is it a period between earthly participation and heavenly acceptance? Or is the person being kept in torturous confinement when, if nature were allowed its natural course, the soul should have been freed long ago? Those who are close to the patient have questions about the best interests of the patient and the greater life plan. While they do not want to admit loss of trust, they do not want to do harm by allowing their loved one to suffer unnecessarily.

We do not really know what occurs on the mental and spiritual plane during vegetative states before death, as we only have few anecdotes and rare claims of personal accounts recorded throughout history. Those of us who have not experienced this state of nondeath assume a superhuman role if we try to judge. The common near-death experiences are reported by people who were resuscitated within minutes of their loss of vital signs. We hope that more near-death experience studies, incorporating blood-chemistry profiles and electrical encephalograms, will give a clearer definition of these various conditions. However, we do know that a long period of coma leads to softening of brain tissue, as would occur, though more rapidly, if the person were already in the grave. This fact—that the portion used for complex thinking actually deteriorates when the personality is not functioning—raises the question of whether the emotional and spiritual quality has left the body rather than remaining dormant, or whether it is rotting without being liberated. Whom are we supporting?

The Phenomenon of AIDS

In the course of the human immunodeficiency virus (HIV) disease known as AIDS, the body's damaged immune response becomes more susceptible to organisms that it usually resists. Thus, *Pneumocystis carinii* pneumonia, Kaposi's sarcoma, and cytomegalovirus are virulent invaders although they are rare in more resistant people. Infections that might otherwise be merely annoying, such as psoriasis, herpes simplex, herpes zoster ("shingles"), candidiasis, intestinal bacterial infections, and athletes' foot, may become magnified, causing as much distress to the patient as the more dangerous complications. Because of these tendencies to develop other infections, AIDS is a dramatic example of the problems that are experienced in any immunosuppressive condition. In the recommended reading section on home care, we have listed references that might be useful for those wishing to understand the cellular changes in HIV-related diseases.

Precautions in caregiving are doubly important in dealing with any of these conditions. Not only is it necessary to prevent the spread of the organism causing the basic disease, it is also important to not introduce potential infections to the susceptible patient. There is no reason to fear crossinfection with any immunosuppressed person as long as precautionary rules are incorporated into all caregiving routines. Using disposable gloves when handling any excrement protects the caregiver. Washing items with a solution of one part chlorine bleach to ten parts water, and air drying, will kill any HIV source. A handy container simplifies cleanup. Two cups of bleach should be added to the regular detergent when soiled linen is cleaned in a home washing machine. Uncapped needles and syringes should always be disposed of promptly in an impermeable container marked for contaminated waste.

AIDS As a Sociomedical Problem

Once it is recognized that precautions are in order, it is easy to develop patterns that are automatically protective. But actions that are normal to adolescent and young adults are potential risks. AIDS affects those who are most needful of companionship. The human species is developed through social interaction. The transmission of this disease, however, is a sociological problem with psychological as well as medical implications.

Learning more about the HIV virus and how to manage it is a primary sociomedical problem facing us today. Resources for basic care may become a problem in the future if the spread is not limited worldwide. Population balances as well as economic and production issues may be altered significantly if an effective check on the spread of the HIV virus is not found and put to use soon.

Young people who are determined to have intimate contact in spite of the risks need personal or social assurance. Drug users who share contaminated needles are seeking to fill a dependency need in the presence of others like themselves. Infants borne to contaminated mothers require emotional and physical nurturing to survive. Young hemophiliacs who require blood transfusions because of injuries often have engaged in risk-taking beyond their known limitations because they wanted to gain acceptance by others. HIV's primary mode of transmission is sexual contact. Since natural behaviors such as mating now threaten individuals who try to fulfill their innate needs for social reinforcement, HIV is a threat to society itself because common interactive behavior is the source of transmission of this death-bearing disease.

Each person with AIDS (or PWA) must answer the question of what his or her fundamental needs are, just as everyone else must do. But the authors have discovered that one element important to many PWAs is the presence of others who care. We single out this group of patients because most continue to want social support. Many of them have experienced some sort of imposed separation. They have been hurt by people who were prejudiced toward their lifestyle or sexual orientation, or by others unable to understand behavior that they felt powerless to change. Many have been rejected by their family and old friends, and even their church, or have been preceded in death by their own chosen mate as well as by good friends too numerous to count.

Although gay men have been the major PWA population in the United States, there is a heterosexual predominance of PWAs in Africa and other parts of the world. These problems are not about sexual issues as much as they are about issues of social relationship.

Most young people grow up feeling different. They seek out others in the same age group to explore similarities or differences as a way of understanding their own natures. When they must confront death before they have fully realized their own potential, they are not ready. How can the intense feelings of separation that are characteristic of an insecure youth be resolved? Many activities that transmit AIDS are used as self-sought rites of passage during the search for adulthood, self-proclaimed independence, or image-building. But promiscuous sex, casual drug use, and personal risks demonstrate only recklessness and disregard for others. Peer reinforcement proves insufficient when illness ravages the body. Plans for successful development and aging have to be modified into the effort to take one day at a time. If serious breaks had previously occurred with the family and the mending of old wounds is neglected, loneliness is intensified because the early comforts are gone.

Resolution of Relationships

Many families who disagree bitterly with their offspring rally in support when serious illness such as AIDS strikes. But if getting along was already a problem, repeated remissions and exacerbations of the disease may exaggerate old arguments about unpredictability, irresponsible behavior, or family dysfunction. Everyone who cares must become as informed as possible about the disease involved, the course expected, and the gains and pitfalls that are part of the process. It is necessary to accept the person who has become the primary light in the patient's private life, whether he or she meets the family's standards or not. Calling upon all available resources shares the load and provides insight into the many dimensions of the loved one about to be lost.

The AIDS Action Committee's buddy system pairs a caring volunteer with a PWA who is in need of support. As with hospice volunteers, training is required before a match is made. Numerous volunteer coordinators have sought comeditation instruction and now include that form of relaxation to relieve symptoms. As in every instruction session, we emphasize adaptation to the receiver's needs and preferences.

Because of the many issues of separation, we have learned that comeditation is particularly valuable for PWAs. Nothing transpires except by the recipient's choice. The session satisfies the need for another's presence without unwanted discussions. Moments of peace may prevail while old problems are set aside. The space needs only to be filled with being. The comeditators join together while remaining separate, and through the helper's caring presence, the recipient may be enabled to extend, in consciousness, beyond the boundaries of the body.

～

The father's only attention was to his son's breath. As instructed, he made the sound precisely as his son exhaled. As they continued, both began to relax their anxieties about this meeting. Their tense muscles became softer. The son began to regain the long-ago peace he had felt as a child when he heard his dad's voice reading a bedtime story. The father discovered that with all his original love he was watching the young child, who had grown into a man. Without discussion, they both experienced unconditional forgiveness.

～

Comeditation has been particularly valuable for someone who is anxious about relationships because the process is personal. It can be taught to a helper and altered as the receiver wishes. In the sharing, the receiver opens a window of confidence. By following the instructions, the giver indicates acceptance. Discussion is suspended. Both become involved in relaxation by focusing on a simple sound. Thus, both let go to a purer level of consciousness, touched only by the other's widening presence and unencumbered by thoughts of conflict.

Of course, sometimes the mere presence of a certain person will stimulate anxiety that cannot be released with comeditation. Rather, the person's effort to become the helper may agitate the receiver more. For example, a helper whose alcoholism offends the receiver will smell and act the part if he has been drinking. A couple who cannot resolve their mutual distrust may be able to reduce their conflict with comeditation, but must still resolve their individual expectations by other means. Comeditation, perhaps with an uninvolved person, does help the letting go process.

~

Simon's girlfriend tried to stand by him after he discovered that he had acquired AIDS from using contaminated drug needles. His illness turned her toward the religious teachings of her childhood, while he continued on his search for spiritual peace by studying Eastern philosophies more than ever before. By using comeditation they were able to experience peaceful moments together, but the gulf between them widened. He became more absorbed in his illness, finding peace on the water while he practiced his trade as a fisherman, not seriously ill but constantly aware of the expectation of death. She was unable to accept her life with him. To correct her own sense of balance, she moved into her own apartment, cultivated new friends, and saw him as a friend rather than as a lover. Thus, both found their own manners of letting go, respectful of each other but not entangled. She no longer chose to be his comeditation helper, but as his symptoms progressed, he found that it was more satisfying to use comeditation with our counseling sessions as a reinforcement, and to meditate alone with the sea.

~

How does one incorporate the ideas of others while identifying with specific concepts of the self? Otto Rank has identified the shadow as a symbol of the soul. Poets through the ages have sung of the completion of oneself by uniting with the lover. Rank found that recognition of conflicting or complementary attributes in each person has been fundamental to belief in the immortal self.[3] We need others, we are fascinated by differences, and we are fearful of losing control to an unknown force.

Rank reported that Chamisso, who created a story about a man who lost his shadow, said to a friend shortly before his own death, "If they were to ask me now [what the shadow signifies], I would answer: 'It is the health which I lack. The absence of my shadow is my illness.'" Psychologists and philosophers have discussed how the double represents an alter ego, an evil or foolish twin, or the yearning for spiritual completion.

The infant's need for a nurturer rapidly becomes a maturing child's need for friends. Many primitive stories represent the search for a mate as a drive to join oneself to one's other natural half. Heroes and holy people are adored because people identify personally with a representation of the good self. In like manner, the appeal of "returning" to the life force (God, universal consciousness, Mother Creator, Yahweh, the fertile void) expresses the awareness of incompletion. In all these examples, each individual is nagged by a lack of the elusive "other." Socialization provides a momentary solution. Nurturing support goes beyond sustenance to assist emotional growth as well. For many, however, only communion with the eternal can satisfy the innate desire for fulfillment.

~

Peter was frightened of the symptoms he had lived through many times before, and he also admitted that he was frightened of the unknown. Thus, we met a young man who had decided he would go home to die rather than continue aggressively fighting his eighth episode of *Pneumocystis carinii* pneumonia. His most difficult times were in the middle of the night, when high fever developed in spite of medicine for inflammation.

He had chosen to come home because he believed he would feel better without drugs that produced nausea, vomiting, and confusion. He wanted control, but his shaking body behaved as if it were completely separated from his mind. Peter despaired of ever dying gently. In his student years, he had basked in quiet, reflective study, and he had incorporated transcendental meditation (TM) into his daily routine. But in his complex adult life, he never thought of his meditation teacher or the principles he had once followed.

We suggested that he could control the effects of the fever with comeditation while giving the anti-inflammatory medication a chance to work. He was surprised by the thought that meditation might reduce his symptoms, but was eager to try. We explained the basic comeditation process to him and assured him that we would adapt the method to his preferences and his personal experiences.

He chose to experience the standard technique the first time. He was thrilled to discover that he truly relaxed. He was impressed by the trust he felt during the session, which was reminiscent of his work with his TM teacher. The next time he allowed the secret sounds given to him by his first teacher to echo in his mind when he heard our counts synchronized to his exhalations. He felt joyous as he slipped into his long-forgotten, now-restored state of calm. He vowed to practice twice a day on his own and to use us to reinforce him when we were available. We taught his sister to act as his coach during our third session. After he had recognized that he could use meditation for his symptoms, he began a routine: At bedtime he took the first dosage of the anti-inflammatory medication. As soon as the fever started he took the second dose of medicine, and he promptly began his meditation. He reported shaking only rarely, and fevers were lower and fell predictably during the sessions.

Peter's dying was long and arduous, for he did have many physical problems, but he felt calmer and more at peace as he gained inner and outer control and spiritual reinforcement. We believe that had his teacher granted him permission to share his sounds, his family could have enabled him to only listen while they uttered the sounds, deepening the effects of his meditation and saving his energy as it waned. He died in peace in his family circle.

~

The desire to complete oneself with the double played an important role for the patient just described. The pleasant memories of his special teacher during his happier years encouraged him to renew his disciple status. Identity with an admired figure, and the promise of higher spiritual attainment, inspired him during his dying as it had during his youth. Many people have a similar experience in a worshipping congregation or when receiving communion. Awareness of any beloved presence addresses the need for union. "No man is an island" when a caring other is present through the final breath.

Denial

We carry many aspects of a dual nature within us, and these warring inner voices cause most of our dilemmas. When one thought whispers "You're okay, just go about as usual and you'll be fine," and another thought counters "You're not okay, you might be in big trouble, maybe no one can help you," which intuition does the person listen to? Is the person expressing fear by asking for help, or fear by not sharing troubling thoughts? Is the person demonstrating bravery by clinging to a resolve to work through everything alone, or bravery by asking for help?

When we suspect that we ourselves are not okay, seeking help is entirely appropriate regardless of the motivation. Fear is a healthy response to a concern. Bravery is an active response to fear. When either is misapplied it becomes a form of denial. Denial that causes one to avoid important issues can be harmful to the self, to loved ones, and to the community. This form of denial has been the focus of various addiction-treatment programs. But in terminal care, as in other living situations, denial can both distort the situation *and* help the person function.

This dualism that each person nurtures within embraces aspects of the same nature—fear and bravery. Although these seem like opposites when relayed as tales of the coward's or hero's behavior, one does not exist without the other. Each of us, as a human infant, awakens to dependency and insufficiency coupled with the drive to survive—to discover and succeed. Through encouragement and praise, each of us, as a developing child, learns to take chances.

On learning to stand and walk, as in all other accomplishments, the toddler experiences failure as well as success. By denying that a fall indicates the inability to walk, the child tries again and again. Fear is reinforced by such things as painful collisions and teasing by siblings. Bravery is reinforced by such things as the sensation of a good balance, praise from parents, and encouragement from siblings. These earliest experiences contribute to our own personal concept of self. They determine our reactions and resistances as expressed through courage and timidity.

Because of these early imprints, humans think of the brave (successful) self as being good. The successful child learns early that denying failure will lead to repeated efforts, producing improvements until success has been achieved. Admiration from others reinforces the person's thrill of success. Pushing on while denying problems becomes a functional habit for many people.

Lingering in any demonstrative mood would be abnormal behavior for a person who has integrated denial into an identity technique. For instance, Joe, whom we met in chapter 6, was a person who always quietly considered the alternatives. In spite of others' efforts to communicate, no one knew what Joe thought until he worked out a solution by himself. Although those who shared his life felt left out and sometimes expressed their feelings by trying to argue with him, he felt he had to weigh all the possibilities before he could announce his viewpoint. If a crisis changed his perspective, he would sometimes readjust his goals rather than engage in the turmoil of the crisis.

When Joe recognized that death was probable, his truthful response was that one can never know exactly when death will occur. Meanwhile, he could complete certain projects and distract himself in various other ways.

Comeditation was especially useful to Joe because it helped him regain control of his relaxed nature when his fear erupted in dreams. These torments were pushed aside when his wife helped him relax and said the rosary to him. But when he returned to sleep, the demons returned as well. He stopped the terrifying dreams after we helped him develop a strategy in which he was able to go to the light as an easy escape during a comeditation session with us. He slept for six hours without interruption, felt refreshed, and was self-assured once again. In later comeditation sessions, he felt comforted when he let himself seek the light or sensed that he was being bathed in blessed holy rays as the rosary was said. Sleep continued to refresh him. Death for Joe was but a gentle exhalation in the midst of a quiet nighttime sleep.

While Joe appeared to be denying how sick he really was, he firmly believed that to show fear would not do anyone any good. He did not think of himself as brave, because he believed that his attitude was just the way he was. Losing his reserve, as he began to do when he had those frightening dreams, would cause him to express the feelings inside. That behavior frightened him and his family more than anything else in his illness. Only a great force, such as a devastating disease, could make him slip out of character. If he had been a victim of such fear in his passage, that would have been a cruel fate indeed.

Yielding to fear is thought of as failure. Badness is related to harm, and we each bear a burden of guilt from associations that hauntingly remind us of our badness (especially childhood pranks) and the fear or sense of failure that accompanied those old memories. Panic occurs when fear manifests itself as physical phenomena such as heart palpitations, shortness of breath, and severe pain (gastrointestinal cramps, headaches, or backaches). This is an extreme reaction of the fight-or-flight response—an innate biological mechanism that protects the being experiencing a fearful situation. This complex reaction to fear is within everyone's biological heritage.

When facing danger, the modern human is expected to suppress innate fear responses and confront the threat by standing firm. The person resists dangers by denying that the fear is so intense that the person is powerless, by asserting his or her will, and by seeing the event through. After the event, assessment of the gains and losses will determine the wisdom or foolishness of the defense, but the person will also be judged (privately and by others) on the bravery displayed. Each time a person experiences a challenge, he or she sets a course that will become a part of the self-identification pattern. For many people, denial becomes a habit.

As changes occur, one's physical reality may be far easier to adjust to than one's own mental identity. Whether a disease will devastate the inner being depends upon what stimulates that person's bravery or fear responses. If appearances are the only meaningful quality that an individual is willing to consider, when there is structural damage (which any of us can expect over the course of a long life) then the person will feel broken beyond repair.

Much has been said about denial as the first stage of the dying experience. In the 1970s, when Dr. Elisabeth Kübler-Ross described the five stages of dying as sequentially normal experiences, health professionals fretted when the patient and/or family did not appear to be moving through the stages properly, when signs of denial continually reappeared. But denial can be a valuable, recurrent response. Denying the absolute certainty of impending death provides the inspiration to try promising treatments, to plan for tomorrow, and to relax one's guard so one day at a time can unfold.

In the following case history, however, the desire for a rapid death held the patient in captivity. Instead of denial being an obstruction to obtaining appropriate help, or a positive response to a dire situation, acceptance of an incurable disease provided a mind-set that no help could penetrate.

~

Appearances were everything to Delores. Her slender figure and her shadowed eyes betrayed her vulnerability. She constantly lived with the conviction that she looked like a dying person. Yet, she did not die until more than nine years after her incurable malignancy had been diagnosed. She attempted to endure the treatment regimen advised by her oncologist, but she interrupted each segment before completion by declaring that she was suffering more than if she were just allowed to die. The more anger she expressed, the more her illusion of a dignified death eluded her.

She raged at her husband that she was suffering unbearably. She refused to allow any relatives or old friends to see her because, convinced that she would never regain her "style," she had stopped wearing makeup. Dressing and bathing were ordeals she avoided as much as possible because she could not bear to think of her body. Her dog was her only comfort, but she banished the pet for a while when the animal bounced on her bed, injuring her chest.

Our relationship with her matured because we were able to draw out her artistic talents without emphasizing physical observation. We were able to direct her nervous energy into activities she could tolerate without being aware that a goal was being accomplished.

Thus, adaptive relaxation methods were helpful, and she actually enjoyed many moments every day during our relationship. But Delores had a hopeless-helpless personality. She constantly thought about dying. Even her sleep was disturbed by distorted dreams. Sedatives, to which she became addicted, did not distract her from the specter. It was as if her concentration on dying was an obsession that had to be kept alive.

We have never known a more miserable person, nor any other who refused so many efforts to accommodate, because she could not allow herself to forget her disease even for a few moments.

~

In this example of a hopeless-helpless personality the issues being denied were those of life. Learning to plan again for tomorrow, and gaining the courage to go beyond the home, would have indicated a reorientation to reality. A qualified adjustment to reality is the measure of emotional maturity. If any portion of the reality is withheld, the holistic balance of individual development is distorted.

The "Oh no! Not me!" denial reaction, which wheels automatically in the mind when one learns of a fatal diagnosis, is a self-protective mechanism. It is an effort to push aside a threatening, unacceptable change in the state of being. If the person refuses to deal with the situation, actually behaving as if the words had never been heard, then the health-care professional must determine whether there was indeed a pathological blocking. The terms used or the manner of presentation may have been at fault; then, the person needs to have the situation explained more clearly and encouraged to bring a companion to the next appointment for interpretation and verification. Initial denial should be expected, but if denial takes the form of ignorance, the responsibility lies with the speaker as well as the listener.

Lyle Miller, et al., distinguish between denial and avoidance, referring to denial as a psychological term for maladaptive "looking away." They say, "Denial can, in fact, be pathological, but only when it prevents us from recognizing and dealing with situations that require action." A more cautious approach to an unclear message, or a dangerous but brief confrontation, might wisely be avoidance.[4] However, withdrawal may become a habit of neglect when it is used passively; conversely, it may provide a person with time to work things through before setting a course. Denial or avoidance, for brief periods, provides appropriate time-out.

Avoidance is a mechanism that reduces the risk of confrontation. Avoiding an argument with an emotional spouse, or with someone whose behavior is crazy (whatever the reason), is a way of recognizing a futile situation and redirecting one's own actions to control the situation better. But avoidance behavior may be a habitual response because of fear or lack of confidence. Then it is necessary to deal with the issues that are the source of anxiety. If a person avoids discussing a terminal illness, it is necessary to learn why, before judging whether this behavior is appropriate.

The most stressed individuals are those who suffer from panic. Ironically, those whose bodies are most reactive to fear actually exercise extraordinary bravery. Every symptom, every uncertainty, leads to internal alarms that signal an impending attack. Such people are prisoners in threatening bodies: the more they need self-control the more aggressively they are attacked from within. Living in a perpetual state of apprehension, a panicky patient has difficulty believing that the next turn will not be far worse than the last.

The surge of adrenaline that nature intends for protection and defense exaggerates the anxiety symptoms. Other related hormone levels are raised as well, with unfortunate effects: increased pain and irritation, and increased sensitivity of vital organs. This sensitized effect lingers for weeks. Thus, a person who is subject to panic becomes more fearful and more symptomatic when engulfed in an illness that exaggerates panicky reactions.

~

Catherine, an invalid when we met her, had turned off her portable oxygen to light a cigarette, trying to control her panic as she accepted bathing and health maintenance by new home-care assistants. While she had reduced her three-pack-a-day cigarette habit to one pack, she continued to use smoking to manage her panicky feelings.

Acute respiratory distress had caused another emergency hospital admission. Her diagnosis was emphysema aggravated by asthma. Because of her reactive anxiety, her doctor had requested home care— but any change in routine aggravated her.

Severe emphysema is a long-term, life-threatening disease in which the tiny lung spaces responsible for air exchange are narrowed, usually because of toughening from tar deposits. Bronchial asthma is a long-term life-threatening disease in which the airway passages narrow in an attack. Asthma attacks are especially provoked by allergens, and they are aggravated by anxiety. Rather than reducing the symptoms of her panic, Catherine had caused more serious symptoms to develop. Now, she had to endure structurally compromised breathing, which caused more anxiety and more panicking, leading to reactive asthmatic symptoms and more dramatic shortness of breath because the lung spaces could not expand.

Because her lungs could not deliver adequately oxygenated blood, her entire body was affected. Walking had become difficult. Her heart was seriously affected by the strain caused by the emphysema. Depressed that her life had been reduced to terror while she awaited death, she had begun to seriously think of suicide as the only way to find peace.

Because she could not allow herself to concentrate on the comeditation process for the full twenty minutes, we taught her about progressive muscle relaxation and gave her a tape to play at her discretion. Follow-up visits gave us the chance to talk about managing the panic symptoms, further reducing her smoking, and adapting the meditative principles to her specific needs and limitations.

Together, we established our goals. By learning to control her panic through accepting death as the ultimate letting go, she could allow deeper, more relaxed breaths to clear her lungs. When her lungs were expanded to their maximum capacity, her circulation improved, her heart had less strain, and her panic lessened. As she gained more control she was able to exercise, improving both endurance and outlook.

～

Catherine will eventually die of advanced emphysema, just as most of us will die of the disease that we acquire in the course of our individual lives. A progressive disease can only be slowed down, but that time is ours to live and to use in the ways that are most rewarding to ourselves. The changes that take place are as important in the mind as in the body. The greatest tragedy, however, is that so many long-term illnesses affect the ability to think and act because of their effects on the brain and central nervous system. Our goal is to help the individual assert and retain his or her choices and to accompany that person through the trials of self-realization while he or she gains personal power beyond the limitations of the illness.

In *The Denial of Death*, Ernest Becker says, "There will never be anything wholly secular about human fear. Man's terror is always 'holy terror'—which is a strikingly apt popular phrase. Terror always refers to the ultimates of life and death."[5] But humankind has always held death in fascination. We have found that the more abhorrent the mention of death is to a person, the more likely that person is to eventually confess suicidal thoughts. They fear themselves and what they might do if their need for control is pushed to the level of desperation.

We do believe that suicide that results from fear of the unknown or of depression must be avoided. Treatments and solutions are available. Rabbi Earl Grollman has said, "In our tumultuous and alienated world, it is the death of love that evokes our love of death. That is why it is mandatory that the . . . community extend continuing love, support and understanding. . . ."[6] We have found that through calm acceptance of death we are able to go past the fears while allowing love, support, and understanding to be manifest.

8
COMMUNITY CONCERNS

~

*Life in the world alone leads to one result, meditation
alone leads to another. So have we heard from the wise.
They who devote themselves both to the life in the world
and to meditation, by life in the world overcome death,
and by meditation achieve immortality.*

—Isha Upanishad, verses 10–11

Is Assisted Death a Patient's Right?

"My freedom should include what I, myself, decide about my own body."

"When I am ill, why must I confront you telling me that I am not allowed to seek suicide when my body has suffered beyond tolerance because progressive cancer is slowly destroying every part of me?"

"Why do you assume that you have more reverence for the sanctity of life if you insist upon seeing me become haggard while suffering pain, and my organs are consuming themselves? When it is my life, I should be the one who knows when my sanctity is threatened."

"Why should your opinion override my family's if my brain is damaged, and I am unable to say, 'Take these damn tubes out; I no longer need fluids and body nourishment.'"

"Semiparalyzed hands, which try to pull the tubes out every time they can get free of binding restraints, should be a clear message that the tubes and their feedings are not wanted."

"'Christian charity' is frequently exercised more on aging pets, who are pitied and 'put to sleep,' than it is on fellow humans."

These and similar sentiments have been expressed many times by patients of various backgrounds who resent the fact that suicide with their physician and/or loved ones present is forbidden in our society. Because being present at a suicide or assisting in one is equated with murder, a person who requests such support is asking the loved one to risk being tried for premeditated homicide. Many believe that being denied this support in dying is an unjust infringement on personal freedom. On the other hand, claiming such freedom takes a toll on the family directly and on later generations, who then question their own coping powers. The greater community shares the family's feelings of guilt and self-blame, of disappointment and betrayal, of loss of time and sharing. Every death extends far beyond the individual who dies, and one must reckon with all those implications.

When death is preplanned by terminally ill patients, it is usually seen as an escape from a dreaded reality. Although their fears are well grounded on experiences reported by others, or on their own acquaintance with pain, very few patients actually suffer intractable pain that requires large amounts of morphine and other drugs. Apprehension over experiencing the side effects of medicines while still having only inadequate control sometimes inhibits people in the search for a medical solution. Other patients are terrified about becoming confused, or losing functional control.

Although depression is believed to be a factor in thoughts of suicide or the wish for euthanasia, many people make these decisions rationally, applying both logic and intelligence to their reasoning. However, the psychological profile of a person who may be potentially suicidal has a range of identifying characteristics and is motivated by a purpose: a rationale that provides justification for the action. Anger may be an expression of alienation because the world cannot give what is needed: health. Believing that it is hopeless to wish for help, the person feels isolated. A strong desire to manipulate—exert control—is likely to be accompanied by a willingness to give up former commitments. Such ambivalence may be due to the loss of physical energy as well as to despondency. When grief is also a factor, the grieving person is likely to have a severely disturbed self-image and no expectation of future satisfaction.[1]

The choice of suicide is never taken lightly. If there is any other way to ease intolerable conditions, most people accept the long wait for nature to complete its processes. The term *euthanasia* was derived from the Greek *eu,* meaning "well," and *thanatos,* meaning "death"; therefore, the term is supposed to signify an easy or painless death.

Questions explored in chapter 1 connect not only with personal issues of the quality of dying but with the greater community's expectations: What is a good death? What are the fundamental needs of the dying person? What state of consciousness is desirable when the person dies? Again, these very personal questions can be answered only by each individual, but the caregivers, the family, and the society influence a patient's point of view and ability to react. If we have been a death-denying society, as many death educators declare, it is probably because we did not want to hear what our dying might tell us.

Emphasis on physical reality is advocated by both science and contemporary religions. While medical ethics may be considered part of philosophy, choosing death has a sociopolitical as well as a moral effect. Our society must examine these questions in order to define solutions for the future. David Meagher, a leading educator in the field of death and dying, has noted concern about the "right of privacy" and the "death with dignity" ideals as conflicts between rhetoric and practice.[2] Society must decide how individual rights will be preserved and restricted. Lois Chapman Dick, editor of the Association for Death Education and Counseling newsletter, *The Forum,* offers ten questions that relate to today's conflicts.[3] We believe they are appropriate for everyone to consider as we debate ethical guidelines to take us into the twenty-first century.

1. Does a person have a right to decide when to end his or her own life, if that person is sincerely acting from personal conviction?
2. Does the state have priority over determining when a person might die, especially if artificial-support systems are used?
3. Should there be a policy of any form of planned death?
4. Should physicians have the right to assist patients in terminating their lives if the patient requests it with fervor?
5. Do family members have a right to be involved in the decision or in the act if a terminal patient chooses to end that life?
6. Should it be legal to allow prisoners who are to be executed to donate organs or to submit to a medical experiment?
7. Is it ethical for death educators or grief counselors to support discussions about euthanasia?
8. Should it be legal for a physician or other medically trained person to offer a method (such as Dr. Jack Kevorkian's system) with his or her support to enable a patient to commit suicide?
9. If assisted suicide is legally respected, must the person be certified to

be in the last stages of terminal illness, or may the person determine personally when life is no longer of value?

10.   What restrictions would be necessary to assure that there are no abuses of any law legalizing a death not of directly natural causes?

The central issue in the debate is how much should the state restrict individual self-determination.

We do not want to become a voice in favor of euthanasia; instead, we want to encourage the expression of views and the development of options so that everyone can anticipate an easy, natural death. These are important problems for our society. Our aging population is likely to require more health-related expenditures. Health-care reform looms as a major issue in the United States. Other countries will be influenced by the economic consequences of these decisions even more than by their ethical implications. But in spite of statistical factors, each question is personally significant. The freedom of one represents the freedom of all; the views of the many determine the ethical boundaries of an individual's right to self-determination.

As modern society has evolved, morality has become equated with practical function and those things that affect personhood. Therefore, a moral imperative of our society has been to protect life, which is represented by the body. Correspondingly, development of the body and enhancements for maintaining the body (such as artificial joints and organ transplants) have become necessities for extending life and happiness. We do not want to lose any medical advances, but we do regret the decline of spiritual awareness. In humankind's earlier history, the expectation of death broadened society's perspectives to include unseen dimensions and speculations about an afterlife that have been virtually ignored by modern philosophers. As society is ever changing, it is appropriate to examine our values, determine how they will be exercised in the near future, and consider the legacy and the debt we are passing to the next generations.

Society, Health, and Responsibility

A person with serious functional and sensory changesto his or her body is likely to ask many questions: What quality of life is left? What will happen? How much suffering will be required? How much can a person be expected to endure? Who will intervene for me if I am not able to assert myself? If a caregiver of patients with progressive illness says that most patients don't consider suicide at some time, one might wonder whether that person is really hearing the most intimate thoughts of the patients. By not listening to "such talk," the caregiver is protecting himself or herself, but the patient learns that the caregiver is indicating his or her own insecurity. Mr. and Ms. Average Citizen who choose to be remote from political decisions about right-to-die issues are suffering from a similar delusion.

The burden of serious illness is a community concern involving issues of responsibility. Many questions surround terminal care. Who will provide the funds for the measures that seem appropriate for the circumstances, and who will provide the caring time? For instance, one reason that hospice was accepted and became a preferred choice for terminal care by insurers was the proof of cost reduction. By signing a contract, the patient gives the hospice the authority to be responsible for all caregiving measures. The contracting organization must plan and execute whatever methods seem appropriate to meet the principles established by hospice standards. The insurer (such as Medicare) is likely to have an agreement with the hospice to pay a specific amount for managing this patient's entire care during the terminal period. An organization that is run by a financially responsible administrator must keep this total price in mind when approving expenses that are beyond the agency's basic policies.

How much does the community value palliative measures (such as radiation and surgery to provide pain relief) when the suffering person is known to be about to die within a short time? The commitment to pay for services is made by those who initially support the insurer—all the subscribers. If curtailment of costs is more important than containing the pain of an individual for a while, then treatment limitations must become part of the policy. Community concerns include the issue of control and whether it results from inadvertent guidelines (such as insurance-payment standards) or court-decided applications of the laws. Of equal public concern are the problems of maintaining the integrity of the patient and family. Most families cannot fully support a patient enduring a long-term, devastating disease without some financial and medical back-up. The availability of health-care and work leaves, and the recognition that some people who are unable to work require financial assistance, are important twentieth-century humanitarian achievements that must not be lost.

Another policy issue is the legally required responses of emergency care. Spiritual denial is a factor in saving life. An emergency team must do everything possible to prevent the cessation of life. Their focus is on vital signs, because any seconds lost will surely jeopardize their patient's physical and mental recovery. They cannot take the time to allow a person losing consciousness to have a near-death experience. They cannot make a judgment about whether a person who has no vital signs would be better off not being resuscitated. When an emergency crew is called, they must apply their best efforts to save the patient's life, even if they are causing trauma to the body after the spirit has left. Most communities have a law that requires police (and therefore a rescue crew, and/or a coroner who may follow up with an autopsy) to be called for any death not attended by a physician. Hospices have had to campaign strenuously to be allowed to have an attending nurse pronounce the patient dead, and to make the necessary contacts so the body can be moved quietly and with respect for the family's and the patient's wishes. For some, this is the strongest argument for choosing hospice over a previously established caregiver relationship.

Many people believe that the spirit does not entirely leave the corporeal form until several hours after the body dies. Therefore, to those who anticipate an afterlife requiring prayerful assistance, it is an offense to assault that transitional phase when the spirit may be confused and is trying to find its way. If our culture valued the spirit as much as the body, in addition to clinics for understanding and managing certain diseases (such as diabetes and stroke groups) there would be programs to learn how to transfer from body consciousness to the "release of the spirit" well before the final event. As a society, all would understand dual goals: body maintenance and care appropriate to any specific physical status, and adjustment to change and preparation for dying. This is a dream of the authors as health-care advocates and as thanatologists.

Sickness and Death As Political Issues

Most of us will not end our lives abruptly. We are becoming a society of aging people. As the population ages, health care becomes more encompassing, more refined, and more responsive to maintaining the individual if the economic resources are available. As research on aging develops, millions of people who want to retard the effects of old age clamor for the most recently publicized miracle.

Through the years, each individual acquires one chronic condition on top of another. Each is treatable. Usually, when managed correctly, any new diagnosis simply means a diet adjustment, perhaps another medicine or two from the pharmacy, and watchfulness to prevent complicating symptoms. Though such health care is costly, when maintenance is so easy it would truly be a sin (or an affront to one's creative source) not to take care of oneself. Thus, compared with past generations, the older we get, the healthier we can become.

But aging takes its toll in physical agility, reaction time, mental outlook, and employment desirability. The person who is past sixty-five is eligible for retirement, and American society is structured so as to subject those who want or need to work beyond that age to job loss. This means those who are using the health-care resources the most are no longer contributing substantially to the financial stability of the system. In the meantime, AIDS—the most rapidly spreading fatal disease the world has known—and traumatic car accidents, sporting injuries, and gunshot wounds are affecting young people who should be at the height of their productivity.

By virtue of rapid transportation and global transmingling, a disease can now be dispersed throughout the planet, corresponding to air-traffic routes, in less than five years.[4] The world is pocketed with murderous civil strife, where thousands of civilians have lost limbs, homes, and families. Natural disasters, local violence, and homelessness demand attention on the home front.

Should the United States align itself with the "civilized" nations of the world in declaring health care for everyone to be a community concern? In the mid-1990s we have witnessed debate over new laws aimed to equalize accessibility to medical services. Those who need the security believe that universal health-care is a moral duty of society. Those who fear they will have to pay more than their share are opposed to government interference. The reality is that whatever the choices, health-care needs are likely to explode before another generation is prosperous enough to assume the debt. Compromises will become increasingly necessary.

Who decides that a ninety-six-year-old man will receive EKG monitoring while carefully ordered intravenous solutions are administered to balance his electrolytes, remove accumulating fluids from his lungs, and stimulate his heart muscles? Having difficulty with breathing, he will require additional oxygen, of course. Not fully conscious, he will require bedside urinary drainage. If he lives more than five days without a bowel movement, he will probably need an enema. If he rallies enough to swallow, he will need assistance with eating. If there is a promise of improvement, a physical therapist and the nursing assistants should work with his legs to prevent clots from forming and to maintain his strength and mobility. Many physicians, most of whom are specialists, will discuss his case at length during hospital rounds. This is an expected and totally appropriate routine for anyone with the symptoms of congestive heart failure. If hospital care corrected a similar occurrence for the same person several months previously, and a few years before that, why shouldn't the family expect the same efforts to be made again?

Discrimination on the basis of age is against the law. Also, many ninety-year-olds are in better physical tone and mental acuity than some who are in their seventies, and many much younger people who have had serious physical or mental damage.[5] But does fully responsive medical care to those who are secure in the system compromise a maimed youngster's opportunity to be fitted with prosthetic devices? A six-year-old whose leg was blown off by stray gunfire, in a civil war or on a city street, will require several prosthetic legs as growth and activity changes occur. And will this youth receive counseling or any other kind of support if his parents can't be responsible? Is it in the best interests of society for parents of ill or handicapped children to discover that they cannot provide for their children's special needs unless they qualify for state welfare by keeping their income below the poverty line? On growing into adulthood, how will those young people who experienced massacres as their neighborhood backdrop assimilate the ideals of a caring civilization?

The child psychologist Alice Miller firmly believed that Adolf Hitler's hatred was a result of his abusive childhood, and that his popular support was largely owed to the frustrations and injured self-esteem of the German people stemming from harsh punishments they had received as children, considered necessary lessons in obedience at that time.[6] We, as world citizens, have been horrified by the pictures and reports of Nazi cruelty and have sworn "Never again." Considering that our child-abuse statistics are higher than ever before recorded, have we actually learned anything about how to prevent inhumanity?

Of what we have learned, are we in any way capable of effecting a change that would alter the way people think before they explode in violence? We have had hopes for mediation workshops that teach dialogue and insight to high-school students and troubled youths because most attendees have expressed changes in their attitudes. It is possible that these programs will be discontinued by a political climate that favors punishment and retribution rather than training and guidance. Is this lessened compassion being reflected in American health-care cutbacks, as well? How will coming changes influence our caregiving methods?

Do we want a society in which the accepted evaluation factor is material possessions rather than spiritual integrity and humane relationships? How do we demonstrate and extract society's demands without being cruel and giving inappropriate instructions to those whose sense of society has been radically distorted? How can we have sincere mutual respect when self-righteous egos are expressed in loud arguments and narrow-minded condemnation of differing attitudes as a pastime, as may be found in many popular radio talk shows?

We are what our most forceful orators would have us be; but weak voices gain strength with meaning. When the frail speak, their thoughts represent experience that can be known only through encounter. When an opinion about a caregiving policy is strong, it takes little energy to dictate or write a note to be sent to state and federal representatives to influence legislation. When family, friends, and acquaintances are included, the message is magnified and the circle expands. In a similar way, decisions to donate to specific causes following a death are simple gestures that extend the ideals of the living, thinking person into the future. Such small actions bear witness to a person's experiences and opinions long after the power to speak has faded.

> *Most of us, as we use life, try to open the universe to ourselves, while Lao-tzu opens himself to the universe.*
>
> **—Ancient Chinese saying**

Even more important than participating in legislative decisions, determining one's own life course is a necessary effort for every adult, healthy or sick. A living will or a durable power of attorney for health issues should be signed, witnessed, and checked every two years with date and initials.[7] Drafting such a personal paper requires both serious thought and deliberate action. Young and healthy people, especially, tend to procrastinate, but our youth are the most vulnerable to accidents leading to long-term, devastating invalidism. The purpose of a living will is to direct health-care providers in the event that you are unable to communicate your choices at the time of need. The paper should show how you wish to be cared for, and name a trusted spokesperson to make decisions for you. By stating exactly what life-sustaining measures are preferred or refused, the individual is represented if permission for medical procedures cannot be personally granted because of incapacitation. Not only is the person able to influence limitations of care, but he or she may express the wish for full support for an extended time if that is the choice. In addition, the desire to be an organ donor (or not) may be included. Communication is the essential factor, but until recently, the patient's wishes were not legally valid because of numerous legal precedents.

Important changes have occurred through legislative and judicial decisions because citizens or their families have persevered against laws they viewed as unacceptable. Karen Ann Quinlan's family fought a New Jersey hospital medical staff through the state court system to have a respirator removed after she had lain in a vegetative state for more than a year following a car accident. The family's suit claimed that prolonged forced respiration with virtually no hope of recovery would have been totally against Ms. Quinlan's wishes. After the New Jersey Supreme Court decided that the respirator was an infringement upon the patient's right to die and should be disconnected, Ms. Quinlan lived nine more years in an extended-care facility without artificial respiration. This landmark 1976 ruling led the way for other patient's-rights claims and caregiving policy shifts.

Florida, and later California, had decisions allowing artificial feeding tubes to be removed. Using the argument for the right to privacy, the first successful appeals were on behalf of persons in persistent vegetative states. But one California case involved Elizabeth Bouvia, an alert and mentally competent quadriplegic. The ruling declared that a mentally competent person has the right to refuse any medical treatment, including life support. Ms. Bouvia later decided to keep the tube when she was better able to handle her pain; the right to refuse was the victory she was seeking.[8]

In the fall of 1985, a former Massachusetts firefighter, Paul Brophy, who had clearly stated that he wished never to be on life support of any kind, was being kept alive by tube feedings for more than two years. His wife, a nurse, and his entire family requested that the feedings be discontinued. Because the tube was already in place, the court ruled that there were no grounds for claiming invasive or uncomfortable interference. The argument to continue feedings was based on the premise that if the treatment did not cause unusual suffering, there was no reason to change what had been an ongoing form of care.

At that time it was estimated that there were about ten thousand patients in the United States who were in a similar condition. The resolution of this case was that the family was allowed to move the patient to a hospital more sympathetic to their position. While receiving full medical support, Mr. Brophy was allowed to die without artificial feedings. Documentation supported that this approach was in the patient's best interests by maintaining his privacy and affirming his expressed choices. At the time, Massachusetts had no law governing a living will.

A decisive court finding occurred when Nancy Cruzan's family lost the appeal to remove a feeding tube from their daughter, who had been in a persistent vegetative state for more than six years. The state of Missouri claimed that its interest was to maintain Ms. Cruzan as a person with a disability. The United States Supreme Court upheld the state's right to take precedence over the family's wishes. The fact that the patient had never left tangible evidence of her preferences was the main argument for giving the state final authority. This decision impelled people throughout the United States to obtain a legal power of attorney in the event of any health-care crisis. For instance, the Massachusetts Health Care Proxy Act was passed in the 1991 legislative session after more than a dozen years of defeats. According to the Patient Self-Determination Act of 1991, each client upon contracting with a health-care organization must be given the opportunity to name a representative and to set limits upon treatment in the event of incapacitation. For some living-will advocates, this was a battle of a lifetime resolved nationwide within a few weeks.

A referendum to legalize assisted suicide was on the ballot in Washington in 1991 and in Oregon in 1992. It passed in Oregon in 1994 but was promptly held in legal dispute. Connecticut is considering similar legislation in 1995. A proposal for California is being carefully worded to assure medical checks and the safety of the vulnerable. The controversy is complex.

On the principle that the desire for assistance with the release of one's own body-confined energy becomes a legitimate need when illness moves slowly and destructively, Derek Humphrey founded the Hemlock Society in California in 1980. Supporters of the society are now worldwide. They hold that belief in a supernatural being or life after death is not universal, and that no group should dictate the actions or penalties of those who do not agree with laws based on differing concepts of reality and moral behavior if no one but the individual is hurt. Right-to-life supporters, on the other hand, express fear that consenting to any "choice" about death will usher in disdain for other lives, as prevailed in Nazi Germany, and that exceptions for individuals will spread to broader interpretations.

While there have been no prosecutions for suicide in the United States since the 1960s, this is partly because a person who successfully commits suicide cannot appear in court. A person who makes an unsuccessful attempt will usually be hospitalized for psychiatric evaluation and treatment. Michigan, unlike most states, has never had a law prohibiting suicide, a position that changed after June 1990, when Jack Kevorkian, a retired physician who specialized in pathology, assisted Janet Adkins, a patient in the early stages of Alzheimer's disease, to take her own life. Much dispute arose over the ethical and legal implications of his actions, and Michigan passed a new law to prevent assisted suicide. A 1990 jury found Kevorkian "sympathetic in his efforts to find a method which would minimize trauma, and provide thoughtful support for the patient."[9] By January 1995 there were twenty-one cases in which courts had found that the patients clearly had sought Kevorkian's services and were determined to end their own lives. In every instance, Dr. Kevorkian has been released based on the patient's right to privacy, but the issues raised by assisted suicide remain controversial.

Whether you wish to have the assurance that another would be available to assist you in suicide if you should need it, or whether you are someone who thinks that everything Kevorkian represents is abhorrent, your position is important as our laws are challenged. The heart of this issue is the practice of terminal caregiving. Recent studies have shown that terminally ill patients voluntarily reduce both food and liquids, usually preferring states of starvation and dehydration because of their symptoms. As long as they are supported in every other way they do not feel dissatisfied.[10] On the other hand, it has been a medical rule that people who were not fed a proper balance of nutrients and were not kept well hydrated were being made to suffer.

The Netherlands is the first country in which physicians have been able to present their case histories in support of patient-requested euthanasia on a basis of medical and ethical standards to the courts for review. Since 1984, hospital-based doctors there have been permitted, following an act of euthanasia, to continue their medical practices without reprimand when their clinical findings, patient-care management, and patient's recorded words were examined both ethically and legally. Other staff physicians are brought into the case before the patient's request is granted so that the burden does not fall on one doctor alone and so that treatment approaches can be attempted from different perspectives before agreement is given.

The patient's motives for wanting to die are examined and interventions to address the problems are tried before the request is acted upon. The patient must express a strong desire to be helped to die at least three times and is required to confirm this intent when the medicine is about to be administered. The doctors believe that a close relationship develops between themselves and the patient during this period, and that they are acting out of love and respect.

Dr. Pieter Admiraal, a founder of the Dutch Society on Pain, spoke at the Seventh International Congress on Care of the Terminally Ill in Montreal in October 1988, on euthanasia as practiced in Holland. Dr. Admiraal, a senior anesthesiologist in Delft, reported that about 10 to 15 percent of their dying cancer patients, and about 5 percent of their total population of dying patients, are assisted to die by physicians. Even though euthanasia is officially illegal in the Netherlands, as in other countries, it is broadly known to be an option.[11] Dr. Admiraal works in a Roman Catholic hospital. In his lecture he referred to the country as being predominantly Catholic as well. But these physicians have their own view of ethics. They believe that passive euthanasia such as starvation and dehydration imposes an unnecessary period of suffering.

The Dutch do not have a separate hospice system but expect general hospital care to include adjustment measures in the care of the dying. The terminal-care program involves a total medical team including nurses, medical specialists, and counselors. Speaking about a worldwide policy, Dr. Admiraal noted that at no time does a doctor study dying, anywhere. In normal medical training, physicians learn only how to stop the dying process, not how to ease it. To address this imbalance in educational and policy practices in medicine, the Soros Foundation, a philanthropic network sponsoring the nonprofit Open Society Institute, has pledged to support "innovations in the provision of care, public education, professional education, and public policy" through the Project on Death in America. Such an endeavor is critical in our approaches to change health-care.

Personal Attitudes

The goal of medical care today, especially of hospice care, is to manage all of the symptoms as well as humanly possible. In actual experience, both causes and effects of pain can be addressed. When receiving full therapeutic support, even the person who claims "intolerable pain" and "suffering beyond belief" will rarely evaluate discomfort or distress (at the moment in which the interview is being conducted) as pain near the maximum level. It is common, though, for the memory of intolerable pain to linger, and the person will not believe that the pain does not continue to pose a threat. Apprehension hovers at the back of the person's mind, causing the fear that pain will return with a vengeance when the guard is let down.

A patient can learn to emphasize a range of different perspectives, however. A declaration of intolerable pain is usually based on fear. Anxiety about the lack of available recourses or about advancing disease causing more distress is often the source of unnecessary suffering. When common hopes must be abandoned, extraordinary hope is essential. The anticipation of being challenged beyond one's capacity can easily become more terrifying than reality. But caregivers and loved ones can suggest ways for the suicidal patient to discover that change can neutralize the fears and find that growth within can enrich and give satisfaction. Although it is a difficult task, all will benefit by having the time and the opportunities to deepen their connections.

~

Walt had led a bitter life, in and out of poorly paying jobs and unfulfilling marriages. He had held the position of chief orderly in a large nursing home by developing the reputation of being strict, efficient, and unemotional. When he developed cancer, his attitude became more gruff. His usual pessimism was turned to inward despair. After he was admitted to an inpatient hospice unit, everyone who came to him found that he would turn to the wall to avoid speaking. Meals were untouched, and even pain medicines were rejected.

Both the pastoral counselor and the social worker had no success getting him to respond. The nurses' aides learned that if they left a basin for bathing he would use it, but if they tried talking he would yell at them to leave. The head nurse, who had tried to accommodate his wishes, finally became determined to break through his barriers. She went into his room, closed the door, sat down, and said, "We're going to have a talk." She started by acknowledging his previous work with sick people. He knew how his behavior would affect the younger staff. She was unimpressed by his rudeness and explained that his symptoms could be addressed if he wished, but his illness was not an excuse for his attitude. Then she asked him to tell her how he felt. What were his wishes? How did he feel about his life? Why was death a threat? They talked for more than two hours.

Every day thereafter, they had a few minutes for private exchange. His needs were listened to, and actions were taken to address his discomfort and other specific complaints. Every symptom and every response was explained as a matter of fact. He felt more comfortable because he discovered that anxiety was okay, and as the issues around the anxiety were exposed, they softened like ripening fruit. Meditative images formed for him. When he wanted consolation he could suck out bittersweet memories. The more he tasted them the more he was able to face his past and let it go.

He began to relate more directly with his girlfriend than he had through any of the five years they had lived together. He asked her to make a call to his son, whom he had deserted thirty years previously. He gave her messages to carry to the Alcoholics Anonymous meetings they had attended (rarely) together. As he let go of old angers that were seated within himself, he could show who he really was: someone who could be respected, someone he could die with. By learning to meditate (an AA principle he had resisted), he could open himself to calmness and forgiveness without having to confront the angry God of his childhood. That anger had messed up his life, and that anger was what he had to let go so he could die as a simple man.

~

Objective self-assessment is the key to developing appropriate responses and communicating with those who can help. Patients who fear psychological and pharmacological therapies can be taught cognitive methods of self-evaluation.[12] Understanding one's own reactions and responses to certain situations, defusing the dangers, using relaxation techniques such as comeditation principles adapted for personal needs, and developing a workable day-to-day pattern helps the patient remain in charge.

~

Rod's cancer of the lung had metastasized to his brain, causing wild behavior when he became fearful of being attacked by bugs that only he could see. When Rod's hallucinations caused him to jump around erratically and yell hysterically, a psychotropic drug was ordered. Also, the nurse talked with the patient and family to help them understand that he was not "crazy" but that the disease had caused a new symptom. She advised the patient to learn to relax when the hallucinations disturbed him, and she encouraged his wife to give him comeditation when he was upset. This action helped him focus on his chosen phrase rather than letting the "bugs" become magnified in his mind. Soon he could just relax and distract himself to maintain control. Then he used comeditation sessions for reinforcement and pain management. One day, Rod signaled the nurse for a private conversation. He confided, "You know those bugs? Well, I've been doing as you said, and I'm able to deal with them a lot better, like my wife said. In fact they hardly bother me at all. But, I think you should know—they are multiplying."

$\sim$

Rod could be cared for at home because he and his home caregivers were able to meet each problem objectively. Hysteria is a cry for help that demands comfort and consolation. The use of comeditation (or any relaxation method) to naturally modulate the anxiety-provoking effects of an illness, combined with medication and the family's ability to reason, produced both pain relief and mental composure. As self-control is regained, trust in the self becomes reinforced and transferred to trust in others. Then, gradually, with spiritual tranquility, trust in an unseen power can lead to letting go when the body is ready. That is, while tiring of the daily challenges, the patient lets time and body changes prepare the way for withdrawal and a gentle transition. Although intimate sharing may reveal private thoughts, most people prefer being able to present themselves as composed as possible. We all would choose to leave memories of our courage in the face of death.

By being aware of the process of change, we gradually develop inwardly because we integrate reality with personal validation. Thus, we experience losses and change while continuing to prevail as ourselves. This letting go of attachments while strengthening within is dual concept. The world can be seen from a broader perspective as personal striving decreases. In the deepest level of meditative consciousness, one may be able to realize that our unique essence is not restricted to the body. The breath is the link between this greater awareness and the body shell. But even the breath is not necessary for the manifestation of this deeper self. When one lets go of everything, completely, the deeper self—the only true treasure—is found.

This message of a soul essence that may transcend earthly boundaries has been the foundation of many religions. And religion has provided a social as well as a spiritual connection for believers. Hindus speak of joining the great "I Am, All That Is." Enlightened Buddhists may enter "the clear light of the void, the true reality." Jewish families recite, "Blessed be God's name, Whose glorious dominion is for ever and ever." Christians are assured of "salvation with the Father, Son, and Holy Spirit"; Muslims include in prayer for the deceased, "To Allah do we belong, and to Him shall we return."[13] Near-death experiences (NDEs) are accounts from people who have been resuscitated after clinical signs indicated that death was occurring. Studies of NDEs report core experiences that include a vivid awareness of going beyond the confinements of the body, the room, and the world (as we know it) into a bright light filled with a presence of love.[14]

The basic subject of this book is learning to let go. The person who is dying needs to allow natural changes to tire the body and calm the mind. We have found that when a person is able to achieve deep relaxation, body tension, emotional anxieties, social separations, and spiritual yearning can be melted away. This is a personal quest achieved inwardly. The extraordinary benefit is that while learning to let go, a person gains control over the self and over adverse disturbances as well. It is a preparation for clear mind, peaceful heart. This waiting period seems to be a natural process as the body closes down; one has but to relax and flow into the spaces.

While we seemed to open this discussion with a completely contradictory message—that some people feel they must have the right to suicide if their condition becomes intolerable—both messages are just different aspects of the control issue. A person who cannot accept the challenges of a difficult life becomes angry because the body is taken over by forces beyond his or her control. By resisting with bitterness and defiance, intent upon self-determination, the person asserts his or her will as anger and unwillingness to compromise. This causes more suffering. Thus, there is even more awareness of loss of control. On the other hand, when the person learns to let go, pain disperses and is modulated through natural body responses. All things are gentler and more harmonious when anxiety is managed. When a person learns to reduce fear, the attentions are freer to let go in the search for safety and peace. This concept is demonstrated in the following portion of a thank-you letter we received from a woman who was present during the last weeks of her sister's life.

> At first [my sister] was quite frightened and fretful, unwilling to comprehend the imminence of her passing. Her mind was burdened and she found it difficult to control her racing thoughts. After a few sessions with comeditation she was able to still her mind and gradually attained a sense of peace and serenity. H. was admittedly quite pleasantly surprised when she experi-

enced such a reversal of moods; she had never meditated before.

She was able to contemplate her passing with acceptance . . . enveloped in the white light of peace, to see herself whole and perfect and full of love. She passed into spirit shortly after one of our comeditations. She was peaceful, breathing softly, and knew she was safe.

This experience was one of the greatest gifts I could ever give myself or my sister. It is indeed a unique and beautiful thing to share with a loved one the intimacy of letting go of this life and passing gently into the realm of the spirit.

Sincerely, in peace and love, Jan

Contrary to many expectations, when inner peace is accompanied by acceptance, a person may have renewed ability to address a resisted task. If quite a bit of time remains before death, earlier anxieties may return out of habit, but they may cause less disturbance. In finding peace and the reassurance of love, the person becomes able to forgive others. He or she may even become devoted to a special cause.

The history of the fight against AIDS is filled with the remarkable energies of men and women who rally from illness to give a speech, or attend a meeting, or sit with a friend. When they are able to find their own center, they become able to give to others. Functioning in a similar manner to some who have had near-death experiences, they feel a drive to contribute in a way that fulfills their lives' purposes. The creative force may be realized outwardly if the task includes others; it may be realized inwardly if the task is within. The creative impulse is our discovery of the divine.

Final Choices

The current general hospice policy in North America is to administer no nutrients or fluids other than those the client wishes to take orally. In practicing total respect for the patient, when the hospice client said, "No, I don't care to eat," or "If I drink, I'll vomit, so please don't make me," hospices began to teach staff and families to never urge what isn't wanted by the patient. They discovered that there are few undesirable effects when natural dehydration occurs. Retention of fluids in the body was reduced in those clients, making movement, respiration, and toileting easier. The patient was more comfortable, especially if incontinence or diarrhea had been a problem previously. Phlegm became less profuse. This meant that many families were not upset with "death rattle" sounds, as often occurs otherwise, and the nursing problem of positioning the patient for lung drainage was not so difficult.[15]

Interstitial fluids that settle in body tissues and lungs when the body is too sick to process incoming fluids causes discomfort to the patient and challenges to nursing care. For instance, the body must be turned more frequently to avoid pooling of fluids at certain resting sites, such as the legs and back, and the skin becomes more fragile. There is likely to be a greater need for suctioning if the patient has been well hydrated. These problems are greatly reduced if natural dehydration occurs.

If a comatose person does not receive intravenous fluids, even if sphincter control has been lost, the urinary output may be so slight as kidney function fails that only pads are needed, thus eliminating the irritation of a urinary catheter. When no fluids are received, bowel activity will lessen. On the other hand, when electrolyte imbalances are present (as may occur with dehydration), weakness, lethargy, confusion, and disorientation can progress to coma before death. Neuromuscular irritation may first be seen as restlessness or faint, random twitching. This is not uncomfortable to the patient and should not alarm onlookers. As in meditation, such activity is merely energy discharge; the Eastern body-mind interpretation is that energy blockages are being opened. Eventually cardiac irregularities develop, leading to heart failure. When the patient's body has been dying for a prolonged time, there is little evidence of change in awareness of pain during the last moments.

Dehydration, as a part of the natural dying process, is probably more humane than the artificial administration of fluids and nutrients for the purpose of balancing the body's requirements. The effect of giving fluids is to prolong the dying and to override nature's method of helping the mind and body enter the realm between consciousness and eternity. On the other hand, the mental effects of dehydration and electrolyte imbalance challenge the choice of our early question, "In what state of awareness do you want your consciousness to be at the time of your transformation?" Contact with a comatose person may be very difficult, and as toxins build within the body there may be hallucinations suggesting scenes of purgatory or happy events. Those unpleasant events can be alleviated somewhat; many comatose patients have appeared to be quieted by cooling baths and gentle assurances.

Sensations such as pain may be realized in coma but are difficult to evaluate, since communication from the patient is uncertain and is perhaps accomplished only by very fleeting signs, sometimes thought to be imagined by the onlooker. It is appropriate to medicate a comatose patient, however, using these signs and previously identified pain requirements as a dosage guide. Analgesics and some other drugs are available as skin patches and/or suppositories, so the patient's inability to take medicines by mouth should not be a deterrent. Injections may also be given, of course, but the patient is likely to feel the shot.

Although the person may have anticipated remaining alert while dying, death approaches each person in an individual way. Some people will stay alert while having no desire for any nourishment for several days. Many will undergo the most elaborate medical checks and balances while slipping into a deep coma. There are many variations between the two extremes; the process of dying is as individual as the manner of living and seems to be a matter of fate rather than plan. Not even our best medical experts can fully direct a patient's progress because the biologically complex interactions of nerves and organs are subject to the developments of disease and chemical imbalances that accompany physical shut-down.

Although more has been learned about brain function during this past century than in all our earlier history, no one has yet determined where the soul resides. Some neurophysiologists and neuropsychologists believe that coma experiences are related to neural static artifacts that activate memory images.[16] The biological process of illness preceding death seems to stimulate numerous chemical variations, which affect mental awareness in many different ways. Might there be a purpose to the altered states of consciousness within the normal process of the dying experience? As there are biological changes at birth that enable the infant to begin earthly life, might the changes that occur when the person is dying facilitate that transition from life to death?

Serotonin produced by the body seems to reduce hyperreaction to pain. Rising serotonin levels during the dying process may contribute to natural pain management and the desire to rest. Intensified, the desire to rest becomes depression, normally experienced as temporary periods in the stages of dying. These natural responses may also contribute to the person's ability to settle affairs and work toward emotional control as he or she becomes comfortable in accepting death.

In other words, it seems possible that the chemicals our bodies produce in response to injury or impending death are necessary to help us complete our tasks and to make the transition into eternity. It has been reported that mental functions occur within fractions of seconds. Although those experiencing sudden death do not have a thoughtful preparatory period, they may still have enough time to be released into the light of peace and love. Of course these concepts are speculation, but so are the skeptical rebuttals.

"Tell me about life after death," requested the disciple of the master.

"I cannot tell you that, only that you must practice clear mind, and peaceful heart," replied the teacher.

"Well, you are a Zen Master, aren't you?" retorted the student.

"Yes," answered the master, "But I am not a dead one."[17]

Hallucinations are not uncommon in people who have undergone mental changes due to chemical imbalances and brain injury. Dr. Ronald Siegel skeptically correlates hallucinatory experiences with the activation of stored memories and the stimulation of optic neurons.[18] Sensory deprivation may occur as the brain receives less oxygen. Exaggerated neural stimulation may be caused by high demands for balancing body systems. Drugs such as morphine, while appropriate to reduce pain, may contribute to mental activity. And toxins collect as vital organs fail. All these phenomena may be linked to the perception of images beyond the ordinary. In addition, a person who has been subjected to extreme trauma may undergo psychological depersonalization, or identify with another persona.[19] This seems to occur primarily in children in abusive situations, however, and we have not found examples in the research literature about terminal illnesses.

Siegel and similar thinkers seem to believe that anything they can examine holds no wonder. But to many others, the more they are able to understand the complexities and relationships between the body and the potentials of the mind, the more awe-inspiring the elements of life—and therefore death—seem to them. Consider the implications of the amazing capacity of our minds. Visions of heavenly escorts, out-of-body experiences, and tunnels leading to bright light, as have been related by many NDE researchers as well as to sympathetic doctors and nurses, impress those who experience them as being more vivid than reality. They know that something special has happened to them because regardless of the brevity of time spent in that exceptional state, it becomes the most powerful event of their lives.

Such speculations about finding a keyhole through consciousness into the presence of God cannot be ignored. Think of the wondrous qualities of our existence. We are constructed as creatures that adapt and emerge from dependency in a fluid environment to air-breathing, two-legged, ego-centered, social beings. Why should we not have the innate capacity to return to the source of our awareness through familiar avenues of assurance?

~

Gus, whom we met in chapter 3, was an example of the people who naturally comfort themselves by making an *ahhh* sound. The use of this sound can become particularly effective when working with those who choose it in comeditation. Gus allowed his body to glide into a deep meditation while he listened. Then he responded rather quickly, as if understanding that it was necessary to assure us that this was exactly what he had needed. When his family returned to his room, he acknowledged them but seemed to prefer to ignore them, as though they were inappropriately distracting.

Suddenly, signs of cardiovascular changes began to be apparent. We recognized these as symptoms that the nurse before us had observed when she reported her surprise that Gus had not died earlier. Knowing that he had come home from the hospital to die, we saw no reason to attempt medical intervention. Instead, judging by his reactions with his family, it seemed evident that he wanted to be allowed to let go. After a few minutes, his eyes widened; and he adjusted the angle of his head as if to improve his vision, looking directly between his son and his wife. His mouth parted in an expression of surprise, and he said, "Well! What are you doing here?" Then he appeared to be listening. He seemed to be responding as he said, "Oh?" "Oh?" "Oh." His head nodded as he spoke; then he finally said, "Okay." We watched as his spirit abruptly left his body.

Gus and his family had battled his disease for many months. They had resisted invalidism and death by trying numerous cures at great expense to them all. But his parting occurred as if it were the most natural thing he could do. After the family adjusted to the shock and expressed their initial grief, his son said, "You know, my father never was a coward; he just always liked to understand what was going on." We had no doubt that Gus's experience escorted him into the next phase of his existence. If our comeditation served to initiate his safe conduct, we could not wish for a more positive example of achieving a harmonious transition. We were grateful to be present.

~

Perhaps there are lessons in Gus's experience when we consider our position in the community as it decides on the limitations and alternatives in health care. Would Gus have been ready earlier if he had not had the opportunity to try various treatments? Would his anxiety have been lessened if comedication had been offered to him earlier? We will never know the answers to these questions about Gus. But we hope to learn more from others who share their experiences and thoughts with us.

Conclusion

A dying patient, for the most part, has a medical condition for which there is no cure. This condition may need to be lived with for several years, or it may last only a few hours. In either case minimizing the symptoms by using various treatments and medications contributes to the patient's quality of life. To the patient, the meaning of that particular disease and its effects, the meaning of personal suffering overall, his or her coping behavior, the sort of comfort or disturbance derived from family or social exchanges, the financial and social implications of obtaining full care, and emotional and spiritual concerns all play roles in working through a serious illness.

Medical ethics is everyone's business. The patient and family can be adversely affected if they do not have an equal relationship with the physician. Who decides the route to take and the treatments the patient will receive? Does the patient have a choice? Are the feelings of the family of no account?

～

Al had been an alcoholic many years earlier. When we met him he was suffering from liver cancer, and his attention sometimes wandered. But immediately, his warm personality and good relationship with his family inspired us. Al wanted to remain as alert as possible throughout the course of his disease. Mental blurring and bizarre behavior frightened him; he felt he had learned those lessons long ago. To help him settle down at night, we taught him and his wife comeditation. They found initially that it helped a lot, and Al liked the fact that his mind cleared.

Al's wife and son were especially upset when he began to have increasing episodes of confusion and wildness because they were so reminiscent of his alcoholic period thirty years ago when he had abused his family. We advised his doctor of these unfortunate changes in Al's status and suggested a medicine that might have enabled him to clear the toxins that were causing the symptoms. We were stunned when the doctor replied, "I don't want him to have anything. That's just the way nature intended it. If the family has trouble handling his craziness that's their problem; we'll bring him into the hospital to let him die." No reasoning with the doctor, by either professional caregivers or family members, would change the doctor's mind. The patient was admitted to the hospital but given no treatments to support him or to correct his electrolytic imbalances. He didn't die for almost two weeks, while the family made periodic attempts to quiet him, fretted over his raging fever, and truly felt helpless and reluctant to visit.

Probably, comeditation would have helped if it had been practiced frequently, and in violation of the doctor's order that no one was to try to contact the patient through his coma. The family felt intimidated, angry, but unwilling to make a change at that period in Al's dying.

～

As a member of society, each person has an obligation to communicate with others. When one is in the midst of conflict, the problems surrounding that situation are most clear, and incentives to improve the conditions are most urgent. On the other hand, when problems seem paramount, one is a tempted to think only of managing one's own day-to-day challenges.

In addition, for both patient and family, there is the emotional requirement to begin backing off. In learning and practicing the philosophy of meditative practice, whatever one's physical condition, the student is advised to let everything become equal in "don't know mind." To let go is to accept whatever is.

As everyone must develop this process in his or her own way, others can only provide support and encouragement. A deceased person leaves many long-lasting impressions of who he or she was, what principles were personally important, and what his or her legacy was. The things acquired during a lifetime are not as important as the refrains of being that influence others and linger in their memories after one passes on. Actions expressing personal sentiments, and efforts to reach out beyond one's own room, are the products of a lifetime but are waves that can be energized during moments of illness and disability, often better than during the busyness of work and achievement. As there is time for sleep, there is time for action; as there is time for meditation, there is time for opinions and solutions to be shared. As there is time to receive comfort and let the comfort move one into a state of peace, there is time to inspire one toward a goal greater than the single moments of discomfort.

Therefore, the sick person and the family should consider that they have dual roles. First, rather than complaining and expressing anger or frustration to the air, they need to divert that energy to effective outlets. They have an obligation to let others know their experiences and their opinions, for a broad consensus derived from actual living, rather than remote intellectualizations, is the only basis on which our society can realistically develop its future. The second obligation of the patient is to prepare to let go into silence and enveloping peace. Then it may be said, "This person's life was worthy, and complete. The resolution was good."

There are many ways to die, just as there are many ways to live. Our theme is that everyone around a dying person adapts to the circumstances, making minor changes as they are required while providing support for every aspect of the person. The right medical advice at the right time, combined with relaxation and movement, and balanced by philosophic and social thoughts, will provide the right blend of qualities and tones when one makes any transition in this life. We would like to share portions of another letter that we received recently.

> I got a call that my brother's fight with lung cancer was about over. The doctor said he had about one week to live. As I prepared to travel to his side, I tucked your little book, Letting Go, into my purse.
>
> His lung cancer made it difficult for him to breathe, but he tried hard to be a gracious host to the steady stream [of people] in and out of his room. His breathing became more labored as he struggled with the pain. On his forehead a vein appeared between his eyebrows in a vertical line. The more he struggled to breathe the more prominent the vein became.
>
> I thought about the breathing exercises in your book [Letting Go]. My brother began to do an exercise. His wife, two sons, a daughter, and I took turns talking him through the exercise, getting him to make the ahhh sound of letting go. He was able to relax in an easier breathing pattern, and the vein in his brow disappeared.
>
> For the next few days we regularly did the breathing with him. The effect was amazing. It not only helped my brother relax, it also helped us stay connected to him at a difficult time. At the very end, he was in an induced

coma. The breathing was again labored, and the vein was prominent once more.

I wanted to establish a connection with him so I started the breathing once more. I really didn't think it would have any effect. I was wrong. Even when he was unconscious it was evident he was responding to us. It helped us stay present with him right to the end.

After his breathing stopped we talked to him, telling him how much we loved him, and sending him on his way. Afterwards, [all of the family] held hands and prayed. This remains one of the most profound experiences of my life. Your book and the exercises in it helped to make it so for all of us.

Thank you, sincerely, C. F.

It is letters like this one, and experiences in our practices, that have energized us through these many years. It is the transpersonal experience that we feel as undefinable energy when we work with the whole person. That whole person is represented by all that ever was and all that ever will be. We know the transition from life to death as part of the miracle contributing to the universal hum, the harmony of the creative source. Every particle in the universe is composed of energy vibrations. Therefore, each of us is a unique combination, which is always evolving and is also leaving a trail. As the body's energies become accustomed to synchrony, the spirit may respond with perfect harmony at the time of transition.[20]

In letting go,
there is gain.
In giving up,
There is advancement.

Do not practice controlling.
Practice allowing.

Such is the mystery of happiness.
Such is the mystery of wealth.
Such is the mystery of power.
Such is the mystery of living and dying.[21]

COMEDITATION GUIDE

~

Comeditation is a process in which a person (the recipient) is aided in releasing all tension by an assistant, who says the cues for progressive muscle relaxation and, focusing on the recipient's breath pattern, vocalizes specifically selected sounds, words, or phrases as the receiver exhales. The effect produced is transpersonal tranquility with a decrease in pain and anxiety, release of muscular tension and mental distractions, and reduction of pain, nausea, and anxiety arising from stress. Full relaxation and meditative peace of mind may be achieved.

By a prearranged sequence of words or sounds (signals from the assistant, cued precisely to the receiver's exhalations), the person becomes aware of his or her own exhalation pattern, objectively. The process of letting go follows.

The recipient must be willing to recline quietly, lying flat on the back with the spine straight, if possible, and with the arms at the side, palms up. The recipient follows the guide without interactive participation other than listening after the plan has been accepted. Changes in position for medical reasons are acceptable as long as the recipient's body is fully supported by bed-position changes and pillows, and as long as the spine is kept straight. Feet and legs should be covered, because the extremities may cool as respiration and circulation slow down.

The assistant should sit in a chair near the ear of the recipient. Light must be sufficient for the assistant to observe the recipient's breathing. Bunching a bit of sheet over the diaphragm area, or placing a tented cleansing tissue at the point of visible movement of the chest and abdomen, may make the breathing pattern more visible.

A third person present may serve as observer and attend to outside interruptions such as telephones and doors. As alternatives, bells can be disconnected, or the participants can agree to ignore disturbances.

To conclude a session designate a signal, such as the recipient raising the nearest thumb, to be used if the recipient wishes the process to stop. Determine the action to be taken after the session, such as securing the house when the assistant leaves, if sleep is desired. At the end of each session, the recipient should rise slowly, if at all, to avoid postural low blood pressure and consequent dizziness or faintness.

A Script for a Comeditation Sequence

Progressive Muscle Relaxation: Phase 1
For the first few comeditation sessions the assistant might ask the recipient—if he or she wishes—to tighten and then release the first few limbs and muscle groups mentioned in order to distinguish between tightness and relaxation. Then the assistant suggests to the recipient, *Repeat each of the following phrases silently to yourself (or"copy them in your mind") as you let your attention rest on each part of the body. Feel your body relaxing as you say the phrase to yourself . . .* Then the assistant begins:

The toes and feet are relaxing.

The assistant should pause for five to ten seconds before beginning each new phrase.

The muscles of the heels and ankles are relaxing.

The muscles of the calves and knees are relaxing.

The muscles of the thighs and hips are relaxing.

The pelvis and spine are relaxing. (Option: *Let the spine fall into the bed.*)

The muscles of the abdomen and stomach are relaxing.

The muscles of the chest and heart complex are relaxing.

The muscles of the shoulders are relaxing. (Option: *Let the muscles of the shoulders fall on the bed.*)

The muscles of the scalp are relaxing.

The muscles of the forehead are relaxing.

The muscles between the eyebrows are relaxing. (Repeat three times.)

The muscles of the eyes and nose are relaxing.

The muscles of the cheeks and jowls are relaxing.

The muscles of the neck are relaxing.

The muscles of the right arm are relaxing, and all tension is leaving the fingertips of the right hand.

The muscles of the left arm are relaxing, and all tension is leaving the fingertips of the left hand.

Progressive Relaxation: Phase 2

Now scan your body, beginning at the top of the head . . .

The assistant should leave a ten-second pause before repeating each new phrase.

The face and neck muscles . . .

The shoulders, chest, and upper back . . .

The abdomen, lower back, and both legs . . .

Let any remaining tension or discomfort go.

Finally, as your body is becoming softer as you move downward, let any remaining tension leave the toes of the right foot, and the toes of the left foot.

Now that your entire body is relaxing, we will begin the sound sequence.

A Brief Comeditation Sound Sequence

Phase 1: Saying *Ahhh*

The comeditator then says to the recipient, *Join with me in the sound of letting go, the sound of* ahhh, *as you would at the end of a hard day when you discard your burdens. For your next three to five exhalations, let us make the sound together.*

The assistant watches the recipient's breathing pattern carefully. If the recipient's voice is barely audible, the assisant should encourage a bit more effort. Confirm the effort by saying *excellent* or *very good* (optional). Through full exhalations, the lungs are cleansed of old air and will begin effective diaphragmatic breathing.

Next, invite the recipient to listen while the assistant continues making the *ahhh* sound, timed with the recipient's exhalations. The assistant can make this invitation in the following way: *Now listen, if you wish, while I make the sound. Nothing else is necessary. Ahhh . . .* Continue this sound on the recipient's exhalations for five minutes or so, or until it is evident that the relaxation is not aided by this sound. If respirations are rapid, go to the next phase. If relaxation is evident, you can go directly onto phase 3.

Phase 2: Counting from One to Ten and Repeat

In phase 2 of the comeditation the assistant counts progressively from one to ten, saying one number upon each exhalation of the recipient. If the recipient regularly hyperventilates because of his or her condition, you may agree beforehand to make the count every other breath or every thrid breath. Continue in this manner for five minutes. If the recipient appears to lose contact, make the voice tone more crisp.

The assistant can begin phase 2 by saying, *I will now begin counting from one to ten following the rhythm of your exhalations. If you wish, you may visualize numbers going down your body and disappearing in the horizon at your feet. I will say the numbers clearly, distinctly. Just listen to the numbers: One . . . two . . . three . . , four . . . five . . . six . . . seven . . . eight . . . nine . . . ten.*

Phase 3: Special Words

In phase 3 the recipient's chosen phrase is sounded, again in time with the recipient's exhalation. The word, words, or prayer have already been chosen by the recipient because of their significance for him or her.

The assistant can move into this phase by saying, *It is time to begin your special words. Just listen; nothing else is necessary.* The assistant can then begin making the recipient's special sound.

This portion may make up the bulk of the session if the client has so requested. Continue for five minutes or longer.

Comeditation Session Conclusion

If symptom management was an aim of the session, plan to include the following suggestion that reduced tension can be experienced whenever it is desired. (Option: [given name], *realize the comfort and peace you feel now. Know that you can signal your body and mind to relax, whenever you wish, and wherever you are.*) Allow a minute for this statement to be processed. Then, proceed with the standard conclusion:

Our session is ending. Become aware, again, of your surroundings. Begin to feel your head on the pillow, your back and legs against the surface of the bed. When you are again in touch with your surroundings, make a fist with the hand nearest me. I will sit here with you until you open your eyes. Please take your time. (Optional, if the client is mobile: *Sit for a couple of minutes before getting up.*)

Caution: Postural low blood pressure may cause dizziness; have the recipient get up slowly.

WORKSHEETS FOR PERSONAL ADAPTATION OF COMEDITATION

~

Please feel free to photocopy these pages and use them to customize a comeditation sequence by entering your own notes or having an assistant enter them. The script in this section essentially follows the one in appendix A but is more detailed and contains suggestions for adding special elements to the meditation.

Preparation

1. Review the procedure to be used, changing the script if desired.
2. Both recipient and assistant should be comfortable; the recipient should lie on his or her back with support as needed, spine straight, arms beside the body with palms up (if comfortable), the lower part of the body covered. The assistant sits near the recipient's ear, using a nondistracting means (such as placing a tissue on the recipient's chest) to determine the recipient's breath pattern.
3. Maintain a nondisturbing atmosphere. A third person, the observer/intermediary, may answer the phone and deal with other interruptions.
4. Determine a signal for the recipient to use if he or she wishes to stop the session.
5. Determine the action the assistant should take if the recipient is expected to fall asleep.

Progressive Muscle Relaxation: Phase 1

The assistant names the part(s) of the body to begin muscle relaxation. This sequence may be introduced by *Repeat each of the following phrases silently to yourself as you let your attention rest on each part of the body. Feel your body relaxing as you say the phrase to yourself.* Specify what you want to be said or omitted below.

_____

_____

The assistant may also suggest that the recipient may wiggle or contract and release the area mentioned to distinguish between tightness and relaxation. This may be done several times when muscle tension is a problem. The process begins at the feet, progresses up the body, and then reviews the body from head to toes. The instructions are spoken clearly and calmly, with enough pausing to allow the person to consciously process each instruction. Indicate specific needs and preferences in the spaces between phrases or cross out suggestions that are not desired.

The toes and feet are relaxing.

_____

_____

The calves and knees are relaxing.

_____

_____

The muscles of the thighs and hips are relaxing.

_____

_____

The pelvis and spine are relaxing. (If the person has back or leg pain, the assistant may insert, *Feel your back fall into the surface.*)

_____

_____

The muscles of the stomach and abdomen are relaxing. (Option: If the gastric system is active, add Stomach noises are our music, let them go.]

_____

_____

The muscles of the chest and heart complex are relaxing.

_____

_____

The muscles of the shoulders are relaxing. (Option: If shoulder pain, neck pain, or headaches are a problem, add Let the shoulders fall into the bed.)

_____

_____

The muscles of the scalp are relaxing.

_____

_____

The muscles of the forehead are relaxing.

_____

_____

The muscles between the eyebrows are relaxing. (Repeat three times.) (This area is very important for people who squint or have tension headaches. The ancient Hindus, referring to this area as the third eye, were probably calming the pineal gland, a trigger for secretions of other glands.)

_____

_____

The muscles of the eyes and nose are relaxing.

_____

_____

The muscles of the cheeks and jowls are relaxing. (This area is especially important for people who have head, face, and/or neck pain due to temporomandibular joint [TMJ] syndrome.)

_____

_____

The muscles of the chin and neck are relaxing.

_____

_____

The muscles of the right arm are relaxing and all tension is leaving the fingertips of the right hand.

_____

_____

The muscles of the left arm are relaxing and all tension is leaving the fingertips of the left hand.

_____

_____

Progressive Muscle Relaxation: Phase 2

The second phase of the relaxation process provides a gradual scanning of the body from the head downward to the feet. The time spent in the second phase depends on the recipient's ability to relax during the first phase, the amount and type of pain being managed, and whether or not the recipient has chosen to have a visualization to facilitate freeing the mind at this time.

Note: for true meditation, visualization is not necessary, as the goal is "clear mind, peaceful heart." The following dialogue may be amended according to the recipient's wishes, using the bracketed suggestions, developing your own images, or cutting as you prefer.

Now that you have relaxed each part of your body, let's review, scanning your body from the head downward to your feet. (If pain is being dealt with, a visualization may be used at this time if the recipient prefers.)

The following is a visualization example:

Imagine, if you wish, that a warming, loving, healing light is bathing your head, and slowly entering your body to provide soothing energies, pushing out irritants and dispersing any intense sensations causing tightening and pain. Feel every fiber soften and float gently in the comforting light. Feel yourself letting go. Nothing else is necessary.

Feel the softness around your eyes, your mouth and jaw, your neck.

If the light image is being used, specify feeling the warm, healing energy on problem areas. The following is an example of working with a person with swallowing difficulties:

As the light bathes your head, every part of your head feels more relaxed. As you think about your neck, allow the healing energies of this loving light to enter your throat. Feel your neck and throat becoming completely relaxed with your next exhalation.

If fever is a problem, a visualization with ice might be tried, such as the following example:

Imagine clear, crystalline ice surrounding your bed. As you breathe deeply, you inhale the cooling vapors of the melting ice, allowing this refreshing air to cleanse your lungs and cool your body. Your exhalations send the fever into space, your body cooling with each breath, melting away anxieties, discomfort, distractions. Letting go into space and time. Nothing else is necessary. Breathe the cooling air, exhale into peace.

Now, relax your shoulders even more, your chest and upper back, your arms.

If light imaging is being used, continue:

Enjoy the warm light as it enters the lungs, heart and vessels. (Additional option: *Feel the healing powers within you as your lungs breathe and your heart pumps, cleansing every cell of your body.*)

Continuing to scan, relax your abdomen, and your lower back and thighs. Just let any remaining tension or discomfort go.

If light imaging is being used:

Allow the light to enfold and enter each organ, correcting imbalances, and clearing impurities.

Finally, relax your lower legs. Imagine any remaining tension leaving the toes of the right foot, and lastly, any remaining tension leaving the toes of your left foot.

If light imaging is being used, suggest:

The light energy is bathing every part of the body, and undesirable energy is leaving the body as the light fills every cell, down into the tips of each toe of each foot. Let all remaining tension leave the toes of each foot.

It is preferable to time the relaxation sequence directly to the recipient's exhalations. Spacing to every other out-breath provides more time.

Now the entire body is relaxing. Experience this soothing relaxation.

Next, we will begin the sounds you have selected.

Comeditation Sound Sequence

In the first phase, the sound of *ahhh* is the most important. It is a universal sound, used in self-comfort by infants and the injured; *ahhh* is an expression of relief and a component of various appeals to the Almighty Spirit. Precisely timed to the recipient's exhalation, it establishes a subtle link between the breath and hearing. This sound sequence should be initiated with a joining of both meditators' voices during the next three to five exhalations of the recipient, at least.

After softening physical tone through progressive muscle relaxation, many people find making an audible sound difficult. But clearing carbon dioxide from the lungs and establishing deep diaphragmatic breathing is basic to the process, as the sounds blend the recipient's and assistant's voices and sensitivities.

The insertion of attention-directing phrases may be said between breaths to give reassurance, direct the attention, and offset distractions. (Examples: *Listen. Listen to the sound. Nothing else is necessary. Clear mind, peaceful heart. Just letting go. It is so good to let go.*)

_____

_____

We will now begin with the choices you have selected. Let us first make the sound of ahhh, *the sound of letting go, ridding the body of tired air as you would when you drop your burdens at the end of a hard day. Sound the* ahhh *with me on your next three [or five] exhalations.*"

_____

_____

The assistant watches the other person's respiration, and together they say, *ahhh,* extending the sound through the recipient's full exhalation. If the recipient's voice is slight or inaudible, the assistant should encourage the next try to be stronger.

_____

_____

Confirm with *Very good.*

_____

_____

After the agreed-upon number of *ahhh*s have been said together, the assistant says,
> *Now you may, if you wish, just listen; I will continue making your sound for you on your exhalations. Nothing else is necessary.* (The recipient may continue if desired.)

_____

_____

If the recipient wishes to continue sounding *ahhh,* the invitation to just listen may be repeated at various times until the recipient feels ready to rest by listening.

_____

_____

If the recipient has an aversion to *ahhh,* they may plan a substitute sound that contains elements to clear the lungs and exercise the throat in the same way, such as *Om* (sounded *ahh-ou-umm*) or *Amen* (sounded *ah-mm-enn*).

_____

_____

The assistant then concentrates upon the person's chest or diaphragm movement to precisely express the sound *ahhh* just as the exhalation causes the fall of the lower chest to begin. This should be repeated for about five minutes. Time: _____

_____

_____

If the recipient obtains comfort through this sound, it may be continued longer or make up the entire session if planned earlier.

_____

_____

The second phase of the sound segment carries an invitation to visualize if the recipient wishes. The process is simply counting the numbers from one to ten, and repeating the sequence several times, continually synchronizing the numbers with the recipient's exhalations. The use of numbers, which are devoid of religious connotation or invasive input, is preferred because of their neutrality. The person is free to drift on the sound while keeping contact with the present by hearing the numerical order. The assistant may say, *We will now begin counting, continuing on your exhalations. I will speak the numbers clearly and distinctly to help you stay in contact. Listen to the sound.*

_____

_____

Add, if planned earlier,

If you wish, you may visualize as the numbers go over your body and disappear at the horizon at your feet.

_____

_____

The visualization may be of numbers flowing from the person outward to an undescribed horizon. The images of light on page 000 may be incorporated in this segment if the recipient requested them when planning the session. It is important that neither the type of scene nor the colors be suggested by the assistant; they should be allowed to be the spontaneous element of the meditative experience. This section may continue about five minutes.

Time: _____

_____

_____

The third phase of the sound segment is the repetition of the recipient's chosen word(s), phrase(s), or sound(s). People often choose simple thoughts such as *peace* or *love*. A portion of a prayer or psalm (no more than ten short lines) and the sound *Om* are other favorites. It is very important that this section be meaningful to the recipient; therefore, the choice must be established at each session. (See appendix C for suggestions.) My choice is:

_____

_____

The assistant makes the transition by saying the person's name, followed by

It is now time for us to say your special words. I will continue with your special thought [sound] on your exhalations only. Listen to your special sound. Nothing else is necessary.

Time: _____

_____

_____

These special words may be repeated for about five minutes when the program is used for daily practice and incorporates the other phases. If they are used as the primary part of the meditation, the recipient may wish to hear only these words for fifteen minutes or longer. If the person is in a terminal state, this segment may be used for several hours if there is evidence that it is helpful. It is advised to plan breaks, however, to allow everyone's basic needs to be addressed.

_____

_____

Conclusion

When concluding the session, sit quietly for a moment so the transition is gradual, then address the person by name, and say quietly,

It is now time for us to end this session, but realize that you can bring the peace and comfort you now have with your renewed energy.

_____

_____

If previously requested,

Take a few moments to identify the posture and easy flow of your body, which you can regain when you let go of tension anywhere, and at any time. (Pause.)

_____

_____

Allow your attention to come back to this room. (Pause.) *Feel your head against the surface, your back and buttocks against the surface, your legs and heels against the surface. When you are ready, make a fist with the hand nearest to me.*

_____

_____

The assistant should touch the recipient's hand when the nearer hand is closing to determine strength and temperature. If the hand is very cold, supply more covering, and perhaps limit the next few sessions to twenty minutes each. If the strength is slow in returning, allow a few more minutes of rest before allowing the person to sit up. Continue the dialogue.

_____

_____

I will sit beside you for a while. When you are ready, you may open your eyes. You may take a moment before you open your eyes if you wish. (Pause.)

_____

_____

When the person's eyes open, say,

When you are ready you may sit up. You must sit for a while before trying to move about because it is normal for you to have postural low blood pressure, as you would if awakened suddenly from a deep sleep. I will stay beside you until you are ready to move.

_____

_____

Before leaving, the assistant must be sure that the person who received the comeditation is free of dizziness when standing. This will take only a few minutes, at the most, unless there was a preexisting condition.

APPENDIX C

Religious and Spiritual Traditions and Texts

~

Traditions

Death is traditionally identified as occurring when the last breath leaves the body and the heart ceases to function. When respiration and circulation are maintained mechanically, a flat electroencephalographic tracing showing no activity is proof of brain death. Yet, observers tend to doubt that the transition has been completed before the body appears changed.

Various traditions have developed to ease the transition from life into death to help both the person who has died and those who are grieving. Our common American practice of visiting the embalmed body in the funeral home before the burial is a modification of the old European wake. In the old tradition, visitors sat with the body from the moment of death, through the night, until the burial one to three days later.

Today, community laws require a medical certificate of death to assure that no treachery took place; and certain sanitation standards, allocated to the mortuary industry, must be maintained. Current technology in undertaking sciences, however, can accommodate many specific family requests to modify the standard procedures, especially if they are planned in advance with the physician, the caregiving staff, and the funeral director.

If the person is kept for a while before being taken by the funeral director, the body should be washed and positioned flat on the back with the limbs straight. Changes will gradually occur. If the skin becomes mottled with gray or purple tones because of oxygen loss, this sign will fade. A creamy skin tone indicates that circulation has ceased. The eyes will be dulled and dilated, the muscles will become limp and heavy. Stiffening of the muscles (rigor mortis) begins about three hours after death but will disappear in about two days. There is no nail or hair growth after death, as is sometimes told in legends, but as the soft tissue recedes from the nails they may appear somewhat longer.

If the body is kept in the home for a while so family members can have a private time with it before it goes to the undertaker, it is appropriate to clear the room of caregiving supplies. Rented equipment may be moved to a rear holding area until the home-supply agency can pick it up at an appointed time convenient for the family. Medicines should be disposed of promptly so children cannot find them. Children can be included in this family time, but precautions must be taken for their safety because adults will be distracted.

We advise that spiritual leaders be consulted (to help understand and choose appropriate readings) by those who are trying to develop a personally meaningful plan for dying, but the following is a simplified overview of various religious attitudes. Our sources are varied, but our major guidance was from *The Sacred Art of Dying* by Kenneth Kramer. We are most grateful for his splendid research, his sifting of texts, and his generosity in allowing us to share this valuable information with our readers.

The Christian anticipates everlasting life. Virtuous behavior and proper repentance for transgressions are believed to appeal to God's mercy for acceptance into heaven. But the unrepentant person or the evildoer who has not been forgiven must expect the threats of purgatory and torments of hell. Christian selections of special words or phrases may be prayers of comfort, reminders of God's care, petitions for forgiveness, or intercessory appeals to Christ, his mother Mary, or selected saints. The Lord's Prayer, a psalm, a favorite hymn, the rosary, or any other liturgical selection may be used, or portions of the selection may be chosen for the repetitive sound.

Jewish traditions require the dying person to repent with confessions of wrongdoing (a rabbi need not be present). The *Sh'Ma* is part of these prayers, and it is desirable that they be the last words of the dying. *Hear, O Israel, the Lord is our God, the Lord is one.* The kaddish is the mourner's prayer: *The Lord gives and the Lord takes away; blessed be the name of the Lord.* Wishes for peace and bliss, grace and mercy, and the recognition of that life by God and through the memories of the living are included in the rabbi's verses. The literature is rich in symbols of corporal death and renewal of spirit.

Islamic faithful also acknowledge and worship one God, Allah, as the creator of all and the judge of all. Believers and unbelievers must face death, but believers grow nearer to the mercy of Allah and their transition into eternity. The soul may expect to be escorted through seven layers of heaven, with the goal of reaching a vision of God. Then it must await judgment day. The purpose of life is to provide tests and trials in preparation for death. Therefore, repentance of sins is necessary to secure eternal bliss and avoid the tortures of the damned. Appropriate suras from the Qur'an may be recited by the dying, but not by others near the deceased. Prayers, however, are recited while standing (no bowing or prostration except before Allah), such as: *Oh Allah, ease him in his matters, and make light for him whatever comes hereafter,* or *To Allah do we belong, and to Him shall we return.* In the practice of fana, the worshiper dies to the self and into God. The Sufis have developed this concept through three stages: the disciple seeks forgiveness and purification, he becomes absorbed in Muhammad's vision of Allah, and everything is then extinguished (including self and Muhammad) into Allah.

Hindu teachings are reflected in most religions as they develop mystical realizations of eternity, similar to the Sufis' fana. The name of Brahman, the ultimate God, means Absolute Reality. The main principles of Hindu thought are that death is ever present within the body and everything within the world, although changes are constantly occurring; the True Self (Atman) is undying; to realize the True Self one must die to fears; Death is the teacher of death; through the full surrender of the self, one may obtain immortality while alive. The sound *Om* is the uniting call to Brahman and should be used in deep meditation and as the final utterance at the moment of death. (Note the similar sound of *Amen,* meaning, "With God's will, so be it.") Various Vedic mantras, prayers, and visualizations may be used by family and friends while the person is dying and immediately after death. The body is cremated to release the astral body quickly.

Buddhist practices separate "attachments" from functions and formulations. The Buddha taught that there is only an ever-changing combination of five aggregates: matter, sensations, perceptions, mental formations, and consciousness. At death these aggregates break apart and later reassemble in a continuous succession. One should do everything in mindfulness (thoughtful awareness without conflict), including contemplating death. The goal is to pass into the state of nirvana, the place of supreme peace beyond death, liberated from suffering, concepts, and desires. Some Buddhists, such as the Burmese, believe the soul remains near the body for up to three days after death. Cremation occurs on the third day, but there is a ceremony on the seventh day for the recitation of sacred texts to assure that the ghost of the person actually leaves, and to cause the spirit world to recognize the dead person's merits.

Zen Buddhist enlightenment is the inner realization that there is no real distinction between states. I am I, and I am the universe (fully alive); and I am not I (dead to notions of conflict and self).

Tibetan Buddhist traditions expect the earth-plane transition into the bardo of the regions of death to occur in stages. The initial service, commanding the spirit to quit the body, takes only one hour after death. The Tibetans continue relay chanting day and night for four days after the death, however. After the body has been disposed of by cremation or burial, specific readings are designed to be offered during a three- to seven-week period. It is believed that it takes the soul forty-nine days to complete the journey through the *bardo* of death. The state of consciousness at the moment of death sets the course. "The clear light of the void" is the ultimate transition. This is awakening to the most subtle consciousness, beyond form. Succumbing to distractions will catch the spirit in a *bardo* state that requires it be born again. This bardo state is believed to be completed within forty-nine days.

References

The Holy Bible; Good News for Modern Man (New Testament in Modern English).

The Book of Common Prayer (ratified by the Protestant Episcopal Church).

Specific selections approved by the Roman Catholic Church: your local priest will provide you with booklets designed to offer prayers for the sick and to assist the planning of funerals.

The Qur'an. Various editions available.

Bhagavad-Gita: As It Is, selections and interpretation by A. C. Bhaktivedanta Swami Prabhupada (Los Angles: International Society for Krishna Consciousness, 1972).

The Tibetan Book of the Dead is the traditional guide for *bardo* passage, translated by W. Y. Evans-Wentz (London: Oxford Press, 1960); Francesca Fremantle and Chogyam Trungpa (Boston: Shambhala, 1975).

The Tibetan Book of Living and Dying, by Sogyal Rinpoche, provides a rich weaving of personal experiences and Buddhist practices (San Francisco: HarperSanFrancisco, 1992).

Deathing: An Intelligent Alternative for Final Moments of Life, by Anya Foos-Graber, is an American story adapting Eastern thoughts to Western practice with before and after death rituals described (York Beach, ME: Nicolas Hays, 1989).

Favored Prayers and Poems

The choice of words, sounds, or phrases should always be determined by the recipient meditator. The following are merely offered as suggestions to aid in your personal search for words of comfort and inspiration.

Single words: *Love, Om* (pronounced *ahh-ou-umm*), *Peace, Amen* (meaning "so be it"), *Understanding, Allah* (no god but God).

The Serenity Prayer: *God grant me the serenity to accept the things I cannot change, the courage to change the things I can, and the wisdom to know the difference.*

The Lord's Prayer: *Our Father Who art in Heaven, Hallowed be Thy name. Thy kingdom come, Thy will be done, on earth as it is in Heaven. Give us this day our daily bread. Forgive us our trespasses, as we forgive those who trespass against us. And lead us not into temptation, but deliver us from evil. For thine is the kingdom, and the power, and the glory, for ever and ever. Amen.*

The Hail Mary: *Hail, Mary, full of grace; the Lord is with thee; blessed art thou among women, and blessed is the fruit of thy womb, Jesus. Holy Mary, Mother of God, pray for us sinners, now, and at the hour of our death. Amen.*

Zen Meditation: *When you become you, Zen becomes Zen. When you are you, you see things as they are, and you become one with your surroundings.* (Shunryu Suzuki, 1970)

Chants and Mantras from Various Religious Traditions

Orthodox Christian chant: *Kyrie Eleison*
English translation: *Lord, have mercy,* or as expanded to the Prayer of the
Heart: *Lord, Jesus Christ, have mercy on me.*

Benedictine Aramaic chant: *Ma-ra-na-tha*
English translation: *Come Lord.*

Jewish recitation: *Hear, O Israel; the Lord is our God; the Lord is One.* (In
Hebrew: *Sh'Ma Yisroel; Adonai eloheynu; Adonai ehod.*) (If desired, add:
*God gave and God has taken away, blessed be the name of God. God reigns;
God has reigned; God will reign for ever and ever.*)

Hindu mantra: *Om-na-ma Shivaya*
English translation: *Salutation to the Lord.*

Islamic chant: *Na-sha-All-ah or Insh' Allah*
English translation: *What God wills.*

Buddhist mantra: *Om-mani-padme-hum*
English translation: *Hail to the Jewel in the Lotus*

Buddist chant: *Gate, gate, paragate, parasamgate, bodhi, svaha*
English translation: *Gone, gone, gone to the other shore, gone beyond, enlightened mind, hail.*

A Traditional Tibetan Buddhist Visualization: (phrases said on meditator's
exhalation only): *Visualize a vast, boundless ocean of light. Place yourself in
the center of the light. With each exhalation, feel yourself flowing into the light.
Merge with the light. There is only the light.* (Clear Light Society, Boston)

Native American Rituals

Native American cultures are numerous, but all share the recognition that
each person's death is a companion staying just to the side. By taking a token
(such as hair) from the body, the family can keep the soul with them for a
short time. The hair is purified by smoke, wrapped, and laid in a special
place. Six to eighteen months later, the family performs a "releasing the soul"
ceremony with special food, prayers, and smoking of the peace pipe. The
hair is buried with token offerings so the soul can depart on the spirit path.

RESOURCES

Associates in Thanatology Representatives

Richard C. Martin, 601-263 Russell Hill Road, Toronto, Ontario, Canada
M4V2T4

Michiee Rolek, 7070 Franklin Avenue, #124, Los Angeles, CA 90020

Carolyn Mullins R. N., 3600 Old Bullard Road, Suite 400, Tyler, Texas
75903

William H. Tallmadge, III, Phillips Street, Berea, Kentucky 40403

The authors will be pleased to respond personally to inquiries about research, training, and group workshops. Write to Associates in Thanatology, 115 Blue Rock Road, South Yarmouth, MA 02664, phone: 508-394-6520; or Learning Center for Supportive Care, 14 Orchard Lane, Lincoln, MA 01773, phone: 617-259-8936.

Note: The term *comeditation* was coined by R. W. Boerstler and H. S. Kornfeld in 1979 and is used by them and by other representatives of the Associates in Thanatology. Other people who teach variations on this technique do so privately and do not represent the authors or their organizations.

NOTES

Notes to Chapter 1

1. Jeremy Taylor, *The Rule and Exercises of Holy Dying* (1652; reprint, New York: World Publishing Co., 1952), 7.

2. Chuang Tzu, *The Complete Works of Chuang Tzu,* trans. Burton Watson. (New York: Columbia University Press, 1968).

3. M. Miyuki, "Dying Isagi-Yoku," *Journal of Humanistic Psychology,* 18, no. 4 (Fall 1981): 38–44.

4. L. A. Govinda, "Impermanence and Immortality," *Creative Meditation and Multi-Dimensional Consciousness* (Wheaton, IL: Theosophical Publishing House, 1976).

5. D. T. Suzuki, *Studies in Zen* (New York: Dell, 1954).

6. David Steindl-Rast, "Learning to Die," *Parabola* 2, no. 1 (1977): 22–32.

7. John Fire Lame Deer, *Seeker of Visions* (New York: Simon & Shuster, 1972).

8. Viktor Frankl, *Man's Search for Meaning* (New York: Pocket Books, 1959).

9. Robert E. Hume, trans., *The Thirteen Principal Upanishads* (Cambridge, England: Oxford University Press, 1931), 3–14, from the *Katha Upanishad.*

10. Abraham Maslow, *Toward a Psychology of Being* (New York: D. Van Nostrand Co., 1968).

11. Elisabeth Kübler-Ross, *On Death and Dying* (New York: The Macmillan Co., 1969).

12. Peter Koestenbaum, *Is There an Answer to Death?* (Englewood Cliffs, NJ: Prentice-Hall/Spectrum Books, 1976), 49.

13. Herbert Benson and R. Wallace, "The Physiology of Meditation," *Scientific American* (February 19, 1972), 84–90.

14. A. D. Weisman, "Psychosocial Considerations in Terminal Care" in *The Psycho-Social Aspects of Terminal Care,* ed. by B. Schoenberg, et al. (New York: Columbia University Press, 1972), 162–172.

15. W. Y. Evans-Wentz, ed., *The Tibetan Book of the Dead* (New York: Oxford University Press, 1927; reprint, 1960).

Notes to Chapter 2

1. Judy Forman, "When 'Natural' Hurts: Caution on Therapies," *Boston Globe* (November 17, 1994).

2. Patricia Carrington, *Freedom in Meditation* (Garden City, NY: Anchor Books, 1978), xviii, 3.

3. Nancy Zi, *The Art of Breathing: Thirty Simple Exercises for Improving Your Performance and Well-Being* (New York: Bantam Books, 1986).

4. Michael Murphy and Steven Donovan, *The Physical and Psychological Effects of Meditation: A Review of Contemporary Meditation Research with a Comprehensive Bibliography* 1931–1988 (San Rafael, CA: Esalen Institute, 1988), 24.

5. Hans Selye, *The Stress of Life,* rev. ed. (New York: McGraw-Hill, 1976).

6. Walter T. Stace, *The Teachings of the Mystics* (New York: Mentor Book, 1960).

7. Stace, *The Teachings of the Mystics.*

8. T. X. Barber, "Physiological Effects of 'Hypnosis'," *Psychological Bulletin* 58 (1961): 390–419.

9. J. B. Earle, "Cerebral Laterality and Meditation: A Review of the Literature," *Journal of Transpersonal Psychology* 13, no. 2, (1981): 155–173.

10. Carrington, *Freedom in Meditation,* 271–273.

11. Anodea Judith, *Wheels of Life: A User's Guide to the Chakra System* (St. Paul, MN: Llewellyn Publications, 1989).

12. Elmer Green and Alyce Green, *Beyond Biofeedback* (New York: Dell, 1977).

13. Herbert Benson and R. Wallace, "The Physiology of Meditation," *Scientific American* (February 19, 1972): 84–90.

14. Green and Green, *Beyond Biofeedback.*

15. Norman Cousins, "The Mysterious Placebo: How Mind Helps Medicine Work," *Saturday Review* (October 1, 1977): 8–12.

16. Norman Cousins, *Anatomy of an Illness: As Perceived by the Patient* (New York: Bantam Books, 1979).

17. O. Carl Simonton and Stephanie Matthews-Simonton, *Getting Well Again* (Los Angeles: J. P. Tarcher, 1978).

18. Bernie S. Siegel, *Love, Medicine, and Miracles* (New York: Harper and Row, 1986).

19. K. R. Pelletier, *Holistic Medicine: From Stress to Optimum Health* (New York: Dell, 1979).

20. Jeanne Achterberg and G. F. Lawlis, *Imagery and Disease* (Champaign, IL: Institute for Personality and Ability Testing, 1978–1984).

21. Jeanne Achterberg and G. F. Lawlis, *Bridges of the Body Mind: Behavioral Approaches to Health Care* (Champaign, IL: Institute for Personality and Ability Testing, 1980).

22. Jon Kabat-Zinn, *Full Catastrophe Living, Using the Wisdom of Your Body and Mind to Face Stress, Pain, and Illness* (New York: Bantam-Doubleday, 1990).

23. Viktor Frankl, *The Will to Meaning* (New York: Random House, 1987).

24. Richard J. Foster, *Prayer: Finding the Heart's True Home* (San Francisco: HarperSanFrancisco, 1992), 117, quoted in Larry Dossey, *Healing Words: The Power of Prayer and the Practice of Medicine* (San Francisco: HarperSanFrancisco, 1993), 69–70.

25. Herbert Benson, *Your Maximum Mind* (New York: Random House, 1987).

26. Foster, *Prayer,* quoted in Dossey.

27. Anthony De Mello, *One Minute Wisdom* (New York: Image Books/Doubleday, 1988).

28. Thich Nhat Hanh, *The Miracle of Mindfulness: A Manual on Meditation* (Boston: Beacon Press, 1975).

29. Jon Kabat-Zinn, *Wherever You Go, There You Are: Mindfulness Meditation in Everyday Life* (New York: Hyperion, 1994).

30. Jon Kabat-Zinn, *Full Catastrophe Living.*

31. Joan Borysenko, *Minding the Body, Mending the Mind* (Reading, MA: Addison-Wesley, 1987).

32. Thich Nhat Hanh, *The Miracle of Mindfulness.*

33. Sogyal Rinpoche, *The Tibetan Book of Living and Dying* (San Francisco: HarperSanFrancisco, 1992), 72.

Notes to Chapter 3

1. Nancy Wilson Ross, *Three Ways of Ancient Wisdom: Hinduism, Buddhism, and Zen and Their Significance for the West* (New York: Simon and Schuster, 1966).

2. James Funderburke, *Science Studies Yoga* (Honesdale, PA: Himalayan International Institute of Yoga Science and Philosophy, 1977).

3. W. Y. Evans-Wentz, *The Tibetan Book of the Dead* (London: Oxford University Press, 1927, 1960).

4. Margo McCaffery, *Nursing Management of the Patient with Pain,* 2nd ed. (Philadelphia: J. B. Lippincott, 1979).

5. Noreen Meinhart and Margo McCaffery, *Pain: A Nursing Approach to Assessment and Analysis* (Norwalk, CT: Appleton-Century-Crofts, 1983), 70, 72.

Notes to Chapter 4

1. National Hospice Organization, Standards and Accreditation Committee, *Standards of a Hospice Program of Care,* 6th revision (Arlington, VA: National Hospice Organization, 1979).

2. Sandol Stoddard, *The Hospice Movement: A Better Way of Caring for the Dying* (New York: Vintage Books/Random House, 1978).

3. Cicely Saunders, *The Management of Terminal Illness* (reprint, London: Hospital Publications, Ltd., 1967).

4. Saunders, *The Management of Terminal Illness.*

5. National Hospice Organization, *1994–1995 Guide to the Nation's Hospices* (Arlington, VA: National Hospice Organization, 1994).

6. D. D. Palmer, *The Science, Art, and Philosophy of Chiropractic* (Davenport, IA: Palmer College of Chiropractic, 1910).

7. Janet Travell and David Simmons, *Myofascial Pain and Dysfunction: The Trigger Point Manual* (Baltimore, MD: Williams and Wilkins, 1992).

8. Dolores Krieger, *The Therapeutic Touch: How to Use Your Hands to Help or to Heal* (Englewood Cliffs, NJ: Prentice-Hall, 1979).

9. Larry Dossey, *Healing Words: The Power of Prayer and the Practice of Medicine* (San Francisco: HarperCollins, 1993).

10. Randolph Byrd, "Positive Therapeutic Effects of Intercessory Prayer in a Coronary Care Unit Population," *Southern Medical Journal* 81, no. 7 (1988): 826–29.

11. Sherwin B. Nuland, *How We Die: Reflections on Life's Final Chapter* (New York: Alfred A. Knopf, 1994).

Notes to Chapter 5

1. Martin Buber, *I and Thou,* trans. Walter Kaufmann (New York: Charles Scribner and Sons, 1970), 89.

2. Elisabeth Kübler-Ross, *On Death and Dying* (New York: Macmillan, 1969).

3. H. S. Kornfeld and R. W. Boerstler. "Anticipatory Grief, Meditation, and the Dying Process," in *Loss and Anticipatory Grief,* ed. Therese A. Rando (Lexington, MA: Lexington Books/D. C. Heath, 1986).

4. Hans Selye, *The Stress of Life* (New York: McGraw-Hill, 1956, 1976).

5. Therese A. Rando, *Grief, Dying and Death: Clinical Interventions for Caregivers* (Champaign, IL: Research Press Company, 1984), 268–70.

6. A. D. Kahn and J. Fawcett, eds., *Encyclopedia of Mental Health* (New York: Facts on File, 1993), 194.

7. Avery Weisman, *Coping with Cancer* (New York: McGraw-Hill, 1979), 56–71.

8. Emily Dickinson, "Hope Is the Thing with Feathers," in *The Complete Poems of Emily Dickinson,* ed. Thomas H. Johnson (Boston: Little, Brown, 1960), no. 254.

9. Michael Simpson, *The Facts of Death* (Englewood Cliffs, NJ: Prentice-Hall, 1979).

Notes to Chapter 6

1. Joan Alevras-Stampfel, "A Burnout Checklist," *The Executive Female* (September–October 1981): 29–31.

2. T. H. Holmes and R. H. Rahe, "The Social Readjustment Scale," *Journal of Psychosomatic Research* 11 (1967): 213–18.

3. Marion Humphrey, "Effects of Anticipatory Grief for Patient, Family Member, and Caregiver," *Loss and Anticipatory Grief,* ed. Therese A. Rando (Lexington, MA: D. C. Heath, 1984), 63–79.

4. Richard Kalish, "The Onset of Dying," *Omega* 1 (1970): 57–69.

5. Ken Wilber, "On Being a Support Person," *Journal of Transpersonal Psychology* 20, no. 2 (1988 : 141–60.

6. Earl Grollman, *Explaining Death to Children* (Boston: Beacon Press, 1967).

7. Sandra Bertman, *Facing Death: Images, Insights, and Interventions* (Washington, D. C.: Hemisphere Press, 1991).

8. Theresa Rando, *Grief, Dying, and Death: Clinical Intervention for Caregivers* (Champaign, IL: Research Press, 1984), 30–35.

9. Theresa Rando, *Grieving: How to Go on Living When Someone You Love Dies* (Lexington, MA: D. C. Heath, 1988).

10. Eric Lindemann, "Symptomatology and Management of Acute Grief," *American Journal of Psychiatry* 101 (1944): 141–48.

Notes to Chapter 7

1. Viktor E. Frankl, *The Will to Meaning* (New York: Signet Classics, 1969).

2. J. E. Knott and Eugenia Wild, "Anticipatory Grief and Reinvestment" *Loss and Anticipatory Grief,* ed. T. Rando (Lexington, MA: D. C. Heath, 1984), 55–59.

3. Otto Rank, *Beyond Psychology* (New York: Dover, 1941), 62–101.

4. Lyle Miller, et al., *The Stress Solution: An Action Plan to Manage the Stress in Your Life* (New York: Pocket Books, 1993), 251.

5. Ernest Becker, *The Denial of Death* (New York: Macmillan/The Free Press, 1973), 150–153.

6. Earl A. Grollman, "A Suicide Occurs—The Abuse of Religion." *The Forum Newsletter* (Hartford, CT: Association for Death Education and Counseling, issue 2, vol. 16 (May–June, 1991), 1, 14, 15.

Notes to Chapter 8

1. Naomi James, "Psychology of Suicide," *Suicide: Assessment and Intervention,* 2nd ed., eds. C. L. Hatton and S. McBride Valente (Norwalk, CT: Appleton-Century-Crofts, 1984).

2. David Meagher, "A Right to Die," Newsletter of Thanatology Program, Brooklyn College (Brooklyn, NY), 2, no. 4 (1984):8–9.

3. Lois Chapman Dick, "To Die or Not to Die—Survey," *Forum,* March–April 1991.

4. Avrion Mitchison, "Will We Survive?" *Scientific American* (September 1993): 136–144.

5. Thomas T. Perls, "The Oldest Old," *Scientific American* (January 1995): 70–75.

6. Alice Miller, *For Your Own Good: Hidden Cruelty in Child-Rearing and the Roots of Violence,* trans. Hildegarde Hannum and Hunter Hannum (New York: New American Library/Meridian Books, 1983).

7. *Choice in Dying, Advanced Directives* (organization brochure, court case studies and support), 20 Varick St., New York, NY 10014.

8. L. A. DeSpelder, and A. L. Strickland, *The Last Dance: Encountering Death and Dying,* 2nd ed. (Palo Alto, CA: Mayfield Publishing Co., 1987), 308–317.

9. Derek Humphrey, *Final Exit: The Practicalities of Self-Deliverance and Assisted Suicide for the Dying* (Eugene, OR: The Hemlock Society, 1991).

10. R. M. McCann, et al., "Comfort Care for Terminally Ill Patients: Appropriate Use of Nutrition and Hydration," *Journal of the American Medical Association* 272 (1994): 1263–1266.

11. Alexander Capron and Pieter Admiraal, *Euthanasia/Euthanasie,* C25A, C25B. Conference tape, 7th International Congress on Care of the Terminally Ill, 1988.

12. Aaron Beck, *Cognitive Therapy and the Emotional Disorders* (New York: New American Library/Meridian Books, 1976).

13. Kenneth Kramer, *The Sacred Art of Dying: How World Religions Understand Death* (New York: Paulist Press, 1988).

14. Kenneth Ring, *Heading Toward Omega: In Search of the Meaning of the Near Death Experience* (New York: William Morrow, 1984).

15. Joyce Zerwekh, "The Dehydration Question," *Nursing* (January 1983): 47–51.

16. Laurence O. McKenney, Neurotheology: *Virtual Religion in the Twenty-First Century* (Cambridge, MA: American Institute for Mindfulness, 1994).

17. Quoted in Philip Kapleau, ed., *The Wheel of Death* (San Francisco: Harper Colophon Books, 1971), 60.

18. R. K. Siegel, "Hallucination," *Scientific American* (October 1977) 132–34.

19. R. K. Siegel, "The Psychology of Life After Death," *American Psychologist* 35, no. 10 (1980): 911–931.

20. Joachim-Ernst Berendt, *Nada Brahma: The World Is Sound* (Rochester, VT: Destiny Books, 1987): 116–117.

21. Doug Smith, *The Tao of Dying: A Guide to Caring* (Washington, D.C.: Caring Publications, 1994): 163.

Recommended Reading

~

Death and Dying

Albery, N., G. Elliot, and J. Elliot. *The Natural Death Handbook*. London: Natural Death Center, 1993.

Bertman, Sandra. *Facing Death: Images, Insights, and Interventions*. New York: Hemisphere Publishing Company, 1991.

Boerstler, Richard W. *Letting Go: A Holistic and Meditative Approach to Living and Dying*. South Yarmouth, MA: Associates in Thanatology, 1982.

DeSpelder, L. A., and A. L. Strickland. *The Last Dance: Encountering Death and Dying*. Palo Alto, CA: Mayfield Publishing Co., 1987.

Enright, D. J. *The Oxford Book of Death*. Oxford: Oxford University Press, 1987.

Feinstein, D., and P. Mayo. *Rituals for Living and Dying*. Ashland, OR: Innersource Publishing, 1991.

Goodman, Lisl Marsburg. *Death and the Creative Life: Conversations with Eminent Artists and Scientists as They Reflect on Life and Death*. New York: Penguin Books, 1983.

Kramer, Kenneth. *The Sacred Art of Dying: How World Religions Understand Death*. Mahwah, NJ: Paulist Press, 1988.

———. Death Dreams: Unveiling Mysteries of the Unconscious Mind. Mahwah, NJ: Paulist Press, 1992.

Kushner, Harold. *When Bad Things Happen to Good People*. New York: Avon Books, 1981.

Lamberton, Richard. *Care of the Dying.* New York: Penguin Books, 1973, 1981.

Meltzer, David, ed. Death: *An Anthology of Ancient Texts, Songs, Prayers, and Stories.* San Francisco: North Point Press, 1984.

Morgan, Ernest. *A Manual of Death Education and Simple Burial.* Burnsville, NC: The Celo Press, 1980.

———. *Dealing Creatively with Dying.* Burnsville, NC: The Celo Press, 1988.

Rando, Therese A. *Grief, Dying and Death: Clinical Interventions for Caregivers.* Champaign, IL: Research Press Co., 1984.

———, ed. *Loss and Anticipatory Grief.* Lexington, MA: Lexington Books/D. C. Heath and Co., 1986.

Grief

Caine, Lynn. *Widow.* New York: Bantam Books, 1974.

Gates, Philomene. *Suddenly Alone: A Woman's Guide to Widowhood.* New York: Harper and Row, 1990.

Grollman, Earl A. *What Helped Me When My Loved One Died.* Boston: Beacon Press, 1981.

Kushner, Harold. *When Bad Things Happen to Good People.* New York: Avon Books, 1981.

Lewis, C. S. *A Grief Observed.* New York: Bantam Books, 1976.

O'Connor, Nancy. *Letting Go with Love: The Grieving Process.* Apache Junction, AZ: La Mariposa Press, 1984.

Rando, Therese A. *Grieving: How to Go On Living When Someone You Love Dies.* Lexington, MA: Lexington Books/D. C. Heath and Co., 1988.

Shapiro, Ester R. *Grief as a Family Process: A Developmental Approach to Clinical Practice* New York: Guilford Publications, 1994.

Staudacher, Carol. *Beyond Grief: A Guide for Recovering from the Death of a Loved One.* Oakland, CA: New Harbinger Publications, 1987.

Worden, J. William. *Grief Counseling and Grief Therapy: A Handbook for the Mental Health Practitioner.* New York: Springer Publishing Co., 1982.

Workbooks

Bisigano, Judith. *Living with Death.* Tucson, AZ: Kino Publications, 1984.

Boulden, Jim, and Joan Boulden. *The Last Goodbye: Bereavement Guide.* Weaverville, CA: Boulden Publishing, 1994.

For Children

Arden, Heloise. *The Transformation of Jennie.* 99 Mulbar Boulevard, Famingdale, NY: Coleman Publishing, 1983. A girl learns her illness is fatal, learns of natural transformations, meets her "comforter."

Goldman, Linda. *Life and Loss: A Guide to Help Grieving Children.* Muncie, IN: Accelerated Development, 1994.

Grollman, Earl A., ed. *Explaining Death to Children.* Boston: Beacon Press, 1967.

Kübler-Ross, Elisabeth. *A Letter to a Child with Cancer.* E.K.S. Center, Route 616, Headwaters, VA 24442, 1979. A simple letter with colorful drawings and metaphors of nature, fate, God, and death.

Smith, Doris Buchanan. *A Taste of Blackberries.* New York: Scholastic Book Services, 1973. The story of a grade-school boy whose daredevil friend dies of an allergic reaction, and the boy's process of working through grief.

Philosophy and Religion

Da Avabhasa (Free John). *Easy Death: Spiritual Discourses and Essays on the Inherent and Ultimate Transcendence of Death and Everything Else.* Clearlake, CA: The Dawn Horse Press, 1991.

DelBene, Ron. *Into the Light: A Simple Way to Pray with the Sick and Dying.* Nashville, TN: The Upper Room, 1988.

Feuerstein, Georg. *Yoga, The Technology of Ecstasy.* Los Angeles: Jeremy P. Tarcher, Inc., 1989.

Fremantle, F., and C. Trungpa. *The Tibetan Book of the Dead.* Boston: Shambhala, 1992.

Govinda, Anagarika. *Creative Meditation and Multi-Dimensional Consciousness.* Wheaton, IL: The Theosophical Publishing House, 1976.

Graham, Billy. *Facing Death and the Life After.* Waco, TX: Word Books Publishers, 1987.

Helminski, Kabir. *Living Presence: A Sufi Way to Mindfulness and the Essential Self.* Los Angeles: Jeremy P. Tarcher, Inc., 1992.

Kamath, M. V. *Philosophy of Death and Dying.* Honesdale, PA: Himalayan International Institute, 1978.

Kramer, Kenneth. *The Sacred Art of Dying: How World Religions Understand Death.* Mahwah, NJ: Paulist Press, 1988.

Kushner, Harold S. *God Was In This Place and I Did Not Know It.* Woodstock, VT: Jewish Lights Publishing Co., 1993.

Prabhavananda, Swami, and Fredrick Manchester, ed. and trans. *The Upanishads: Breath of the Eternal.* New York: Mentor Books (with Vedanta Society of Southern California, copyright 1948), 1957.

Red Pine, trans. *The Zen Teachings of Bodhidharma.* San Francisco: North Point Press, 1989.

Reincourt, A. *The Eye of Shiva.* New York: William Morrow, Co., 1981.

Ross, Nancy Wilson. *Buddhism: A Way of Life and Thought.* New York: Alfred Knopf, 1980.

Singer, June. *A Gnostic Book of Hours: Keys to Inner Wisdom.* San Francisco: HarperSanFrancisco, 1992.

Suzuki, Shunryu. Zen Mind, Beginner's Mind. New York: John Weatherhill, 1970.

Meditation, Relaxation, and Inner Growth

Benson, Herbert. *Your Maximum Mind.* New York: Times Books/Random House, 1987.

Blakney, Raymond B., trans. Meister Eckhart. New York: Harper Torchbooks, 1941.

Borysenko, Joan. *Minding the Body, Mending the Mind.* Reading MA: Addison-Wesley Publishing Co., 1987.

Dossey, Larry. *Healing Words: The Power of Prayer and the Practice of Medicine.* San Francisco: HarperSanFrancisco, 1993.

Jampolsky, Gerald. Teach *Only Love: The Seven Principles of Attitudinal Healing.* Toronto: Bantam Books, 1983.

Kabat-Zinn, Jon. *Full Catastrophe Living: Using the Wisdom of Your Body and*

Mind to Face Stress, Pain, and Illness. New York: Delta Publishing Co., 1990.

———. *Wherever You Go There You Are: Mindfulness Meditation in Everyday Life.* New York: Hyperion, 1994.

Levine, Stephen. *Who Dies? An Investigation of Conscious Living and Conscious Dying.* Garden City, NY: Anchor Books, 1982.

———. *Healing into Life and Death.* Garden City, NY: Anchor Press/Doubleday, 1987.

Murphy, Michael, and Stephen Donovan. *The Physical and Psychological Effects of Meditation: A Review of Contemporary Meditation Research with a Comprehensive Bibliography 1931–1988.* San Rafael, CA: Esalen Institute, 1988.

Thich Nhat Hanh. *The Miracle of Mindfulness: A Manual on Meditation.* Boston: Beacon Press, 1975.

Miscellaneous Therapies

Achterberg, Jeanne, and G. Frank Lawlis. *Bridges of the BodyMind.* Champaign, IL: Institute for Personality and Ability Testing, 1980.

———. *Imagery and Disease.* Champaign, IL: Institute for Personality and Ability Testing, 1978, 1984.

Arlin, Mirean. *Science of Nutrition.* New York: Macmillan, 1977.

Balch, James, and Phyllis Balch. *Prescription for Nutritional Healing.* Garden City Park, NY: Avery Publishing Group, 1990.

Caudill, Margaret A. *Managing Pain Before It Manages You.* New York: The Guilford Press, 1995.

Chopra, Deepak. *Creating Health: Beyond Prevention, Toward Perfection.* Boston: Houghton Mifflin Company, 1987.

Kenny, Carolyn Bereznak. *The Mythic Artery: The Magic of Music Therapy.* Atascadero, CA: Ridgeview Publishing Co., 1983, 1989.

Krieger, Dolores. *The Therapeutic Touch: How to Use Your Hands to Help or to Heal.* Englewood Cliffs, NJ: Prentice-Hall, 1979.

Lacroix, Nitya. *Massage for Total Stress Relief.* New York: Random House, 1989.

Puntillo, Kathleen A. *Pain in the Critically Ill: Assessment and Management.* Gaithersburg, MD: Aspen Publishers, 1991.

Siegel, Bernie. *Love, Medicine, and Miracles: Lessons Learned about Self-Healing from a Surgeon's Experience with Exceptional Patients.* New York: Harper and Row, 1986.

Simons, David G. *Myofascial Pain Syndrome Due to Trigger Points.* Cleveland, OH: Gebauer Co., 1987.

Simonton, Carl, Stephanie Matthews-Simonton, and James L. Creighton. *Getting Well Again.* New York: Bantam Books, 1980.

Home Care

Bernstein, Lawrence. *Primary Care in the Home.* Philadelphia: J. B. Lippincott Co., 1987.

Billings, Andrew J. *Outpatient Management of Advanced Cancer.* Philadelphia: J. B. Lippincott Co., 1985.

Cassileth, Barrie R., and Peter A. Cassileth, eds. *Clinical Care of the Terminal Cancer Patient.* Philadelphia: Lea and Febiger, 1982.

Duda, Deborah. *A Guide to Dying at Home.* Santa Fe: John Muir, 1982.

Eidson, Ted, ed. *The AIDS Caregiver's Handbook.* New York: St. Martin's Press, 1988.

Friedman, J. *Home Health Care: A Complete Guide for Patients.* New York: Norton and Co., 1986.

Jones, Monica Loose. *Home Care for the Chronically Ill or Disabled Child: A Manual and Sourcebook for Parents and Professionals.* New York: Harper and Row, 1985.

Kirchheimer, Sid, and the editors of Prevention Magazine Health Books. *The Doctors Book of Home Remedies.* Emmaus, PA: Rodale Press, vol. 1, 1988; vol. 2, 1993.

Lewis, Angie. *Nursing Care of the Person with AIDS/ARC.* Rockville, MD: Aspen Publishers, 1988.

Little, Deborah Whiting. *Home Care for the Dying: A Reassuring, Comprehensive Guide to Physical and Emotional Care.* Garden City, NY: The Dial Press/Doubleday, 1985.

O'Brien, Mary, and Phyllis L. Pallett. *Total Care of the Stroke Patient.* Boston: Little, Brown, and Co., 1978.

Parker, Page, and Lois N. Dietz. *Nursing at Home: A Practical Guide to the Care of the Sick and the Invalid in the Home, Plus Self-Help Instructions for the Patient.* New York: Crown Publishers, 1980.

Powell, Lenore S., and Katie Courtice. *Alzheimer's Disease: A Guide for Families*. Reading MA: Addison-Wesley Publishing Co., 1983.

Prichard, Elizabeth R., et al., eds. *Home Care: Living with Dying*. New York: Columbia University Press, 1979.

Zimmerman, Jack M. Hospice: *Complete Care for the Terminally Ill*. Baltimore: Urban and Schwarzenberg, 1986.

Psychology and Brain Function

Beck, Aaron. *Cognitive Therapy and the Emotional Disorders*. New York: New American Library, 1976.

Borysenko, Joan. *Guilt Is the Teacher, Love Is the Lesson*. New York: Warner Books/Time Warner Co., 1991.

———. *Fire in the Soul: A New Psychology of Spiritual Optimism*. New York: Warner Books/Time Warner Co., 1993.

Douglas, Jack D. *The Social Meanings of Suicide*. Princeton, NJ: Princeton University Press, 1973.

Frankl, Viktor E. Man's *Search for Meaning: An Introduction to Logotherapy*. New York: Pocket Books/Simon & Schuster, 1959/1963.

———. *The Will to Meaning: Foundations and Applications of Logotherapy*. New York: New American Library/Times Mirror, 1969.

Hampden-Turner, Charles. *Maps of the Mind: Charts and Concepts of the Mind and Its Labyrinths*. New York: Collier Books, 1982.

Hatton, Corrine Loing, and Sharon McBride Valente. *Suicide: Assessment and Intervention*. 2nd ed. Norwalk, CT: Appleton-Century-Crofts, 1984.

Hooper, Judith, and Dick Teresi. *The Three Pound Universe*. New York: Dell Publishing Co., 1986.

Jung, C. G. Modern *Man in Search of a Soul*. New York: Harvest/Harcourt Brace, 1933.

May, Rollo. *The Meaning of Anxiety*. New York: Pocket Books, 1977.

McKinney, Laurence O. *NeuroTheology: Virtual Religion in the Twenty-first Century*. Cambridge, MA: Institute for Mindfulness, 1994.

Miller, Lyle, and Alma Dell Smith with Larry Rothstein. *The Stress Solution: An Action Plan to Alter the Stress in Your Life*. New York: Pocket Books, 1993.

Murphy, Michael, and Steven Donovan. *The Physical and Psychological Effects of Meditation: A Review of Contemporary Meditation Research with a Comprehensive Bibliography 1931–1988.* San Rafael, CA: Esalen Institute, 1988.

Rossi, Earnest L. *The Psychobiology of Mind-Body Healing: New Concepts of Therapeutic Hypnosis.* New York: W. W. Norton Co., 1986.

Sheehan, Davis V. *The Anxiety Disease.* New York: Bantam Books, 1983.

Weisman, Avery D. *Coping with Cancer.* New York: McGraw-Hill Book Co., 1979.

————. *The Coping Capacity: On the Nature of Being Mortal.* New York: Human Sciences Press, 1984.

General

Baer, Louis Shattuck. *Let the Patient Decide: A Doctor's Advice to Older Persons.* Philadelphia: Westminster Press, 1978.

Berendt, Joachim-Ernst. *Nada Brahma: The World Is Sound—Music and the Landscape of Consciousness.* Rochester, VT: Destiny Books, 1987.

Brilliant, Ashleigh. *I Feel Much Better, Now That I've Given Up Hope.* Santa Barbara, CA: Woodbridge Press, 1984.

Hamel, Peter Michael. *Through Music to the Self.* Longmead, Shaftesbury, Dorset, UK: Element Books, 1978.

Huxley, Aldous. *Island.* New York: Harper and Row, 1962.

Moore, Thomas. *Care of the Soul: A Guide for Cultivating Depth and Sacredness in Everyday Life.* New York: HarperCollins, 1992.

Sahtouris, Elisabet. *Gaia: The Human Journey from Chaos to Cosmos.* New York: Pocket Books, 1989.

Smith, Doug. *The Tao of Dying: A Guide to Caring.* Washington, D.C.: Caring Publications, 1994.

Spring, Beth, and Ed Larson. *Euthanasia: Spiritual, Medical, and Legal Issues in Terminal Care.* Portland, OR: Multnomah Press, 1988.

Stace, Walter T. *The Teachings of the Mystics.* New York: A Mentor Book/New American Library, 1960.

Van Bommel, Harry. *Choices: For People Who Have Terminal Illness and Their Families.* Toronto: NC Press Limited/New Canada Publications, 1987.

Near-Death Experiences and Rebirth

Cranston, Sylvia, and Carey Williams. *Reincarnation: A New Horizon in Science, Religion, and Society.* New York: Julian Press/Crown Publishers, 1984.

Moody, Raymond A., Jr. *Life after Life.* New York: Bantam Books, 1976.

———. *The Light Beyond.* New York: Bantam Books, 1988.

Ring, Kenneth. *Life at Death: A Scientific Investigation of the Near-Death Experience.* New York: Coward, McCann, & Geoghegan, 1980.

———. *Heading Toward Omega: In Search of the Meaning of the Near-Death Experience.* New York: Quill/William Morrow and Co., 1984.

Rogo, D. Scott. *The Return from Silence: A Study of Near Death Experiences.* Wellingborough, Northamptonshire, UK: The Aquarian Press, 1989.

Zaleski, Carol. *Otherworld Journeys: Accounts of Near-Death Experience in Medieval and Modern Times.* New York: Oxford University Press, 1987.

Articles by the Authors About Their Work

Boerstler, Richard W. "Meditation and the Dying Process." *Journal of Humanistic Psychology* 26, no. 2 (1986): 104–124.

———. "A Meditative Approach to the Dying Process." *Unity* 167, no. 6 (1987): 42–45.

Boerstler, Richard W., and Hulen S. Kornfeld. "Harmonizing the Transition from Life to Death." Proceedings of International Conference on Paranormal Research (July 1988): 482–491.

———. "Letting Go." *Newsletter,* Association for Transpersonal Psychology, no. 3, (Summer 1983): 5–8.

———. "Meditation as a Clinical Intervention." *Journal of Psychosocial Nursing* 25, no. 6 (1987): 29–32.

———. "Comeditation: A description of How It is Used in Terminal Care." *Illness, Crises, and Loss,* 1, no. 3 (1991): 56–60.

Fasko, Daniel, Jr., Ph. D., Michael R. Osborne, M.D., Geri Hall, M.S.W., in consultation with R. W. Boerstler and H. S. Kornfeld at Morehead State University, Morehead, Kentucky. "A Study of Pulse and Respiration Rates when an Auditory Stimulus Is Synchronized with Respiratory Exhalation." *Perceptual and Motor Skills* 74, (1992): 895–904.

Kornfeld, Hulen S. "A Holistic Case History: A Lesson in Letting Go." Beginnings. *The Official Newsletter of the American Holistic Nurses' Association* 8, no. 1 (1988): 1, 4.

Kornfeld, Hulen S., and Richard W. Boerstler. "Anticipatory Grief, Meditation, and the Dying Process." *Loss and Anticipatory Grief,* ed. Therese A. Rando. Lexington, MA: D.C. Heath, 1986. 131–143.

———. "Addressing the Fundamental Needs in Caring for AIDS Patients." *The Forum Newsletter: Association for Death Education and Counseling* 16, no. 1 (March–April 1991): 7, 12.

Articles About the Authors and Their Work

Callaghan, Thomas. "Comeditation." *Thanatos* 10, no. 3 (1991): 56–60.

Cochran, Tracy. "Co-meditation." *Omni* 9, no. 7 (April 1987): 113.

Delear, Frank. "Tibetan Meditation Helps in Caring for the Terminally Ill." *The Register,* South Yarmouth, MA, January 26, 1986.

Drexler, Madeline. "The Co-meditation Cure." *Boston Sunday Globe Magazine,* August 8, 1993.

Little, Deborah W. "Letting Go." *Home Care for the Dying.* Garden City, NY: Dial Press, 1985, 274–276.

Miller, Olivia H. "A Sharing of Breaths." *The Quest* (autumn 1991): 65–69.

———. "A Sharing of Breaths." *Yoga Journal* (March–April, 1993): 136, 124.

———. "A Sharing of Breaths." *Earth Star,* 14, no. 95 (December 1993–January 1994): 96–98.

Pease, Theresa. "Helping to Slow Down the Waterfall Mind." *Tufts University Criterion* (winter 1993): 23.

Swain, Bruce. "A Tibetan Breathing Approach to Dying." *East-West Journal* 18, no. 4, (1988): 32–37.

About the Authors

RICHARD W. BOERSTLER, PH.D., is a practicing thanatologist and psychotherapist who conducts seminars and workshops in transpersonal counseling, death education, and assistance in grief and loss for hospitals, churches, universities, and hospices. In recent years, he has been especially concerned with both HIV/AIDS and aging-community services on Cape Cod. Author of *Letting Go: A Holistic and Meditative Approach to Living and Dying*, he has published articles of related interest as well as being the subject of numerous published and television interviews. He is currently associated with the Learning Center for Supportive Care, which offers programs for patients, families, and caregivers dealing with life-threatening illnesses. He is founder and director of Associates in Thanatology, which offers discussion groups and comeditation instruction.

HULEN S. KORNFELD, R.N., M.A., developed a graduate program concentrating in hospice studies, medical ethics, symptom management of the terminally ill, and the psychology of loss. Hulen's nursing specialty is care of both chronically and terminally ill patients, with emphasis on pain management. She is a faculty member of the Division of Continuing Education and Community Services of Northern Essex Community College, Haverhill, Massachusetts. She also functions as director of the Learning Center for Supportive Care, offering consultations and programs for lay and medical caregivers. She is a certified death educator, a certified hypnotherapist, and is presently completing certification in pain management. She and Dr. Boerstler have presented more than two hundred lecture-demonstrations of the comeditation method they developed, adapting it to people with many different physical, emotional, and philosophical needs.